glad to be dad

A CALL TO FATHERHOOD

glad to be dad

A CALL TO FATHERHOOD

by Tim J. Myers

*"A truly rich man is one whose children run into
his arms when his hands are empty."*
—Anonymous

Published by Familius LLC, www.familius.com
Familius books are available at special discounts for
bulk purchases for sales promotions, family or corporate use.
Special editions, including personalized covers, excerpts of
existing books, or books with corporate logos, can be created
in large quantities for special needs. For more information,
contact Premium Sales at 800-497-4909 or email
specialmarkets@familius.com

LCCN 2013935814
ISBN 978-1-938301-01-8
eISBN 978-1-938301-00-1

Printed in the United States of America

Book design by Clarise Insch and David Miles
Jacket design by David Miles
Edited by Hannah Vinchur

10 9 8 7 6 5 4 3 2 1

First Edition

Dedication

What would I give you, child, if I could?
Myrrh and amber and sandalwood;
dolphins painted on Cretan walls
in blues and greens and pale yellows;
a house built deep in a forest of green;
a horse in a stable; a bubble machine;
gold that Inca royals wore;
moonlight through an open door;
toys and books; a dog and a cat;
music that rises; rain in a hat;
the aquamarine of Hawaiian seas —

or maybe I should just give
me.

Contents

Foreword i

The Way It Is 1

Two Hours in the Life: A Cautionary Sample................................23

Homelife: The Benefits to Men..33

So You Think It's Easy? 51

Your New Stress Chart 73

Lost Children 79

Your Child 87

Your Kid's Development: The Important Stuff............................109

Men at Home: Action and Inaction 123

Home Management: Some Do's and Don'ts.................................135

The Male As Domestic Wanna-Be...................................165

Men and Women: Domestic Differences 181

The Smoking Ruins of Your Sexual-Romantic Life....................207

The Male As Domestic Warrior......................................221

Our First Goodbye 245

Afterword..253

About Tim J. Myers...254

Foreword

I FIRST CAME ACROSS THIS BOOK about fifteen years ago, when it was still in an early draft. My wife and I and both our daughters adored it. We found it touching and tender and it prompted many happy and humorous memories of our children's young lives. I've now reread the book in response to Tim Myers's gracious invitation to write a foreword to it. I loved the book the first time I encountered it and I love it now. It is remarkably fresh and relevant.

Let me confess my predisposition to love a book like this. Being a father to my, now grown, daughters has been the greatest joy of my life. That's probably true for most people about parenthood. But in my case it was easy. My daughters are genuinely wonderful. They came into the world that way. I've always said, "Anyone could love these kids." I've met other people's kids with whom I couldn't spend a weekend, let alone a lifetime.

Despite the unalloyed joy I've experienced as a parent, I couldn't escape a rueful sense as I read this book. It reminds me of the things I could have done as a parent and didn't. I have tended to believe that my failings as a parent were mostly failures of omission rather than failures of commission. I have few regrets about any bad behavior on my part but I do regret the things I didn't do that I could have done. The hikes I didn't take, the books I didn't read to them, the math homework I didn't help with, perhaps even not sharing fully and passionately enough with them my love of history, sailing, and moonrises.

When I read this book again, it made me wish I had read it and absorbed its wisdom the day my first child was born. Had I done so, I would have worked harder at not missing anything in my children's growing up. I treasured and still treasure every minute with my children, but now I wonder if I feel that way in part because I didn't spend enough time with them. As Tim points out, with wry humor, all kids have bad moments. That I can remember so few of them with my own children makes me wonder all the more if I shouldn't have been spending more time around the house.

Two vivid memories underscore the point. When my older daughter was about twelve, I called home on a summer afternoon and asked her if she would like to go climb a nearby mountain with me. I had recently finished working on my PhD and now had more free time to do spontaneously exciting things like this with my kids. My daughter was delighted. And when I arrived home a short while later, she was sitting on the front steps waiting for me. She was wearing a pair of black high-top sneakers and shorts that highlighted her long, skinny legs. That afternoon, we hiked to the top of a small mountain in the Adirondacks. I remember thinking to myself that our time together for these special moments was really just beginning. But it wasn't.

The teenage years were about to dawn on our world. There would be precious few days in the future where she would simply be waiting at home for a call from me to go climb a mountain. Soon the house would be filled with other teenagers; too many of them would be boys. Many days she would not be home at all—sometimes she would even be out with one of those boys. We still did things together, often simply taking a quiet walk on a summer evening holding hands. But her childhood was ending, even as I thought it was entering the full flower of early summer. Now I know the lesson: There were too many missed summer afternoons. If I had read and really absorbed Tim's book earlier, I would not have had to learn that lesson the hard way.

I learned a second lesson about parenting, this time in a more timely manner, but also quite accidentally. When my younger daughter was about two years old she caught a bad cold. Every night that winter at about two o'clock in the morning, she would wake up and need hot tea to relieve her congestion. Since I was still working on my dissertation at this point and staying up late anyway, I would just wait for her to awaken and sit with her in the quiet of the dimly lit kitchen of our graduate school apartment. She would sit in silence and look at me with her big, soulful, trusting brown eyes, while I spoon-fed her the hot tea. This went on every night for about two weeks. I have never gotten over the realization of the bonds of tenderness that grow between a parent and a vulnerable and grateful child in the middle of the night.

Because of the path he chose, Tim's life must have been filled with many more of these moments than mine has been. But even in my case, the outcome was powerful. For the rest of her childhood, when my daughter felt sick at night, she would come and get me. I imagine there were nights when I really didn't want to get up, but as I look across my life now, I know that she gave me a great gift. Those were precious moments and I continue to relive them as precious memories.

Tim Myers's book not only brings me closer to my children, it brings me closer to my wife as well. His depictions of the workload and demands of running a household and being a loving parent, often while working outside the home, leave me with awed admiration for the women who have always managed these roles, including my own wife, who performs them so superbly well. Too often women do all of this with little awareness of their extraordinary accomplishments on the part of the men who live with them and perhaps, more sadly, with even less open expression of gratitude and respect from those men.

Reading this book is a blunt reminder to me of how much more help I could have been and still could be to my wife in the shared responsibilities of living together. At a purely practical level, the book makes me think I should learn to cook well enough so that my wife would want to eat what I prepare. (I'll eat pretty much anything, which means that her gourmet cooking is largely wasted on me; friends eat at our home and wonder why I don't weigh 300 pounds.) Given my orientation to food, I may never be the family cook. But Tim writes a lot about vacuuming. Surely I could do more of that going forward. Thanks, Tim, seriously.

If you are a man, read this book and learn. If you are a woman, read this book and encourage the man in your life to learn from its insights; doing so will enrich both of your lives.

Frequently, I wonder if there is a view of family life that doesn't have the barbed and edgy humor of a TV sitcom, like *Everybody Loves Raymond*. Programs of this sort remind me of Eugene O'Neill's play *Long Day's Journey Into Night.* Or perhaps even more fundamentally, a Greek tragedy moved to the American suburbs, with good comedic gag lines instead of bellowing. But the gags and barbed humor still wound and diminish. We laugh while the bonds of family life get reduced to the accretions of resentments, rivalries, and needs for dominance and subterranean psychological control.

Of course, we human beings are complex and nothing perhaps is ever precisely what it appears to be. The dynamics of love and family are multilayered and contradictory. Yes, I get that. But sometimes I long for a narrative in which children's problems become opportunities for new ways for parents to create the conditions in which love grows. Tim Myers' book does just that. His book is not simpleminded; in fact, it is sophisticated, albeit in a disarming and lighthearted way. Nevertheless, the book answers that longing and strives to light a path to the most hopeful human capabilities.

The renowned developmental psychologist Urie Bronfenbrenner observed that, "the future belongs to those societies that make the greatest investment in their young." Tim's book is intelligent, loving and wise. It will help all of us as parents to brighten and deepen the commitment we make to our children's well being. It is a commitment that matters decisively to our children—and to the future we all hope for. Now as a grandparent, his book has new resonance for me.

Finally, though, you simply have to love a book that makes you laugh, makes you think, brings swelling emotion to your throat, and makes you want to be a better person. You also have to love an author, who when referring to his young daughter, can say things like "no problem, it's only urine" and then quote the poet Yeats to his wife of many years while they fold laundry together. Isn't this what Dostoevsky really meant, when he wrote about the true meaning "of active, living love?"

Tom Moran
June 4, 201

CHAPTER ONE

The Way It Is

*"I had been studying the way various peoples bring up
their children, who takes the responsibility for them and
how that responsibility is understood, since this seemed to
me a place where a people frees or enslaves itself."*
—Ursula LeGuin, *Four Ways to Forgiveness*

*"The ruin of a nation begins in
the homes of its people."*
—Ashanti proverb

AT THAT POINT BACK IN THE 90s, my wife and I found ourselves excited. Years of hard work and careful decisions were soon to bear fruit. Our two sons were in middle school, and she was at work on her dissertation and therefore close to finishing her degree. Family life was running smoothly and on schedule. We had Big Plans.

But that September all hell broke loose. Suddenly my spouse and I learned, in the most direct way possible, that abstinence is the only 100% effective form of birth control. (And we'd never been big on abstinence.)

Actually, "all hell broke loose" is exactly the wrong way to say it. After nine years we were pregnant again, which was more like a bit of heaven breaking into the world. Only we weren't prepared for it. A friend said it was as if we'd been sitting at a poker game with a royal flush when a gust of wind blew down the door and scattered the cards. I told people God had decided to throw a kegger at our house—but forgot to tell us.

(You should see the popping eyes of complacent couples in their thirties and forties when I tell our little "story"; I've sent so many guys to the urologist I ought to be getting a percentage from the AMA.)

Our daughter—whom I'll call "Shilly-Shally," for reasons soon apparent—was born that May. She was, and is, one of the most beautiful creatures I've ever seen, a falling star we happened to catch, a bright, wild, funny, utterly lovable kid. But this Blessed Event brought disruption and difficulties in its wake. My wife, finishing the dissertation only through herculean effort, finally got her PhD, which meant she had more earning power than I did. So I became our daughter's primary caregiver—"Mr. Mom," as people so stubbornly insist on saying—and found myself called on to develop skills and attitudes I'd only *begun* to learn when I'd stayed home with my sons for a short time years earlier. Living that life, and watching other families go through similar struggles, led me to write this book.

A surprise pregnancy isn't the norm, of course, and as a stay-at-home dad I'm certainly in the minority of American men. But the general circumstances of our family life have been just what, from many indications, most American families continue to face, and which the American family in general has been facing for *decades* now. If you're reading this book, you're probably also going through it, or are about to. The basic problem? There simply isn't enough time and energy to go around. (Money, of course, also plays its customary role.) The tug-of-war between work and family has many if not most parents worried, frustrated, and physically wiped out. Add to this the other, less publicized conflict parents inevitably face in balancing their own needs and desires with those of their children. And measure in the ominous news, based on a University of Michigan study reported in the *New York Times*, that "the time squeeze felt by parents trying to juggle the demands of work and family is increasingly being transferred into their children's lives."

Well, maybe the word "parents" is only partially accurate here. The truth is that in many cases it's *women* who bear the full brunt of this. And the problem has been compounded in a number of other ways too. Sociologist and economist Paula Rayman, according to Ellen Goodman, has found "'common ground agreement' between Americans of all incomes, races and locations on the interlocking crisis of the economy, the workplace and the family." A "Harper's Index" from 2006 shows that newly-married women have a 17% rise in housework activity—while newly married men come in at *minus* 33%. Many of us believe that some of the old ways just aren't working any more. And the strain is showing in lots of marriages.

The wide interest in Allison Pearson's best-selling novel *I Don't Know How She Does It* should be, I think, even wider. The novel's heroine, a working mother with two children, begins to surmise through the chaos of her life that such a set-up may be a "one-generation-only trick." "We are living proof," Kate Reddy says, "that it can't work, aren't we?" One reviewer emphasizes that the book's climatic "come-uppance" directed at men "will be deeply satisfying to any working woman who's ever wondered when men are going to Get It." In the real world beyond novels, Kathy Thompson of Albany, Indiana, had a similar experience. An ordinary housewife, she was fed up with taking care of everything at home while her husband was off fishing, so she went on strike, simply posting a sign in her yard to that effect—then was astounded when her story garnered world media attention. She shouldn't have been surprised.

And consider for a moment how many *Fatal Attraction* movies have come out over the last couple decades. In the '50s we saw droves of science-fiction flicks about invasions from outer space; fear of monolithic Communism and nuclear war gave these movies some of their power. In a similar vein, the driving force in '90s films like *Sleeping With the Enemy, The Hand That Rocks the Cradle*, etc., may be our dread fascination with *intimate* enmity, the fear that people we love and trust may suddenly go psycho on us. It strikes me that what Hollywood is using here (in its usual half-sleazy, half-vital way) is the profound tension in many male-female relationships today. This is perhaps why studio execs believed we were ready to see a new version of *The Stepford Wives* in 2004. And why so many tune in to watch the inept, selfish husband and usually angry wife on *Everybody Loves Raymond*. Such tension in marriages reveals itself most obviously in divorce and spouse abuse—but it can hurt any couple. And one of the main points of contention has become the division of domestic responsibility, the seemingly simple question of who does what.

When I was ten or eleven, back when my friends and I still played King Arthur with broomsticks and trash-can lids, my dad announced one night at dinner that the boys in the family would no longer be required to do dishes or housework of any kind. We were stunned. Up to that point, we'd cleaned up after dinner one week, the girls the next. Suddenly, by imperial edict, we were free. *Our* job from now on would be yardwork; that was what made it fair. Never mind that we lived in Colorado, with no lawn-mowing for most of the year and not all that much snow-shoveling. *And don't forget*, my brother Mike and I added hotly when our sisters protested, *we go out for sports—which is hard work!*

Jane, the oldest daughter, sputtered at this. *You guys play sports for fun!* she insisted. (I only learned years later how much she resented, rightfully, the family's intense focus on male athletic involvement in those pre-Title IX times.)

It's not just fun! we countered angrily. *In sports we fight for the family honor!*

With this heroic-sounding phrase rolling so pleasurably off our tongues, my brothers and I were utterly convinced of our righteousness.

So the girls took over the dishes—and dishes for a family of 13 are nothing to sneeze at. But it didn't matter if they were mad; it didn't matter that Mom herself disagreed. The Lion had spoken, and we boy-cubs secretly congratulated ourselves, puffing up our scrawny grade-school chests. My sisters still remember that day with something like the bitterness the Irish feel for Oliver Cromwell. But we boys had been handed a role—and we were fine with it.

The only immediate effect was that, with our sisters still in the kitchen after dinner each night, we got the best places on the couch to watch *Bewitched* or *The Carol Burnette Show*. But there was, of course, a much deeper dynamic at work. The girls resentfully gritted their teeth; we boys accepted the "fact" that work in the home had nothing to do with us. This was a defining moment for my family—and it defined us by splitting us apart, male from female.

And that, it seems, is where some of us still are. The mainstream American family is, obviously, under stress. Mothers who work outside the home are knocking themselves out trying to run two shows at once; for many of us, daily life has become "routine panic." And the most logical resource to help deal with all of this remains largely untapped: men. We need more than time-worn images of fatherhood that focus only on taking kids fishing, or teaching them how to play catch, or baking the occasional casserole. We need more than humorous, self-deprecating admissions of non-involvement and domestic ignorance. We have to go to the depths of the thing—because that's where we find purpose and a guiding vision as to the real breadth of what fatherhood can be.

At this point, though, you may be thinking, *Okay, but none of this really applies to me. I'm already involved with my family.* And maybe you are; more and more men are evolving along these lines, and millions can legitimately claim to be committed, involved fathers and husbands. But are you involved *enough*? Remember how you laughed when your wife had no idea what sports terms like "birdie," "rabbit ears," "swinging for the fences" or "covering the flats" mean? Domestic life has its own jargon too. So take this little test—then compare your score with hers. All you have to do is define the terms:

DOMESTIC VOCABULARY QUIZ

1. board book
2. fabric softener
3. a "double ender"
4. cubby
5. pre-K
6. DPT
7. retainer
8. roseola
9. tippy cup
10. sippy cup

EXTRA CREDIT:

Translate the following sentences:

1. "She has no tolerance for anything but Amoxycillin, Doctor! Suprax just isn't an option!"

2. "I was getting him a roll-up when he started chewing on the grapes in his pop-up—but that was no reason to send him to time-out!"

(ANSWERS AT END OF CHAPTER)

Don't feel bad if you didn't measure up all that well. The last thing I want to do is add to the reflexive male-bashing we hear far too much of these days. Everyone should realize that being domestically involved is not always a simple matter for American males; this can be a challenging and complicated issue.

For one thing, most American men obviously haven't been trained to make this kind of commitment. For generations, at least in our culture, a father was isolated from his own family almost by definition. When I was a kid, no one used the term "absent father" —even though we pretty much all had one. The breadwinner role helped create this isolation, since, at least from the time of the Industrial Revolution, fathers have tended to leave home for work. But there were other reasons too—the worst of which, I think, was the idea that adult males are reasonable, level-headed people but nobody else is. The pomposity and emotional gridlock this attitude created are satirized beautifully in, of all places, Disney's *Mary Poppins*—but maybe that comic portrait doesn't go far enough. The poet Robert Bly speaks of his father's continual "brooding," which Bly came to understand as a form of grief. This, I think, tells us much more about the dark reality of the isolated father.

Today, of course, TV and magazine ads regularly feature fathers holding infants (these "fathers," of course, are bronzed shirtless hunks in their early twenties) or *Father Knows Best* types tousling the curly heads of older kids. With a few exceptions, we didn't see such things when I was growing up. But although things have begun to change, there's still a lot to do. The image of father and child isn't considered negative in Western culture, of course—but it simply hasn't been evoked much, in marked contrast to the sacred image of Madonna and Child. Imagine a Christmas card showing Jesus in *Joseph's* arms, with Mary nowhere in the picture. People just haven't tended to think that way.

This kind of social change comes slowly. Even today, according to Michael O'Donnell of the Center for Fathering at Abilene

Christian University, there are more than 70,000 books on mothering—but fewer than 1700 on fathering! Men who hunt will read about deer and ducks, men will pore over car magazines or the sports page. So why shouldn't a guy who has children actually read about parenting, including his partnership with the woman he's sharing this life-task with?

And most men are already working very hard at demanding jobs in a highly competitive world. Many are also genuinely confused about their changing roles. Besides, men *have* made progress. Millions of American men have willingly taken on their share of the work (and the joy!), becoming true partners and responsible fathers. Approximately two million have even become full-time, stay-at-home dads. And there are plenty more, I suspect, who *want* to change but don't quite know how, or don't know how to work past the obstructions some wives set up against their full participation. (On a lighter but still important note, consider this: In 1996, 14 of the 100 finalists for the Pillsbury Bake-Off were men, and Kurt Wait's Macadamia Fudge Torte took the grand prize—the first time in history a male has done so. Dick Boulanger won one of the prizes in 2006. Baking isn't parenting, of course, but such sweet examples show a new openness in men to valuing the domestic.)

We can see real success, too, in the way women's lives are changing. A friend of mine, formerly in the Coast Guard, tells a true story that illustrates how far, and how fast, we've come. A Coast Guard commander was presiding over a staff meeting when the subordinate officers noticed that "the old man" was acting strange. The commander had never looked so pale and shaky, and paused from time to time to breathe heavily for a moment— then resumed the discussion as if nothing unusual had occurred.

Finally one of the subordinates realized what was happening. "Excuse me, sir," he ventured in a quiet voice, "but I think you're in labor."

He was right. The commander was pregnant with her second child. She'd been induced for the first, already had an induction scheduled for the second, and so assumed that her contractions were just Braxton Hicks. But at that moment her stiff upper lip was no match for her uterus, a vessel no longer under its captain's control. She later gave birth to a healthy baby girl. And who can guess what seas that kid will cross?

But as a society, it seems to me, we haven't fully kept up with these changes. My sister Jane, now a gifted and compassionate counselor, deals every day with families in crisis, and one negative she encounters again and again is the absent father. "Get this!" she told me the other day. "I'm doing a session with a family who have a six-year-old boy in in-patient psychiatric care. This is supposed to be a *family* session. So where do you suppose the father is? Out in the parking lot sleeping in his car." Of course there may have been psychological reasons for this man's absence; maybe he felt marginalized in the family. But in the final analysis it all amounts to the same old problem. And this anecdote is only part of a world-wide reality; a Dutch research group found in a recent study, the AP reports, that "young children are rarely in the sole care of their fathers, regardless of the culture." Guys have begun to change, yes, but—to put it in more familiar terms—we're still playing catch-up ball.

I couldn't begin to list all the examples I've collected of references to parenting that simply leave men out completely. A few will suffice to establish the general tone. Under a 2003 newspaper headline about the role of parent labor in the national economy comes the opening sentence, "A mother's work is invisible when it comes to the gross domestic product"—that classic unspoken assumption that caregiver men simply don't exist. An article that mentions "the people most influential in determining the course your whole adult life takes" goes on to say, "Of course there's Mom, and sure to be others, but don't forget . . . [college] admissions officers . . ." It's as if fathers have been "erased" by some Soviet-style ministry—in favor of college admissions officers! A report on a study of maternal influence on teenage girls is at least more forthright, and, presumably, practical: "The effects of fathers were not addressed because fathers were not interviewed." In an even more heartbreaking example, an article in my local paper called "Mothers of U.S. Casualties Share Grief" focused on the mothers of American soldiers killed in Iraq; the piece mentions "relatives," but fathers are, incredibly, absent.

I think the time has come for *all* husbands and fathers to be fully involved in the lives of their families, and for American culture to see this as normal and desirable. It's only fair that males do their share, and are valued for that. But to me there are even stronger reasons than equality and domestic practicality. Many men are beginning to understand just how much they're *missing* by not being domestically involved, and how much they themselves can learn and grow when they are. This is part of what author Warren Farrel refers to when he says, "Instead of a women's movement or a men's movement, we should be working on a gender transition movement." One of the most beautiful things I learned by being a father was simply that it made me so profoundly happy.

But before going on, I should try to define the situation in a general way. "Being Dad" is a broad term, and it covers a variety of circumstances. This book isn't just for men who consider themselves "primary caregivers"; far more American men regularly spend hours per day with their kids but aren't officially "full-time."

Some fathers work nights or odd schedules and care for kids in their time off. Some work part-time; some work in the home; some have schedules that defy description. Many are divorced and care for their children during visitations, or between visitations as custodial parents. Some are unemployed or recently laid-off and have become domestic figures temporarily. And of course lots of guys are at their jobs full-time during the work day but still look after their children while their wives work or go to school or travel. Any of these situations can include significant childcare and other domestic duties.

And even men who work long hours or travel extensively can still be true partners to their wives and true fathers to their children.

So even though American fathers statistically spend little time with their children (that figure is apparently going up), millions of men are already caregivers, and millions more may find themselves spending serious time at home as economic and social patterns continue to change. And even if you aren't part of a dual-income family, these issues are probably still a basic part of your day-to-day life.

Another important point here is the nature of what we call "family." Statistics cited by Stephanie Coontz, an expert on family life, show that 50% of American children live with their biological mothers and fathers, with an additional 21% in stepfamilies; this book is aimed primarily at all such two-parent homes. But the word "family," according to sociologist Jan Bernardes, can have over 200 different meanings; we're learning that it has much more to do with how people *feel* than with any particular structure. I define family as a group of people living together in love on a more or less permanent basis. My focus in these pages is on the two-parent heterosexual family, but that doesn't mean this traditional and majority form is the only real or important one. I don't mean to suggest, either, that there's anything wrong with couples who choose not to have children at all.

So why *should* men be domestically involved?

First, I think it's clear by now that many men must change for the sake of their wives. Most women I know are working way too hard trying to balance work and family. I read how increasing numbers of women have grown disenchanted with the "Superwoman" role, mainly because they're exhausted. I see how my own wife, an incredibly efficient and hard-working person, still has trouble meeting all the demands in her life. And I note how, when women are breadwinners, there's generally no such thing as withdrawing from the domestic sphere as some men do.

And this isn't just an American or Western phenomenon. *Parade* Magazine reports that 45% of the women on Earth (ages 15 to 64) are working. (That actually means *working outside the home*; those of us who have been "homemakers" are a bit sensitive about these terms.) *Parade* adds that while women in "developing countries" devote 31 to 42 hours per week to housework, men only do 5 to 15.

Second, I think men must change for their children. In her column for the *Boston Globe,* Ellen Goodman has written magnificently about all these issues, and quotes the scholar David Blankenhorn on this crucial point: "[There is] an emerging consensus across political lines that the fragmenting of the family is the principal cause of declining child well-being." Goodman goes on to say that "[f]athers are no longer peripheral to this discussion. They are central." Historian John Gillis discusses "the central contradiction—that modern society and the modern economy are not really family-friendly." As evidence, consider this statement by an investment-banking bigwig, paraphrased by the *New York Times* as "confirm[ing] that there is little room in the . . . field for men or women with strong family commitments." Clamorous titles of articles in national magazines reveal our growing concern: "Putting Kids First"; "Who's Taking Care of the Children?"

Some Americans seem to believe that, when it comes to balancing work and family, you *can* get something for nothing, that merely cutting corners is a way to have it all. But we can't have it all—at least not all at once. The hard truth is that raising a family carries a personal and professional cost for parents. And if you don't pay now you'll only have to pay later. The work, love, and self-sacrifice you "spend" on your children will make them happy and productive adults, and will make them closer to you, all of which will make you happy too. Skimping on them when they're young usually means you end up paying in some form of heartbreak—yours and theirs. As one horrible and extreme example, consider Oregon Senator Gordon Smith, whose adopted son committed suicide at 21; Smith wrote a book about it called *Remembering Garrett*. And as my local paper reports, Smith "especially was consumed with guilt because of the large amount of time he spent away from home pursuing his business interests and political career."

We must remember, too, that this isn't just about our individual families; men must change, in my view, because no less than the fate of the nation depends on it. A society is no more than the individuals who make up the whole. And some of the most critical issues facing us today are being played out in our individual domestic circumstances. David Murray speaks eloquently about the crucial significance of the parent-child bond, which achieves, among other things, " . . . the orderly transfer of social meaning across the generations." " . . . [C]hildren are the ultimate illegal aliens," he continues; "[t]hey . . . must be socialized and invested with identity, a culture . . . " In other words, our society is not merely affected by child-rearing—it *is* child-rearing. And this is true in the practical as well as the broader sense; as the title of an Ellen Goodman column has it, "Economy Hinges on Family, Not Vice Versa."

Still, there's much confusion. A review of a new scholarly book about the almost 31 million two-income marriages in America reveals, I think, some of it:

> The first myth shattered by their new study [the authors say] is that everyone in the family is happier if Mom stays home. . . . Being at home with small children all day and taking care of the household can be drudgery . . . [The authors cite] studies of women who did just that in the 1950s . . .

The article then quotes one of the authors as saying

> We're fighting this myth that women are terribly happy at home. What we know is that home contains more dangers

to their well-being than work. Housework is worse than being on the assembly line at Ford.

This is big news? Please. Anyone who's ever seen an "I HATE
HOUSEWORK" bumper sticker suspects already that homelife
isn't exactly Club Med. Of course it's absurd to assume that wom-
en are automatically happy in domestic life. But many are. And
we can't conclude that domestic responsibility itself is therefore
something to be avoided at all costs. Time spent at home often *is*
drudgery—but if done right, it's an inspired drudgery, and crucial
to the human enterprise. There's a certain amount of drudgery in
running a business, writing a novel, or training for the Olympics.
There was drudgery in the day-to-day labor whereby Michelan-
gelo illuminated the Sistine Chapel. Our desire for equality between the sexes shouldn't lead us to belittle the hard work and
self-sacrifice that parenting naturally demands of us.

Part of this attitude may be a general negative reaction to the
sentimental paeans to domestic life the Victorians are so famous
for. That kind of soupy exaggeration bugs me too. And such sen-
timentality isn't accurate, at least in my experience. "Domestic"
comes from the Latin "domus," a house. Not a whiteframe sub-
urban mansion with a parlor and horsehair settee—just a house,
a shelter. Perhaps a more accurate image would be that of a
campfire burning in a cold benighted wilderness. If you want to
know what home really means, go backpacking in the Rockies
for a week. Or try living on the street. In its essence, home isn't
some fancy middle-class pipe-dream; it's one of humanity's single greatest achievements, the human instinct for sheltering and
protecting shaped into something much deeper: a place of safety
and freedom for being our deepest selves. Sure, domestic life is
often mundane and boring. But it's *always*, whether we recognize
it or not, sacred.

Our general attitude toward fatherhood, too, appears to be
in limbo these days. Most of us, it seems, don't really believe in

the old machismo (though there are still plenty of men trying to live that way). And yet we can't seem to envision a good father as anything more than a supporter or sometimes-helper, with Mom as Coach and Dad as mere bat-boy.

A recent book called *How to Dad* is advertised as helping "all fathers fine-tune the skills they'll need for parenthood—the right way to roll a snowball, skip a rock, how to whistle through a blade of grass or tell a joke . . . " I like all that stuff, believe me, but I'm uneasy about this approach. What—these little tricks are what it means to be a *father*!? Maybe back in Mayberry when Aunt Bea was doing all the dirty work, but certainly not here, not now. Other titles suggest a similar vision of marginalized fatherhood, like *Why My Wife Thinks I'm an Idiot: Keeping the Baby Alive Till Your Wife Gets Home.* Even Bill Cosby's best-seller *Fatherhood,* as I read it, presents the male as a kind of half-parent, hard-working and concerned but still basically floating around the edges. I'd never claim a man has to stay home full-time to be a good father—but it seems to me he does have to feel the same responsibility toward homelife that we've always expected of women.

How would the world change if all men suddenly took this responsibility seriously? Would Barry Bonds show up on *Good Morning America* with a recipe for tuna bisque? Would Little League fathers start screaming when their sons' souffles collapsed? Would the Hell's Angels all have little roll-a-crib trailers behind their choppers?

Probably not. But the real changes would be, I think, no less amazing than these, and would strike far deeper into all our lives.

It won't be easy; it can't be. And I don't claim to be an all-knowing expert. Consider the following incident (which also explains, by the way, why I'm calling my daughter "Shilly-Shally").

One morning before my wife left for work, she "suggested" (in that leaning-on-me-hard kind of way) that I make our daughter a grilled-cheese sandwich for lunch. I wasn't sure Shilly-Shally, four years old at the time, would eat grilled-cheese; she'd been fussy all morning. But I dutifully asked her—and yes, she did want one! Her enthusiasm knew no bounds. And lo, she even stopped fussing—but only long enough for me to get butter into the pan. Then she started crying so loudly I thought the cops might show up. Why was she crying, I asked? Because, she blubbered, she was hungry. So I coaxed her into her chair and managed to finish making the sandwich.

When I set it in front of her, though, she freaked. First she screamed that she'd never wanted it. Then she pushed it off her plate with profound disgust—you'd think I'd offered her a dead rat. She then started pounding the innocent sandwich into the table with the flat of her hand, to the rhythm of I—DON'T—WANT—GRILLED—CHEESE! I—DON'T—WANT—ANYTHING!!

I had to send her to her room, of course (the fourth time that morning)—and all my later efforts to comfort her, read to her, play with her were to no avail. After half an hour or so she finally calmed down (which I correctly predicted would mean five used tissues stuffed carefully back into the kleenex box in her bedroom).

During that half hour, though, I faced a vexing dilemma. At first I'd been ready to throw the offending sandwich right out the front door; I hated this disruptive, war-mongering sandwich. But I couldn't bear to throw it away—because that would mean all the trouble I took to make it was suddenly rendered useless. Which was something I just couldn't stomach. But I could stomach a grilled-cheese sandwich—even if it'd been pounded flat and was probably soaked with bitter tears. What the hell, I thought—it still smelled good. And after all, we're talking melted cheese here. So I ate it. Nicest thing to happen that whole morning.

Later my darling came down from her room all red-eyed but smiling weakly. I found myself thinking in a prayerful way, *Maybe the tizz is over! It could be a good day after all!*

Rookie naivete! My daughter had a request. Smiling wanly, she said in a quiet voice, "I want my grilled-cheese sandwich now."

"You . . . want your *sandwich*!?" I sputtered. "But you said . . . !"

With amazing speed, her voice leapt from normal speaking level to full-blown scream: "I—WANT—MY—GRILLED—CHEESE—SANDWICH! . . . "

The point here is that there's no ready formula to help you deal with such things. My family was preparing for a cross-country move; Shilly-Shally was deeply stressed, as only a kid living partly out of boxes and dreading a major life-change can be. There wasn't much I could do except be patient—and even with all my experience, I still made the stupid mistake of eating something she might eventually want. But it's all part of the challenge, the craziness, and the happiness of family life, which is, after all, only a bit less frenzied and dangerous than bull-riding.

That's why this book isn't a "manual" with neatly alphabetized instructions on how to do this, that, or the other. Being domestically involved isn't a step-by-step process like bicycle repair or learning to type. It's much more about who you are as a person and what you truly value, about that kind of growth—and it has far more to do with attitude than with skills. As poet and writer Wendell Berry says,

> "It may be that when we no longer know what to do, we have come to our real work, and when we no longer know which way to go, we have begun our real journey."

So good luck, brother. This is your real work. If you're just starting out, stay cool and stick with it; you'll do fine. If you're already in it, maybe you can do better. Hope I can help.

ANSWERS TO DOMESTIC VOCABULARY QUIZ

1. **board book**—picture-book for very young kids, made of heavy laminated cardboard to withstand being mouthed by child.

   IMPORTANCE: This is what your infant will chew on—and spit up on—for months. Cleaning wet spit-up unpleasant, but scraping the dried form off regular pages even more so.

2. **fabric softener**—those gauzy little sheets you put in the drier to make clothes soft and less static-y.

   IMPORTANCE: Don't forget, or your kid will whine all day that her Esmerelda the Gypsy sweatshirt is "scratchy!"`

3. **a "double ender"**— Isabel Avery's term for when a kid has vomiting and diarrhea simultaneously, a body-storm so violent it will consume a closetful of bed linen (including, of course, that on your own bed) in a matter of hours. And every kid gets to this point at one time or another.

   IMPORTANCE: Not to be confused with a "double-header," since that's good and this is very, very bad. You'll be up all night. And believe me, that's the *least* of it! (Your wife may not know this specific phrase, but she knows the concept.)

4. **cubby**—the little shelf-box at pre-school where your kid keeps his lunch box, sneakers, etc.

   IMPORTANCE: The place you have to check every day, when picking kid up, for half-eaten food, mud-encrusted shoes, used emergency-underwear, and important notices about minor things like head lice.

5. **Pre-K**—educational term for children still too young for kindergarten, or for schooling below the kindergarten level.

IMPORTANCE: "Pre-K" denotes the whole world of early childhood—in other words, the time in your life when you're most likely to say to childless couples, "Have you really thought about what it means to have children?"

6. **DPT**—One of the scheduled vaccinations your child must receive, this one to prevent diphtheria, pertussis and tetanus. Oh, and they won't let 'em in school without it either—and you definitely WANT them to go to school, for reasons not limited to the educational.

IMPORTANCE: You even have to ask!? Your kid's getting a *shot*— is likely to freak out and scream like a stuck pig while the nurses give you that scornful "You've spoiled her!" look. And then she may be sick for three or four days, turning your life into a chaos of sleeplessness, cabin-fever, and cartoons.

7. **retainer**—an astoundingly expensive dental device which federal law requires every American child to wear for at least five years.

IMPORTANCE: The "home-improvement"-type guy may think this has something to do with concrete and split-level lawns, but no. A retainer is that delicate little assemblage of wire and plastic which your kid will take out and forget at the pizza place, forcing you to wade through the "ball room" and pick through the dumpster in search of. As your wife will pointedly remind you, "You wouldn't just not search for a thousand dollar bill, would you?"

8. **roseola**—a reddish rash, which often indicates rubella (German measles).

IMPORTANCE: No, this is not that good-looking waitress down at the Mexican restaurant. Although classified as a "mild infectious disease," there's nothing mild about the impact of a kid with measles—particularly since most kids take the attitude that making their parents miserable will somehow make *them* feel better.

9. **tippy cup**—a cup with a cover and a rounded bottom to prevent toddlers from spilling.

IMPORTANCE: A tippy cup is very helpful. That is, *if* you can *find* the top, and *if* the kid hasn't chewed the top to shreds, and *if* the kid doesn't chuck the weighted cup at you—and *if* you, while washing the cup, don't get depressed thinking how, since you have a toddler, this is the only rounded bottom you've had your hands on in a while.

10. **sippy cup**—for 2- to 4-year-olds; an ordinary cup with a cover that has protruding suck-holes.

IMPORTANCE: You'll go nuts trying to keep these washed so your kid won't spill juice etc. all over the house. But then she'll whine till you let her drink with the top off (because she's such a "big girl"). Might as well go get the carpet cleaner.

EXTRA CREDIT

1. "She has no tolerance for anything but Amoxycillin, Doctor! Suprax just isn't an option!"

These are antibiotics. And kids, confound their complexity, are sometimes allergic to stuff, including medicine. The difference between these two medicines, at least for Shilly-Shally, is the healing of a major ear infection that's turned her into a howling banshee—or adding to that a bout of heavy vomiting. With such consequences, one learns the vocabulary rather quickly.

2. "I was getting him a roll-up when he started chewing on the grapes in his pop-up—but that was no reason to send him to time-out!"

The parent is bringing the kid a snack (a fruitlike substance pressed into a sheet; very popular with children) when the hungry kid begins eating the life-like fruit in his "pop-up" (i.e. "paper engineered") book. Since eating paper isn't something we encourage, the parent considers disciplining the child by depriving him of activity, having him sit for a minute or two in a pre-established place—but then realizes that, because of the paper-engineering's lifelike quality, this isn't really a punishable offense.

CHAPTER TWO

Two Hours in the Life: A Cautionary Sample

THE PHRASE "EASIER SAID THAN DONE" applies with particular force to certain activities, things like bungee jumping, sky diving, or Formula-1 racing. Spending time at home with kids, it turns out, falls into the same category, and not all men are fully aware of this. Those who think it's a piece of cake are simply ignorant; unless you have first-hand experience, it's hard to know just how "challenging" this job can be.

The following, therefore, is an account of one cold January afternoon I spent with my four-year-old daughter Shilly-Shally (not, I promise, her real name). It represents a more or less typical day—well, actually about two hours. (I considered recording a whole day but then realized that might be too frightening.) You may think I've selected for high drama, but I swear I haven't exaggerated, cross my heart and hope to survive.

So remember, comrade: Whatever you may feel when reading this, I'm really giving you only a thin slice of the pie. To get a true taste, multiply these two hours by the ten years or so it takes to turn a kid from a restless, curious, whining, monkey-like, self-centered little consumption-machine into something approximating human character.

Then come the teenage years.

> **1:00 p.m.**—Feeling restless after a morning of housecleaning and the thrills of making lunch, I attempt to convince Shilly-Shally that we should put on our snow clothes and play in the backyard. She's always loved to do this; in the past it's given her hours of delight. But at the moment she's utterly forgotten her former pleasure. I attempt to remind her. I fail.

> **1:05**—After refusing to go outside, Shilly-Shally lies under the dining-room table playing with the "squirrels" she made out of strips of cardboard and paper. As I continue my attempts to convince her, she states categorically that she *hates* to go out in the snow and will *never* agree to do so.

> **1:10**—I mention that the little boy next door may go out too. Her eyes brighten. She *loves* to go out and play in the snow! Will I *please* get her dressed in her snowsuit?

> **1:15**—First we argue in the kitchen about why she can't wear a dress under snowpants. Then I go up to her room and get her some clothes. Once I convince her to stand still—which takes some doing—I dress her in her socks, her boot socks, her long underwear, her shirt and jeans, her snowpants, her boots, her coat, her mittens, her hat, and her scarf. Then she

has to go to the bathroom. I take off her scarf, her hat, her mittens, her coat, her boots, her snowpants, and her jeans.

1:20—I put back on her jeans, her snowpants, her boots, her coat, her mittens, her hat, and her scarf. Then I dress myself hurriedly to repeated choruses of "Come *on*, Dad! I'm *hot!*"

1:25—We go outside. The little boy next door isn't there. We discuss this. The discussion ends with one of us crying in a loud and blubbery fashion. I return to the house for kleenex.

1:30—The little boy next door comes out. The tears dry on Shilly-Shally's suddenly joyous cheeks. Then the little boy next door says stubbornly that he doesn't want to play with Shilly-Shally. I go back in for more kleenex.

1:35—Shilly-Shally and the little boy next door start to play (his memory, it seems, is a lot like hers). I'm shoveling snow to make a sled ramp for them. Shilly-Shally pretends to be the Grinch Who Stole Christmas, roaring and saying mean things to everyone. The little boy next door asks me if he can be the guy from the video game Mortal Kombat. I agree.

1:40—They're still playing. The little boy next door asks me four times if he can be the guy from Mortal Kombat. I agree each time.

I happen to cut my hand on the snow shovel. Shilly-Shally always cries piteously when she gets little scrapes and cuts; thinking this a perfect teaching oppor-tunity, I show her mine. "See?" I say, "It's bleeding, but it doesn't hurt much. Just a little cut. No big deal."

"That's right," she says. "Just a little cut."

"Yes!" I echo, surprised and pleased at her maturity. "Nothing to worry about."

"That's right," she agrees. "*I'm* not hurt. So nothing to worry about."

1:45—Shilly-Shally and the little boy next door have a fight. He's upset because the Grinch keeps screaming in his ears. I ask the Grinch to crank it down a notch, but she refuses. I insist—which results in my having to go back into the house for more kleenex. I return to start mopping-up operations on the Grinch's face. As I do so, the little boy next door asks me three times if he can be the guy from Mortal Kombat. I agree each time.

1:50—The fight is not only over, but they've forgotten it ever occurred. That's because there's a new fight now—over who gets to swing on the swing. (Even with two feet of snow on the ground this is still the Holy of Holies.) I talk to them about sharing and taking turns, going so far as to sing the appropriate song from *Barney*. Shilly-Shally actually refrains from crying; I consider this a victory and a small step toward maturation. (Of course I made sure she got the first turn; I don't have to fetch Kleenex for the little boy next door.)

1:55—While he's waiting to swing, the little boy next door asks me five times if he can be the guy from Mortal Kombat. I agree each time.

2:00—I continue to shovel snow. Shilly-Shally and the little boy next door begin to play separately. For the little boy next door, that means coming over to me and asking four times if he can be the guy from Mortal Kombat. "YES!" I roar, then add, "Why do you keep asking me that?" His answer? He looks away for a moment and then says, "Hey, Tim—can I be the guy from Mortal Kombat?"

I quietly agree.

2:05—Shilly-Shally wants me to find her plastic football. It's buried somewhere in the ocean-like depths of snow that cover our sizeable backyard. "Are you *sure* you have to have that plastic football?" I ask her. "It's going to be *really* hard to find." She looks stricken. "Dad! It's my *puppy!*"

This is true; she's lavished hours of attention on her plastic football (though the "puppy" has been pretty much on its own in the snowy wilds since last summer). I let out a long sigh, which she accurately translates as "Okay—I'll do it." When the little boy next door begins to ask if he can be the guy from Mortal Kombat, I shout "YES!" before he finishes the sentence. He looks at me for a moment. Then he laughs. I realize I've made a serious error; he *likes* this new game.

2:10—After much snow-shoveling and a lucky guess, I fish Shilly-Shally's plastic football up out of a snowdrift and hand it to her. Then I go back to building the sled ramp. For all of thirty seconds, Shilly-Shally pours motherly and canine affection over the plastic football. Then she drops it and says her feet are cold. I'm not stupid; I know the signs of apocalypse when I see them.

So I stop shoveling and start pulling Shilly-Shally and the little boy next door around on the sled. I figure this will keep them happy and maybe even warm them up a little. Huffing like a plow horse, I drag them back and forth, swinging wide on the turns to make them giggle. They enjoy this immensely. But no passion, as Yeats said, can burn forever in so frail a lamp as man. In three minutes they're tired of it. As Shilly-Shally loudly reminds me about her cold feet, I hear that ominous note of serious displeasure in her voice. Again, with the pride of the professional, I attempt to forestall the inevitable. I show them how to sled on the half-finished sled ramp.

2:15—The little boy next door remembers to ask if he can be the guy from Mortal Kombat. Realizing now that a shout will only make him laugh, I quietly agree. He interprets this as permission to ask four more times. Then Shilly-Shally falls off the sled and does a face-plant in the snow. I go back into the house for kleenex. (In my male stupidity, it never occurs to me that I could just put a wad of kleenex in my pocket and so avoid these increasingly annoying trips back into the house.) With enormous effort and a cheerful energy worthy of Richard Simmons, I manage to calm her down. But a major hissy fit may be only moments away.

2:20—Disaster strikes. After asking me five more times if he can be the guy from Mortal Kombat, the little boy next door manages to twist his foot on our three-foot-high sled ramp. He starts to cry. By the time I come back out with more kleenex (all right, I admit it—I caved), he wants to go home. This throws the already frozen-faced and icy-footed Shilly-Shally for a complete loop. She desperately wants the little boy to stay out so they can play; she also desperately wants to go in and get warm. This emotional dilemma, like the pressure of magma deep inside a volcano, must be vented somewhere.

2:25—The little boy next door says goodbye, but not before asking if, when we play tomorrow, he can be the guy from Mortal Kombat. When she realizes he really *is* going in, Shilly-Shally lets out a howl of anguish that practically melts the snow. "THEN I'M GOING IN TOO!" she half-shriekingly declares, and stomps up the porch steps as if mortally offended.

2:30—Once we're inside, I brush all the snow off her and help her take off her hat, her mittens, her coat, her boots, her snowpants, her shirt, her jeans, her long underwear, and her boot socks. She's still upset, but at least now the kleenex is handy. Because she's recently stopped napping and is very tired at this time of day—and because she always has a hard time when the little boy next door goes in—and because she did a face-plant in the snow—and because she generally has strong feelings about things—and for whatever other reasons—she's feeling bad. Very bad. Her pretend-Grinch scowl has become the real McCoy. (I'd describe her as "fit to be tied" but that would reveal some of the inappropriate strategies flitting through my mind at the moment.) Even putting on a new dress (the third of five that day) fails to provide her with its usual boost. A series of demands and complaints and a deeply furrowed little forehead indicate that things are turning ugly. I note the storm warnings; I've seen before just how quickly a tropical low can turn into a hurricane.

2:35—Full-blown flip-out occurs. She's screaming, weeping, refusing to do anything I ask, shouting terrible things like "I DON'T LOVE YOU!! I'M NEVER PLAYING IN THE SNOW AGAIN!! YOU'RE NOT A VERY GOOD FATHER!! I *HATE* BARNEY!!" (a child's equivalent of taking the Lord's name in vain).

I offer to play blocks with her, read her a picture book, color, whatever she wants. "I HATE ALL THOSE THINGS!" she bellows. After many attempts to pacify her, I find myself thinking about Hitler and Neville Chamberlain. So I tell her firmly that if she can't stop screaming and crying, she'll have to go to her room. She continues; I say "Go to your room." She finally complies, at approximately 50 mph and 90 decibels, but only after I approach her with the intent of picking her up and carrying her there. The slam of her bedroom door echoes through the house like a sonic boom.

In the suddenly quiet kitchen I wonder: Is the little boy next door even now asking his mom if he can be the guy from Mortal Kombat?

2:40—I start feeling bad for Shilly-Shally. After all, she's had a rough twenty minutes—and she hasn't eaten for over an hour! Deciding to be Super-Parent, I make "tea" to take up to her room. A PB & J cut into squares becomes petit-fours; I fill her pink plastic tea kettle with apple juice. (A truly loving father, of course, would have gone out and bought her one of those kid-sized, actually-motorized Malibu Barbie Fun Jeeps.) Then I carry the whole thing upstairs on a tea tray, with napkins, pink plastic cutlery, apple slices, the works. She's going to love this!

I've also made myself a cup of hot chocolate and suddenly realize, rather wistfully, that it's the first thing I've done for myself since I brushed my teeth in the early a.m.

2:45—Shilly-Shally's delighted. As we picnic on the floor of her room, her passionate sorrow melts into ecstasy. She wants to play the Three Little Pigs. She'll be Penny, the oldest, smartest pig. I'm Paulie, one of her less intelligent younger brothers come to live in the wolf-proof house she built. This, of course, makes her "the boss." "Can I really be the boss, Dad?" she asks, wanting to be very clear about this. The question has a dangerous ring to it. I hesitate, knowing what such a political precedent can mean. But we're still too close to the recent crying fit to risk a re-engagement over what's really only a negative possibility. "Yes," I say, "You can be boss—if I can be the guy from Mortal Kombat." She laughs.

2:50—For the next five minutes we know sheer, undiluted happiness. For five minutes we live just like the parents and kids on TV commercials. I savor it like an elixir.

2:55—The phone rings. Before I go downstairs to answer it, I caution Shilly-Shally *not* to carry her little teacup full of apple juice anywhere. With a parent's eternal vigilance against messy spills, I've noticed she's a little shaky handling the cup, so I insist she stay seated if she's going to drink from it.

I answer the phone. Luckily, it's only one of those annoying telemarketers—not someone asking if he can be the guy from Mortal Kombat. But my relief is shattered when I hear a cry from upstairs.

3:00—On reaching Shilly-Shally's room I learn that she's not only "moved" her little teacup, she's spilled it—*and* the entire plastic tea kettle full of apple juice. Simian restlessness of youth! Tears well up—but I suppress them. Of course Shilly-Shally's crying too. When I gently remind her that she did *exactly* what I asked her not to, the floodgates of the deep are opened. I look around; naturally, the kleenex box in her room is empty. But that's no problem; I'm on my way downstairs to get rags and carpet cleaner anyway. The spills shouldn't be all that tough to deal with, since she's only soaked about 50% of the carpet surface. Besides, my housemaid's knee has been pretty calm lately. I'll have all this cleaned up in, say, twenty minutes or so.

But first I've got an impromptu lesson about "not crying over spilt milk" to give, and a troubled angel to soothe—whose happiness is, after all, one of the main reasons for my existence on this planet.

CHAPTER THREE

Homelife: The Benefits to Men

"Life is so short that we must move very slowly."
—Thai proverb

"We know what we are, but not what we may be."
—Shakespeare

FOR THE LAST THREE OR FOUR CENTURIES at least, men in our culture have generally spent most of their waking hours outside the home. And for many men, this has become a basic orientation; even in those few hours when they *are* home, some, as their wives and children would tell you, "aren't really there."

My dad was a doctor, but, as our family's standing joke had it, he was the last person to go to if you were sick or hurt. "Ask your mother," was his standard reply; he wouldn't even brush you off with a band-aid or the traditional aspirin. And he certainly didn't want you to call him in the morning. Some guys seem to think of their homes as a place to crash and recover, like a motel along the interstate.

As an experienced parent and all-around hard-working guy, I can understand my dad's response, especially since my wife and I have our hands full with three kids, while he and my mom had to deal with eleven. And as is true for many of the old-fashioned "providers," my father worked himself like a draft animal. I'm passionately grateful for all the things he provided for us. But when he was home, he rested, and I'm sure he wasn't the only man to set up "Ask your mother" as a buffer between himself and domestic demands.

There were a couple of problems with this, though, however understandable it might be. For one thing, my mom never had *any* time off. Period. When he was resting, she was still working.

Then there's the fact that we didn't see Dad very often, or do things with him, or even talk to him much. I didn't really get to know him until I was an adult. In the love and friendship I now feel for him, and in the sadness for all we missed in those earlier years, I've learned how profoundly a father is rewarded for things like putting band-aids on his children.

The old habits of the distant, workhorse father die hard. The good news, though, is that there are *plenty* of reasons for us to spend more time at home and be more fully engaged when we're there.

If you ask the average guy to list some benefits, though, he may draw a blank. Men are changing, of course, even as we speak. But the typical male, it seems, still has something of a gap in his thinking when it comes to home life, a nearly empty space somewhere between preoccupation with sex and a free-floating devotion to professional sports teams.

From my point of view, at least, this is somewhat surprising. You might think the men it applies to would be a little embarrassed. A guy who's uneasy admitting he doesn't know what channel-locks do may blithely declare his ignorance about toddlers or basic house-cleaning. And considering the intense nature of family experience, you have to wonder how certain fathers actually avoid at least *some* domestic awareness. Because I've stayed home with all three of my kids, domestic life has become an essential part of who I am, deepening and strengthening me in ways I couldn't have imagined. I am, in part, what being home with my children has taught me to become. And you don't have to be a stay-at-home father, of course, in order to reap these benefits.

I learned of one such benefit in an issue of *Working Mother* magazine, which gave the results of a University of Nebraska study on supportive husbands. The researchers looked at over 2,000 married people, concluding, the article reports, that "[h]usbands who are supportive of their wives' careers and share in household chores are happier with their marriages than other men . . . " Non-supportive males, in contrast, tend to "feel threatened and resist change, which causes *more* stress in the marriage." It only makes sense, I think, that men who *give* more to marriage actually *get* more from it, in that old and sacred paradox whereby in giving we receive.

Another benefit springs immediately to mind: the practical education home life can provide for a male, an antidote to that learned helplessness many men acquire when it comes to this most basic part of living. (Just how bad can we guys get? When I read a draft of this chapter to a small group, one woman sputtered with surprise and burst out "I didn't know any men even *knew* how helpless you all are!")

Of course it's true that some guys learn, as bachelors, how to manage their own domestic affairs. But the independence of bachelorhood is no guarantee that a man has learned basic domestic skills and attitudes. For one thing, a bachelor only takes care of himself, which is a far cry from caring for a family; bachelors are notorious, of course, for going into marriage with entrenched self-centered habits.

Besides, the bachelor's approach to domestic life is often crude, to put it mildly. Plenty of my college dorm-mates, for example, took a less than labor-intensive approach to their laundry. A guy would wear his clothes until they were simply unwearable, then throw them on his closet floor and choose something else. In this spirit of homage to Huck Finn, he'd go through his wardrobe piece by piece. By the end of the semester you'd see him wearing slacks, dress shirts and sports coats, both to class and to parties and bars—not because he wanted to look formal but because those were the only clean clothes he had left. When even his dress clothes were filthy, he'd push the whole moldy, odorous pile into his laundry bag and take it home to Mom—or give it to his girlfriend, if their relationship had reached that romantic point.

A divorced friend of mine, in his forties, used the same "strategy" for doing dishes. Whatever he used he'd stack in the sink, washing all his cups, glasses, plates and cutlery in one great burst when nothing clean was left. On Friday nights you could usually find him eating with a spatula off one of those ribbed microwave trays.

But not only do men tend to be domestically ignorant to begin with—some of us duck even more of our responsibility by depending on women to take up the slack. This is a dependence many mothers actually encourage in their sons! It's true, of course, that young males can be stubborn and mindless when it comes to helping around the house. But when frazzled parent "enables" stubborn and lazy kid, the process of training a helpless male adult has begun. Memories of my own adolescence make me hot with embarrassment. One scene sums up just how out to lunch I was. "Now, Tim," my mom told me seriously one day, "I need you to do something for me. I need a package of frozen hamburger. Go downstairs. Open the big freezer. Just to your left will be a wire basket. The frozen hamburger is *not* in the basket, it's *under* it. Not *in*, but *under*. So lift the basket out. Right below you'll see a package. Don't get me anything but *ground beef*. That's *ground beef*. Okay?"

"Sure!" I said cheerfully, then tromped downstairs, opened the freezer, and stopped. "Mom?" I called up tentatively. " . . . Uh . . . what did you want?"

Most wives will have their own anecdotes to add here, some more far-fetched and dramatic, most less so. But even the little things can build up, and a pattern of continual domestic ignorance is not only bad for the marriage but also for the man himself. That typical *Honey-where-do-we-keep-the . . . ?* dependency can lead to resentment in both partners, since *she* feels put upon and *he* feels inadequate and humiliated. (I'm still fighting the problem, in fact. Once you contract this disease, there's no cure, really—you can only manage it.) And this kind of learned helplessness takes larger and more general forms too; far too many men, it seems, actually reach an almost total dependence on their wives for everything from meals to emotional expression.

Men, I think, should acknowledge their often hidden embarrassment about this and let it guide them to new skills. And if by some chance a guy doesn't feel embarrassed about being a domestic ignoramus—maybe he should learn how to.

Our society values the well-rounded individual. But "well-roundedness" should include domestic as well as other abilities. Many times, after admitting that I don't change my own oil, I've had to endure an auto mechanic's look of scornful surprise; why is it, I wonder, that men don't feel the same about sewing on buttons? I have a kind of typical-male belief that I won't really be well-rounded until I can do things like sail a boat or attempt simple carpentry. Such skills, which I don't possess, strike me as basic abilities everyone would do well to have. In my life, though, there aren't many occasions when I need to cross large bodies of water or build huts. But a man is usually home with his kids on a daily basis; it's many a recklessly yanked-on button I've seen go flying. Running a house and caring for children are fundamental life skills; how can a man justify not knowing anything about them?!

And all we have to do to break the cycle of dependence is get in there and learn. For fifteen years I "helped" my wife with our grocery shopping, week in and week out. "Where's the pizza sauce?" I'd ask her. "What aisle is Pop Tarts?" It was only when she became ill for three months that I finally learned the layout of the store—simply because I had to do the shopping myself. That's all it took.

And what advantages a little domestic knowledge can bring to a guy! Like any skills, these engender a certain pride and personal satisfaction, expanding both our knowledge of human experience and of ourselves. They can help bring husbands and wives together. They can also lead to the kind of anchoring humility everyone needs.

Besides, being able to take care of something yourself is a hundred times more convenient than always depending on her.

A second general benefit is that time at home allows a man, in psychologist Herb Goldberg's phrase, to "step out of harness"—to escape, however long, from the narrowness of the male-achiever role. In the high-pressure world of the working male, emotional expression is often frowned on, achievement at any cost is championed, and a man is judged by his earning power, his social or sexual dominance, and his material wealth, often denying his own genuine desires and frustrations. Wordsworth said it perfectly, I think: "Getting and spending we lay waste our powers."

In *The Hazards of Being Male*, Goldberg lays out with great force and clarity just what rigid male sex roles have cost the many patients he worked with as a therapist. (Dr. William Pollack of Harvard has even more up-to-date and research-based things to say about this same problem.) "The male . . . " Goldberg writes, "is out of touch with his emotions and his body . . . Our culture is saturated with successful male zombies . . . [who] have confused their social masks for their essence . . . Only a new way of perceiving himself can unlock [a man] from old, destructive patterns and enrich his life." This isn't true about all guys, of course. But for those to whom it applies, I say: Fess up, at least to yourself. We should acknowledge our hidden slaveries, our hang-ups, the deep hurts and false assumptions that can so terribly limit us.

Time at home is a precious opportunity to live in exactly the opposite way. The work-horse can step back, take a breath, begin to savor his life. All those stereotypical behaviors of male mid-life crisis—pursuing sex, living in the fast lane, preening to recapture lost youth—are shallow and bound to fail, since they're only the "reward" behaviors of the man in harness. But a man can learn to remake himself, to awaken things within him, if he lets quieter, stronger things begin to grow. Many men I've talked to, on hearing that I stay home with my kids, have expressed wistful envy for my position. "Man, what I wouldn't give . . . " they'll say, looking off into the distance. Perhaps they're naive about the difficulties of full-time fathering; perhaps not. But many would clearly love a break from the type of work-life that stifles some of their humanity. "I kind of like, at this point," a father from New Jersey says, "*any* occupation that isn't full of politics, stress, white shirt/ties, and joining the good-old-boy network." Similarly, in the blue-collar and service sectors, heavy demands from above, monotony, struggles with co-workers or bosses, or the constant feeling of being expendable can lead to the same strong desire for escape—and not just to kick back and take it easy, but to take stock.

Many men, Goldberg says, "discover that they are shadows to themselves as well as to others." But one of the most powerful ways for men to step out of this shadow-life, this practiced grief, is right under their noses. In their own homes, with their own children, men can move toward becoming the full selves many are struggling to be.

And another advantage flows from this pausing to catch your breath: the small magic of just slowing down.

I often use clouds as a gauge of my own life-speed. Sometimes people have to hurry, and hurrying isn't necessarily bad in itself; it can even be enjoyable. But on every side I hear complaints about the frantic pace of modern life. It's clear that many of us, at least, are overdoing it. Clouds aren't like that. They flow across the sky at their own Tao-like pace, steady and rhythmic, usually so unhurried we must consciously slow ourselves even to notice their movement. Sometimes I stop in the middle of a busy day and just watch. If slowing myself to their pace, to the pace of the natural world, the rhythm of wind and water and the deep slow life of the land—if doing this frustrates me too much, and I want to break away before I've really seen the perfect motion of the clouds—then I know I'm living too fast. But not necessarily in terms of physical speed; clouds tell me I'm going too fast on the inside. It's usually our inner velocity, more than our outer, which drives us too hard.

But still, we're only human, and our bodies dictate much of our interior life. Since many jobs include high stress and pressure, we often respond by internalizing that endless anxious race to get things done. Being home is different. I don't mean that it's paradise, that you won't be busy, pressured, or frustrated. But the overall pace, and the nature of many of your new tasks, will begin to slow you down.

As a Thai proverb has it, "Life is so short that we must move very slowly." An American's first reaction to this statement is likely to be confusion; if life is short, shouldn't we go faster, to experience more? No, Thai wisdom tells us. You must learn instead to fully savor what you do. This aspect of being home with children provides another precious opportunity for men, especially since some of us live in an unnatural fear of idleness, having been taught to be relentless engines of achievement. Time with kids isn't "idleness" by any definition, but it does impose a more organic kind of life-rhythm on a parent. And the child's life-rhythm will do even more to shake you out of a rigid attitude toward time—that is, if you let it.

Life at home will always be challenging in its own way. But there will always be those other times too: Shilly-Shally and I lying on our backs in the grass, talking quietly or just drinking in the silence, watching clouds (and for once I don't have to check if I'm patient enough). Me holding her, pressing my face into her fragrant hair with its little-girl smells. And here I am on hands and knees picking up strands of plastic Easter grass, because she *had* to have her Easter basket from the attic, since Belle from Disney's *Beauty and the Beast* carries a basket in some scene...but suddenly she jumps down without a word, leaving her snack at the table, and begins to search the rug carefully, snatching at stray pieces of plastic grass and carrying them to the trash, both of us laughing when she can't get the sticky grass off her fingers. Or she's standing in the backyard at twilight, gazing at the evening star, when the automatic sprinklers suddenly come on, and she screams—the closest sprinkler thirty feet away from her—and I come running, pick her up, within seconds she's smiling, wiping tears away and telling me, with big solemn eyes, the story of the startling sprinklers . . .

The truth is that, at home, such beautiful little miraculous times happen far more often than the maddening disasters do. And this leads to another profound benefit. Being home with a child is a magnificent opportunity for adults to reconnect themselves to a whole set of abilities we seem to leave behind in childhood. Emerson says bluntly that most adults take on a kind of blindness: "To speak truly, few adult persons can see nature. Most persons do not see the sun." A fundamental ability to look at the world with wonder, to really see what's before us, lies sleeping through many people's lives, a distant memory they've all but forgotten. That's one reason most of us treasure certain childhood remembrances; it seems a golden time not so much because things were so perfect, but because we had an orientation to existence that allowed us to see the world that way. This orientation—without the sometimes frustrating limitations of our childish minds—is still available to adults. It's what haiku poetry is based on, and is in fact the aim of much art and spirituality—a re-establishing of direct connection to experience.

And what a banquet of "direct experience" being home can set before you! With your child's behavior as a model, a kind of lens to peer through—and beyond the frantic pressures or numbing boredom of much of the work world—you can set about really looking at things, really tasting food, smelling smells, hearing sounds. With time enough, and your own willingness—and with the continual example of your child's wonder-driven heart—you can actually re-learn how to be a human animal in the sensual flow of the natural world. You might even discover again how to see the sun.

But not all the benefits of staying home are so philosophical. A while ago, having called our HMO to see a doctor, I was sitting there, phone on my shoulder, putting in the apparently mandatory half-hour it takes to make an appointment. As I waited, I found myself half-listening to the disembodied recorded voice on the other end reciting health tips. But I perked up when it started to talk about laughter and health. Children, the voice intoned mechanically, laugh 400 times a day—while adults only manage 15.

Now you've got to wonder how they counted this; I picture some labcoat following a kid around and marking a clipboard, then doing the same with a tax accountant. Still, we all know kids laugh a lot more than adults do, and we hear more and more these days about the health benefits of laughter and a positive attitude. Being home with children is a natural way to bring more laughter into your life. For one thing, kids love comedy as much as they love candy, if not more, and any parent who doesn't use it, both to teach and to control, is wasting a precious resource. Your children are the perfect captive audience, eager, interested, and always there. In addition, the slower, warmer atmosphere of home life naturally allows more laughter. For although humor is essentially a spontaneous phenomenon, it occurs more often in certain environments—and it can be pursued. And those who pursue it are happier than those who don't.

So how to pursue it? You open yourself, you value it, you consider its preciousness, you practice it, you embrace it whenever you can, you consciously look for it in everyday situations.

I was complaining to some friends once about a big gash I'd gotten on my shin. In that typical "trials of parenthood" mode, I launched into the story of how, to calm a sleepless Shilly-Shally, I'd slept on a futon on her bedroom floor—had woken in the wee hours with a terrible backache—had crept down to the living-room couch so I wouldn't wake my wife, setting my alarm on the coffee table—and then, when it went off, had jumped up in a stupor not remembering where I was, banging my leg on the table in a frantic effort to hit the button.

But as I told the story, I found myself, in characteristic Irish fashion, I suppose, warming to it, gradually realizing the humor it afforded. By the end of the little narrative my friends and I were laughing, and I'd come to see the night's events in a whole new light. That's when I suddenly thought about my dad.

It's from him, and from my mom, that I first learned the profound and simple art of enjoying life as it happens; his status as a workhorse didn't keep him from that crucial ability. I found myself remembering the night Dad recounted to us, with utter delight, how he'd put his necktie on *over* his shirt collar before 6:30 Mass that morning—and then had gone blithely through his day, confused by all the strange reactions until someone finally took him aside. This certainly wasn't high comedy; there was no punch line or hilarious climax. It's just that he got such a *kick* out of it, out of the little incongruities of being human, and saw so instinctively—as he almost always did—the funny side of things.

It's easy to underestimate the power of this approach to life, this instinct for humor in ordinary experience—which constitutes, in fact, a kind of wordless faith in our daily existence. Of course there are things too horrible ever to be laughed about. But in most cases, finding humor is to humans what agility is to cats. People who know how to do it tend to land on their feet. And being home with children is an ideal opportunity to develop this skill.

Besides, kids are funny—sometimes when they try to be, more often just by virtue of who they are. Some examples:

> Shilly-Shally has named her index fingers. "Stinkypan" and "Lady-o" are a pair of giraffes who constantly bicker and insult each other, acting out Shilly-Shally's negative impulses. The other day they actually attacked *her*, pulling repeatedly at her braids and calling her ugly names. It was better than pro wrestling.

• • • • •

> When my older son was little, I showed him a map of the Milky Way. "This is our galaxy!" I said, "and this is our sun—one of billions of suns! And somewhere close to the sun is our planet, the Earth!"
>
> "Hey, Dad!" he exclaimed, caught up in my excitement. "I can see our house!"

• • • • •

> My wife was explaining delicately to our younger son, in answer to his earnest question, how human flatulence can sometimes help doctors make diagnoses.
>
> "You know," she said, plainly embarrassed, "the... frequency, and . . . uh . . . odor . . . "
>
> Our little boy looked up at her with big serious eyes.
>
> "Does it mean anything if it's . . . loud?"

• • • • •

To explain the seasons to the boys when they asked about them, I got out an orange and a ping-pong ball.

"This orange is the sun," I told them, "and this ping-pong ball is the Earth. The Earth revolves around the sun"—here I moved my models, delighted to see the boys entranced, their wide eyes fixed on my substitute sun.

"Now—can you see how it goes?" I asked proudly, convinced I'd given them the gift of wonder. For a moment they were silent. Then the younger asked brightly, "Dad—can I have that orange?"

And it's not just the outright humor that can lift and re-direct you, but also the sheer zaniness. Living with kids is like running a kind of asylum for very sweet patients—but patients nonetheless. Things are different in a house with children. Shilly-Shally's bathtub, for example, is often full of balloons, even during the daytime. She loves balloons (which are among the most commanding passions of the pre-K set), endlessly demands them, and delights in filling her bathtub with them. I walk past the bathroom and notice a rainbow-like profusion in the tub, and part of me wants to do that parent thing and PUT THOSE TOYS AWAY. It's like an itch I can't ignore. I want order, I want control, those balloons are bugging me, all huddled up together in there like a little group of escaped cartoon creatures.

But then I stop and think. Balloons! Hell, I love balloons too! It dawns on me that I'm lucky to have a tub full of balloons to walk past each day, a reminder of what the world can be, the strange delights our lives present to us. I'm lucky that someone keeps trying to tell me, in the language of balloons, how to loosen up a little about controlling the house, how to let it be a place where life isn't merely organized but actually *happens*—how to let delight rise up out of the world even as I impose order from above.

In all of this I keep seeing a beautiful light in things, one I only glimpsed before I spent serious time with my children. Humor is much more than a moment of relief, a physical release, belly-laugh and then back to the grindstone. Garrison Keillor knows it for what it really is:

> "Humor is not a trick, not jokes. Humor is a presence in the world — like grace — and shines on everybody."

Keillor put this truth into words for me. But in fact I'd learned it long before, wordlessly, from Shilly-Shally, and from her brothers before her, and from my own parents and siblings before that.

Of all the benefits of spending time at home, the next is, I think, the most obvious: It's the only way to really know your kids. We live in an age when the absent father (in the many forms such absence takes) seems to be crippling whole swaths of our society. How many fathers, I wonder, have secretly gotten teary-eyed or come close to it, sitting alone in their cars as Harry Chapin's "Cat's in the Cradle" played on the radio? The irony of this has struck me many times: We plod on as a society, with fathers in so many families all but separated from their children, men at work or on the road or living in other cities or locked away behind the fortress of a newspaper — but they hear this song, we all listen. We know it's true: Kids grow so fast, but we're too busy. We keep putting off our plans to spend time with them, we keep running, and then one day they're gone and there's no real connection, no strength of love and shared experience, only a skeletal version of what family life should be. But the system goes on as it always has, the disk jockeys keep playing that song — and moments of tenderness that should be shared by fathers and children actually take place in cars or offices or hotel rooms where men, alone, sit and wonder who their children are.

How can it be that we let ourselves drift from the center of our lives out to the edges, and then spend most of our time there? How can the family, the human grouping most essential to all of us, become just one more item on our to-do lists? "In America you raise your children; in India we live with ours," an East Indian once said. His statement strikes me as an over-generalization, but there's certainly some truth in it as a description of much American family life.

In the time you spend at home you get to know your kids on a whole new level. And this knowledge will run much deeper than a mental catalogue of favorite colors and who likes what for lunch. No human being, in fact, not even a spouse, can know another as intimately as parent knows child. This will not only make you a much better parent—it'll also make you happier. And if you really know your own flesh and blood, maybe you won't find yourself sitting in the car one day wondering if your life has any center, awash with sorrow and guilt as you're transfixed by Harry Chapin's words about a father who watches his own life pass without ever spending real time with his son.

For some men, in fact, time at home with children will be part of a necessary education in learning to love. Some simply haven't learned how, and some love deeply but can't express it. Others feel love but don't channel it into responsible and nurturing action. Whatever his own background, a man won't find better teachers in the art of loving than his own children. By their very nature they demand, beg for, insist on, wither without his love. And he too will wither, may already be withering, until he learns to give that love freely, until he grows to that point where giving is as joyous as getting.

You don't think you've got a "feminine side"? Don't think you can handle that much homelife? Hey, cast your mind back: You didn't like the taste of beer the first time either, and now look at you. Contrary to prevailing stereotypes, men *are* adaptable.

In *The Tunnel of Love*, Peter de Vries says "The value of marriage is not that adults produce children, but that children produce adults." Although some marriages are an exception, in most cases a man can learn all this at home. The love in him can be

more than a mere aching dependency, or dark need, or mute cry
buried in the self. His love can blossom out into the world, an
overflowing that enriches his own life, the life of his family, even
his community.

And another thing. Most males are what you might call "rec-
reation-oriented." We like to play. Guys hang little basketball
hoops in their bedrooms and offices and shoot sponge basketballs
at them. We stack beer cans, throw snowballs, lay bets on who
can catch the most peanuts out of the air in his mouth. We tend to
make games out of almost any activity. So what does being home
have to do with this basic masculine urge? Simple: If a guy's willing to get down on his hands and knees, he'll find that a kid is the
greatest interactive toy ever invented.

One final point, which I've hinted at throughout this chapter. There are plenty of reasons for men to be committed fathers.
Some, though, are easier to grasp than others, particularly since
certain truths can only be fully understood through experience.
How does an adult, for example, explain sexual love to a child?
Since this experience is outside the child's conscious awareness,
any description is inadequate. To a child it may sound silly, even
crazy (I recently saw a kid's "Letter to God" that read, "My brother told me where babies come from—but it doesn't sound right").
Most likely, though, the kid simply won't relate to it, with boredom or indifference as the result. And yet some day this same
child, now something more than a child, will find these longings
stirring in his or her own body, and the human birthright of sexual love will become central to that life. Sometimes telling men
about the advantages of home-life is similar.

To learn these deeper truths, men must be willing to let things
happen to them—things they may not understand yet. Why
should a man truly commit himself to fatherhood? A final, and
profound, reason: to find himself.

I'm not lost, you say; *I know where I am, who I am.* And maybe
you really do know some of who you are. But how completely do

you know yourself? How fully have you expressed your potential, explored all your capabilities, felt all your inherent feelings?
How freely have you fulfilled all the roles in your nature?

I'm at the computer working, hurrying, concentrating on the
task before me. I'm a provider, a do-er, an adult, I have plans,
ambitions, I move from point A to point B. Just then Shilly-Shally
quietly opens the door, having woken from her (always brief) afternoon nap. Then she comes to me quickly, climbs onto my lap,
and I hold her—and the suddenness with which she's come into
my arms is like the suddenness with which she came into our
lives. This jars me from my narrow-minded focus, lifts me instantly past it, and I'm filled with astonishment: This child, this human
being, having come out of nowhere, out of the depths of space,
non-existent but now here, warm, on my lap, those little-girl
smells in her hair—I marvel wordlessly at her, and passionately
thank the powers that brought her to us.

In that moment I'm not anything else but someone who loves
her completely. I'm a father, just that, feeling nothing extraneous,
nothing shallow or transitory, nothing that isn't true to the depths
of my being. There in the midafternoon light, with the computer
still on before me (soon to be reluctantly shut down for the day)—
with the silence in the house about to be hurled away, with hours
of dish-washing, laundry-folding, table-setting, crayon-wielding,
block-building, picture-book-reading and storytelling ahead of
me—with her in my arms, I realize, surprised, that I'm most who
I am—my deepest, truest self.

CHAPTER FOUR

So You Think It's Easy?

"Experience is what you get when you
don't get what you want."
—Dan Stanford

"A model dad demonstrates [that] time is love."
—Shana McLean Moore

ONE OF MY BROTHERS was married a few years ago, and soon his wife was pregnant—with twins.

Although I rejoiced with them, I was also a little concerned. I know what it takes to raise a kid, and I can multiply by two. In some cultures twins are considered good luck, an indication of divine favor. But I'll bet a whole pile of cowrie shells the *men* believe this more than the women do. My brother married after a long bachelorhood; did he really understand what was coming down the pike?

For the first six months after the birth of his daughters, he'd always say things were fine. Two wasn't really twice as much, since you already had a system going. I knew he was becoming a terrific father, but I wondered about the fatigue factor, which is even more important in parenting than in sports. I couldn't help thinking about "the Bear."

If you've ever run track, you probably know about the Bear. I heard it from the older guys on our high-school team. "It's like this," they'd say. "You're doing a quarter-mile or whatever, and you're kicking hard for the finish—you're right about there . . . "—they'd point to a spot three-fourths of the way around the track—"...when all of a sudden the Bear comes up out of the ground and jumps on you. Your legs turn to lead, you can't breathe, you get dizzy—the finish line suddenly looks a hundred miles away . . . "

"The Bear," of course, is that phenomenon whereby a runner making maximum exertion suddenly feels exhausted. Young runners nod when they hear about it, but they don't really understand. Just listen to them, though, once that beast sinks his claws into their backs. *Oh man! I was starting my kick and all of a sudden . . .*

I wondered if something similar was in store for my brother.

Then one day he called me, sounding a little down in the dumps. The twins had just turned eleven months. "How's it going?" I asked.

"Well, okay," he said, the weariness plain in his voice. "It's just . . . well . . . it's pretty *constant* . . . "

Bingo, I thought; the Bear claims another victim.

Like any worthy labor, spending time with your kids can be exhausting, frustrating, and downright tedious. It is, as my wife says, both overwhelming and underwhelming at the same time. In addition, and in contrast to most jobs, this one is grossly unrewarded in terms of money and status, with the extra wild irony that some people don't even consider it *work*!

Most mothers, of course, know all about such ironies. But some men don't realize just how brave they'll have to be in this new world. The level of difficulty, of course, depends on your individual circumstances. But a man needs to go into this with his eyes wide open—and his heart. How hard can it be, you wonder? You'll find out.

For starters, try this little readiness quiz. It's designed to enhance mental preparation for the new father. All the examples are taken from real life—I kid you not. Answer each question "yes" or "no." And be honest.

DOMESTIC READINESS QUIZ

Your toddler is, as your wife tells the neighbor, "not such a good sleeper." Once he's weaned he stays up till 11:00 or 12:00 at night for about six months, waking at 5:30 each morning, and often during the night. You're seriously sleep-deprived and beginning to hallucinate; your boss has begun to look sympathetic and kindly. Even the bags under your eyes are getting bags. Finally the kid cycles around to a normal bedtime. You enjoy the luxury of a week's worth of semi-adequate sleep.

Then Daylight Savings Time kicks in, and he's right back to midnight.

ARE YOU READY FOR THIS!?

This same kid, a little older now and the world's lightest sleeper, has just settled down for a nap, and you *desperately* need the break. Once he's asleep, you get ready to tiptoe out of his room— but like a fool you can't resist putting a few toys away first. With little plastic tractor and farm animals in hand, you creep to the toy barn where they're kept—but you've already opened the barn door before you remember it "moos." Your kid sits bolt upright. "I'm done with my nap, Dad. Can I play farm too?"

ARE YOU READY FOR THIS!?

You have a guest for dinner, an important guy who works with your wife. He's an older bachelor. In the middle of dinner, a number of things happen at once: The phone rings and your older son goes to answer it—the doorbell rings and your younger son takes care of that—the timer goes off in the kitchen and your wife jumps up to check the dessert—and you rush upstairs, having heard a thump and the unmistakable shrieking of your four-year-old. Your guest is suddenly completely alone at the table—and in the middle of a sentence. And once you've calmed your screamer down, you're going to have to explain why.

ARE YOU READY FOR THIS!?

It's Christmas day; you want to take the family to church. But your three-year-old NEEDS a bath. You've got one hour before the service starts. Before she can get into the tub, however, she has to move EACH of her TWELVE cardboard-cut-out "squirrels" up the stairs to the bathroom. And that means lifting each "squirrel" one stairstep at a time. When you try to hurry her, she protests. "They're only *little* animals, Dad!" Total elapsed time: thirty-three minutes.

ARE YOU READY FOR THIS!?

First your kids got "Lite-brites," thousands of tiny colored plastic reflectors they're supposed to arrange on a pegboard to make pictures with. What they prefer, of course, is to scatter the damn things everywhere. For *years* you clean up Lite-brites. Then your wife brings home an "Indian dress" for your daughter, which is covered with beaded fringe, bits of which are constantly falling off the dress. Soon you can't take a step in the house without encountering this new form of litter. Then, just when you think you've finally vacuumed up the last beaded fringe, Grandma comes over with a pink feather boa for your daughter. Within hours your living room looks like a psychedelic henhouse. Grandma, of course, is long gone.

ARE YOU READY FOR THIS!?

At 1:00 you're going to a local photo studio for a formal family photograph. Your kid needs lunch, but you've learned that feeding *any* semi-solid food to a child under five automatically means a complete change of clothes (for both kid and yourself). So you carefully avoid pudding, jello, yoghurt, ice cream, spaghetti-o's, applesauce, peanut butter and jelly, mashed potatoes, canned fruit in juice, cereal in milk, etc. But you learn rather quickly that some foods normally considered "solids"—like graham crackers—can easily cross into the semi-solid category. Lunch is over, your kid looks like a pig after a good wallow, and the clock now reads 12:34.

ARE YOU READY FOR THIS!?

You've been working your tail off all day for your kid, doing cosmically-important things like finding lost coloring books, trying to wash off a fairy-tale DVD so the picture won't keep hanging and pixelating, and hooking up the back of her doll's incredibly tiny dress. You're right in the middle of some similarly devilish task, and pulling it off beautifully, when you wife comes in from work. Your kid looks up and instantly bellows, "Mom, will you come here and do this better than Dad?!"

ARE YOU READY FOR THIS!?

SCORING:

If you finished this quiz without serious thoughts of abandoning your family, you've passed. If, however, you answered "No" to four or more questions, you should probably stick with your current method of birth control.

Spending more time at home inevitably presents a number of specific problems. It's not easy on a number of fronts.

Some of these problems, of course, are practical difficulties whose major impact is on your life as an adult. Your career, obviously, will be affected (like a telephone pole is affected when a car rams into it; can the pole take the shock, or is it coming down?). This is unavoidable; even if men suddenly had years worth of legal paternity leave, a committed father is still taking himself out of the loop to some degree. For some, this is just a bump in the road; for others, it can lead to serious frustration, even bitterness.

Every man has to make such decisions for himself. But there are a few clear principles here. The first is that well-known one about people on their deathbeds not wishing they'd spent more time at the office. The second is that you have to make up your mind and stick with your choices, even when things get rough. To me it's simple, though difficult: Love is more important than anything else. My family needs me, and I simply won't let my career aspirations keep me from being a happy and loving father and husband. I have my frustrations, but the compass of my heart keeps me pointed in the right direction.

A second disadvantage is the financial drain of lost salary, resulting either from a man's giving up a job (or a better job), or from not putting in the longer hours often required for promotion and higher salary. Some couples work around this; you can certainly save money on childcare. But it's no road to riches. My family continues to struggle; our "Tupperware collection," to use one small example, consists mainly of old whipped-cream and margarine tubs. Eating fast food is about as high-toned as our celebrations get. We rent; we have no savings; we worry. But we make do.

These problems arise, obviously, because your family commitments keep you from devoting all your time and energy to your job. Most men can easily imagine that kind of frustration.

But being with kids also has its own unique difficulties, which some guys seem to have no real sense of.

The biggest shock to the uninitiated, I think, is the endlessness of this job (as my brother recently learned firsthand). Even long hours at a day job can't really prepare you for being "on" *whenever* you're with your kids, or, for the stay-at-home dad, 24/7. And if you think that means time off for meals and sleep, think again. There *are* kids who sleep all night and take long naps, but there are others who almost never sleep—and even the good sleepers need less as they grow older. Besides, few kids have the moral decency to match their sleep schedule to yours. And your kids will soon teach you what mealtime really means: While they're at the table, you spend your time either serving them or watching to make sure they don't indulge in those creative disasters they're so good at. And once they finish, you're still eating, and stuck in one place so they can easily find you to present requests, demands, complaints, and passionate dessert preferences.

Almost nothing in domestic life is ever truly finished. A New Jersey stay-at-home dad says that "trying to clean with two children in the house is like trying to empty a bathtub…with a sieve." The basic rule? If your kids are awake, the house is getting dirtier by the minute. Children relentlessly seek attention, entertainment, and animal satisfaction, and this isn't something they can control. Even my teenagers don't get it when I finally turn off the vacuum and sardonically announce, OKAY, THE HOUSE IS NOW CLEAN—TIME TO GET IT DIRTY AGAIN. They just look up with blank stares like you see on zoo animals—that "Don't bother me if it isn't feeding time" expression.

And don't kid yourself that carrying around that egg-baby for a week in your high-school health class was any real preparation. Taking care of an egg, to mix metaphors, is a piece of cake. Parenting *never* stops. Family life is a kind of mindless force to which you, with your selfish need for things like sleep, peace and quiet, personal space, etc., must continuously adapt. How many times, while running around madly trying to get things done, have I found myself praying to get back some of the time I wasted in my youth, like listening over and over to all 17 minutes of Iron Butterfly's "Inna-gadda-da-vida"?

I experienced a similar feeling of endlessness when, as a six-teen-year-old, I started work at a grocery store. I was a bagger (or "courtesy clerk," as management insisted on calling us). On the first day I spent eight straight hours watching groceries come down the belt, then piling them into paper sacks. Somewhere during that eternity it occurred to me that this whole process was truly unending; people would always need food, would get hungry and come back to the store over and over, groceries would keep coming down the belts, bags would be ceaselessly filled and emptied and filled again. That night, in the refuge of dream, my teenage mind thrilled as some beautiful faceless girl began taking off her bikini top. But once it slipped from her shoulders, I saw not the treasure I expected—only groceries pouring out in endless streams, apples, bread, canned fruit, cookies, cartons of milk, as if from some horrible cornucopia.

Domestic life is, unfortunately, quite similar. A parent can't conceive of his role in terms of days, weeks, even years—he has to stretch to decades. This is the reality of family life.

And of course it gets boring. Sometimes I wonder exactly what the difference is between having small children and being under house arrest. Despite the considerable amount of work and endless attention-switching, there's also a lot of "down time"— which can get to be "bring-you-down time." And the world of kid culture is often less than reviving. I once took my sons to a Care Bears movie. As the story unfolded—fuzzy little bears oozing ditties and plotting cheerfully, among rainbows, clouds and uni-corns, against a nasty wizard—I felt my boredom reach crushing proportions. "This," I thought, "is Hell. It's like Sartre's *No Exit*. Hieronymous Bosch has nothing on these bears."

You can glimpse the inherent boredom of domestic life in what my wife and I call the "Kathy at Farrraday's" phenomenon. Long ago, in that now mythic time before we had children, we went out one night to Farraday's, a local pizza place, with my sister and some friends. My sister introduced us to Kathy and her husband; Kathy was a housewife, with two small kids at home. This meant nothing to me at the time. But Kathy's behavior certainly made an impression. She drank too much beer, talked too loudly, kept laughing and whooping it up—in fact, she couldn't seem to get enough of anything. And this was at a family pizza place where the wildest possibility was plunking a quarter into the player piano. It pains me to admit that I looked down on her a little for this; I mean, you'd think she'd never gone out before!

But Allah is merciful; if justice were automatic, He would have struck me down then and there. My karma finally rolled around years later, when I became the housewife, and went out one night with some people, so delighted to be free of my duties, so thrilled with adult company, that I drank too much, talked too much, laughed too hard and too long, like a sailor on shore leave or a prisoner after a jailbreak—acting, in fact, just like Kathy at Farraday's.

Only if you've known the hours of ticking clock, the half-coherent twists and turns of a pre-schooler's conversation, the endlessness of laundry and dusting and sandwich-making, only then can you understand why parents sometimes get a little crazy out on the town.

And the nature of the child, of course, adds to the challenges. Kids really are wild animals; I don't think Miss Manners understands them nearly as well as Charles Darwin might. Emotional instability is a natural and essential part of childhood. A good parent accepts this, but that doesn't make everything easy. For one thing, kids tend to communicate through noise and action rather than through language. A screaming child is to life at home what Old Faithful is to Yellowstone. She wants this or that; you say no. Suddenly she becomes an air raid without planes, a rock concert without melody, an invisible jack-hammer assaulting your cochlea. When she gets a good one going you're sometimes tempted to run out into the street. You know it's your job to put up with this, so you go to comfort the little car-alarm, but silence has become your drug, and you crave it with a junkie's despair. If you have more than one kid, they'll look after each other, right? Sure, occasionally—except for those times when they all scream at once, keening like lost souls, endangering your own. Or those equally priceless moments when, as your pre-schooler is shriek-ing with the force of a North Atlantic gale, your teenager blithely asks, "Dad, could you make me a sandwich?"

I'm not making that up.

If the two of them were mad cows, you could shoot them. But they're kids—and *you don't shoot kids*.

This, however, is only one of the things that can drive you nuts. At times this life takes almost insane twists. Yesterday, just as I'd picked up the full laundry basket AND the ten shirts on the multi-clothes hanger and started up the basement steps, the phone rang. *All right*, I told myself with jock-like determination, *I can do this*. So I rushed up the steps, balancing the basket on one hand and carrying the multi-hanger with the other, in a flurry of flying socks and underwear. But I had to pause at the top of the stairs; our refrigerator is so close to the basement door we have to lift the laundry basket *over* the fridge to get it out of the basement. This is usually a two-handed job, but I managed to do it with just my left. More clothes went flying, of course—and the phone rang a second time.

Still balancing the basket, I pulled the shirt-heavy multi-hang-er through the tight space and quickly hung it on the refrigerator door handle. Its weight, however, pulled the door open, and with that movement the flashlight on top of the refrigerator crashed down, bouncing off the door-shelves and into the refrigerator. *I can leave it there!* I told myself. *Surely no one would eat a flash-*

light!—and the phone rang a third time. I dropped the laundry basket, pushed the refrigerator door shut, and sprinted for the living room.

But when I picked up the phone—take a wild guess.

What kind of person calls a house where kids live and lets it ring only *three* times?! I slowly replaced the receiver and closed my eyes. *The bastards!*

(It was partly my own fault, I suppose—I'd so desperately wanted to hear another adult at the end of the line, be it telemarketer, survey-questioner, or phone evangelist. Hell, I would have settled for a robo-call.)

An experienced parent learns that you can never predict the craziness this life will bring. You just have to roll with it. Why should I get upset when my young sons have removed every book from our five-shelf book case and piled them on the living-room floor? Why should I lose patience as Shilly-Shally belts out her forty-third identical verse of "The Song That Never Ends"? And surely I'm not the only parent in America who stands picking peppercorns out of the sliced salami for my sons' bag lunches, dropping the foul things into the trash can where they belong. They feel no compunction whatever in saying, *We hate salami with peppercorns—but we like how it tastes when they've been picked out* . . .

A further problem with life at home is the way your own needs and desires are often crushed under your parenting role. Committed parents can't avoid feeling, at times, like overworked servants. This is an intrinsically thankless job. For one thing, it takes twenty years just to find out how you did! And thanklessness goes with the territory. Children just aren't capable of understanding parental behavior, and by the time they're teenagers their own developmental needs tend to overwhelm any appreciation they might feel. Parents have to more or less check their personal lives at the door. I sometimes find myself mutely crying out, in an immature yet heartfelt way, *But who'll take care of me?*

Our recent experience with the "evaporating week" is a good example of this.

On the morning of our anniversary, my wife and I sat at the breakfast table "talking calendar." It was a rather pitiful discussion; money-wise and time-wise, all we could squeeze out for this august occasion was a quick dinner-date ("Anywhere but Mac's!" my wife pleaded). What we really needed, of course, was a weekend's worth of the various blisses available in any decent Montreal hotel, just an hour north of us. But that was okay; the whole situation, in fact, struck us as funny, and we laughed. (Of course we still had all the Saturday house-cleaning to do, which wasn't quite as humorous.)

So how did we manage to be so accepting, so unselfish, when we hadn't been on a date together since Grandma Moses danced disco? Parental altruism, you ask? No. It was partly because we had no choice, and partly because we had a much-better-than-average week planned.

But then we started talking details.

My older son had agreed days earlier to babysit Tuesday night so I could go hear the Pulitzer-Prize-winning feminist journalist speak at the university (my wife had to work; ironic, eh?). But a time-check revealed the talk didn't start till 8:00 p.m. I'm Shilly-Shally's bedtime guy; she simply *won't* sleep till she's gotten two picture books, a story, and usually a lullaby out of me. If I don't get back till ten, she'll be up till at least eleven, and we'll all pay for that the next day, her most of all. Besides, I'm not comfortable with the irony of supporting feminism by disrupting my little girl's life that way.

But that was okay—my wife and I had planned to catch a jazz concert on Wednesday night, and our younger son, mirabile dictu, *volunteered* to babysit. But then we find out it's a 7:30 start (normal enough for everyone in the world except the parents of small children with sleeping problems). And I just remembered I have to give a talk to an out-of-town group on Thursday night, which

Shilly-Shally will *have* to deal with. Two late nights in a row, and their inevitable fallout, just aren't worth it.

"Hey," I say to my disappointed wife, "maybe the *boys* could go to the lecture and the jazz concert."

"Uh, Dad?" the younger says, with a charming smile (quite aware of the brownie points he'd earned by offering to babysit). "I'm broke. Could you guys . . . pay for my tickets?"

In less than five minutes, a week we'd looked forward to for some serious adult fun simply . . . evaporated. There's no other word for it.

But then that's pretty much the way it is, once that plastic stick in the home pregnancy test turns blue. Parenthood is by definition an exercise in selflessness. But even parents are only human, so it also becomes a difficult kind of balancing act. Marguerite Kelly and Elia Parson's wise words about mothers can be applied equally to committed fathers:

> "Motherhood brings as much joy as ever, but it still brings boredom, exhaustion, and sorrow too. Nothing else ever will make you as happy or as sad, as proud or as tired, for nothing is quite as hard as helping a person develop his own individuality—especially while you struggle to keep your own."

Another of the hard realities of domestic life will probably surprise some men: Being with kids is a surprisingly complex undertaking. Despite a lot of ignorance on this point, the job actually requires great skill, and experience can make a huge difference.

I learned this the hard way. When LeBron flies toward the hoop, he makes it look easy; Jimi Hendrix would fling off those amazing guitar riffs with a fluid power that seemed simple. In the same way, what *looks* uncomplicated in domestic life is usually the grace of the experienced professional.

I love this caption from a picture, in *Baby Talk* Magazine, of a father feeding an infant : "Feet and hands in motion, Maggie eagerly downs her cereal. She's a neat eater unless she can get her hands on the bowl. Then it's all over." You want the bowl as close to the mouth as possible, for obvious reasons, but that of course puts it in the danger zone. If you fail, guess what? Wipe down the highchair, mop up the floor, launder the clothes, and bathe the kid. And keep in mind—they eat more than once a day! Talk about pressure; it's worse than a potentially game-winning free throw. Another section in the same article features a mother's struggles to get her two daughters to nap at the same time; the difficulty of this task is matched only by its intense desirability from a parent's point of view. Think about it: Just how *do* you get such a thing to happen? It's possible, I suppose—but you need at least the patience and skill of a bonsai gardener to ever win any success.

Some examples will underscore the point. The following chart is my attempt to bring some order to Shilly-Shally's drinking cups. (Encyclopedic knowledge like this has always been tucked away in the already overcrowded brains of hard-working mothers.) And remember, there's more than a little at stake here. Kids love routine; they crave it, demand it, go crazy without it. Offer your charge the wrong cup at the wrong time and you'll hear about it. And if you're callous enough to insist that "it doesn't really matter," your monkey may freak on you.

CUP NAME	PREFERRED LIQUID	PLACE OF USE	STRAW USE
sippy cup	apple juice, water	universal	can't
"fishie" cup	apple juice, milk occasionally	bedtime snack or dinner	*always* causes spills, so sometimes

"walking cup"	apple juice	outdoors	sometimes
Alice in Wonderland cup	milk	bedtime snack	never
tea-set cups	apple juice	tea parties	the very idea!
ordinary cup	whatever I'm drinking, which she will then want	anywhere, anytime	Oh no! That would prevent her from back-washing!

What—don't tell me you thought *one* cup was enough!

And note well: Straws are a *very* big deal. At last count, Shilly-Shally had the following types: regular, bendy elbow, dolphin, turtle, and four kinds of crazy (a phrase which, coincidentally, describes Shilly-Shally herself). And her straw preferences can be as intense and whimsical as those for cups.

But this is nothing compared to footwear.

Raising kids is a kind of perpetual war, with battles breaking out suddenly after long periods of boredom and slogging work. But the World War III of dealing with pre-schoolers is footwear. Yesterday, for example, I gently suggested that Shilly-Shally wear her tennis shoes to school. But she insisted that her hiking boots "look Indian" and match her Pocahontas dress. The fact that the boots no longer fit was irrelevant—that is, until she couldn't get them on and started to cry and it was suddenly all my fault.

And yet there's one thing worse than these almost daily battles—and that's your usually doomed attempts to actually buy *new* footwear. If I had my way, we'd all have our kids' feet sprayed up to the ankles with some kind of heavy porous polyurethane—

hand-washable, teflon-coated, and grip-soled—that could be re-
sprayed on a yearly basis.

But there's really no way around the hell of buying shoes for
kids; it's just something you have to do.

The situation: Shilly-Shally in a shoe crisis. Her tennis shoes
are too short; she screams. Her sandals are too tight; she screams.
Her "aqua-socks" are not only losing their inner pad (the only
thing that keeps them from actually being socks) but have begun
to smell like dead things on the beach. We won't let her wear
them; she screams. She's worn her black dress shoes twice; now
they pinch her feet. She screams. We kiss that forty bucks goodbye, suppress screams.

So we go out to buy new shoes. But don't let the simplicity of
that statement fool you.

Walking into the store, we're met with a vision of footwear
paradise. There are rows and rows and rows of shoes for kids.
Our hearts brighten; surely we can find *something* in this Store of
Wonders!

But once each of the interested parties has asserted its own
demands, the actual number of possible purchases shrinks dramatically—the interested parties being, of course, myself, my
wife, and Shilly-Shally.

You might think Shilly-Shally is underrepresented in this process, or at least out-gunned by parental authority. Nothing could
be further from the truth. We have the authority, but she has the
lungs. And we're in public. Although we're the ones who usually *initiate* legislation, Shilly-Shally exercises her ear-splitting veto
quite freely. It constitutes a kind of final vote.

My wife is, naturally, the Prime Mover. But her ideas about
what to buy are fairly complex. She knows we need something
that (a) fits, and (b) Shilly-Shally's little magpie-heart will love
enough to actually wear. But my wife entertains other notions
too, dangerous ones, to my mind, about style, matching color, sea-
son-appropriateness, and the like. This complicates things enor-

mously. When our daughter's godparents sent her a tri-colored sweatsuit with matching troll-doll barrette, for example, we had to find sandals to "go with" the new outfit. The pair my wife decided on fairly bristled with straps and buckles; they looked like little strait jackets. I cringed to imagine the tearful, scream-punctuated scenes each morning as I struggled to get Shilly-Shally into these sandals-from-hell and then buckle all those tiny buckles with my thick dumb male fingers. But my wife insisted, and she had an incontestable principle on her side: The sandals *matched* the outfit. There's a federal law about it somewhere. How could I possibly object?

You may have already surmised *my* only request when it comes to children's footwear: Velcro. I feel nothing but pity for parents who lived before its invention; they were ignorant savages, and they suffered for it. Mount Rushmore should have five heads: those four political guys and the NASA hero who invented this miraculous material.

My wife's reaction to this enthusiasm for Velcro is very interesting; in fact, she's downright ambivalent, though she hates to admit that. On one hand she'll dismiss the whole topic as one more example of male laziness. And she has a point. If left to themselves, many men would live without the "finer things": no pictures on the wall, no curtains at the window, no flower beds, no holiday celebrations. My wife has helped me see how sad this actually is, and how parents must continually enrich family life with rituals, celebrations, niceties—all the special touches. I agree with her, though of course I can only take it so far. To her, my insistence on Velcro is akin to my affection for old torn sweaters or a steady diet of hamburgers and tater tots. From a certain female point of view, men *are* pretty much like dogs.

I've come to understand and appreciate her perspective on this, and I'm grateful to her for teaching me. So I try to apply the general principle in my fathering. But buying shoes for a pre-schooler is, by definition, a crisis. So I go with Velcro every chance I get—and watch with amused detachment how my wife sometimes waffles on her principles as the pressure at the shoe store builds.

Standing there in the aisles, we're hoping to get our kid a sensible, long-lasting, convenient pair of shoes with a decent fit. (We also dream of world peace and an end to the budget deficit.) Our daughter, though, takes one sweeping look, immediately fixes on the Princess Jasmine sandals, then grabs them and won't let go.

You people at Disney—what the hell's the matter with you?! Did you have to design these cheap plastic sandals, encrust them with rhinestones, and then slap HER picture on the side?! It's like a box of chocolates in the middle of a broccoli farm. Every little female in North America was currently going weak in the knees over that cartoon Madonna, parents standing pitifully behind, wringing their hands. And the sandals themselves! Somewhere under all that glitter is a pair of truly crappy shoes. They pinch, they don't stretch, the plastic rubs—have mercy on us! Do we have to start blindfolding our kids in the shoe aisle like we do in the cereal aisle at Safeway? We go to your movies, buy your videos, your t-shirts, pajamas, what not; couldn't you give us a break on the plastic sandals?

It takes ten minutes to talk Shilly-Shally out of the sandals—and we have to muster all the pre-school reasoning we're capable of. But those ten minutes take their toll. Shilly-Shally's emotional resilience, never that strong to begin with, is wavering. She looks like she's about to use her veto . . . !

But suddenly my wife spies a pair of white loafer-type sneakers. No snaps, buckles, laces, buttons, or deadbolts. The slip-on kind! Can it really be true? Yes! They fit! And the kid wants them!

We take them home—she still loves them! That is, for twenty-four hours. The next day she decides they don't fit and she hates them. She screams. And we have to face facts: If a kid doesn't like the shoes she won't wear them. So we drag ourselves back to the mall (stopping on the way to buy rum and coke for the aftermath).

"I've learned my lesson," my wife declares. "We just can't buy cheap shoes. That's why they don't fit." (Forgive us, oh mighty American Economy, for our reluctance to drop $40 or $50 on a pair of shoes this weed will grow out of in two months.)

At the pricier store we find a pair of sandals. Velcro straps—I'm satisfied. Big black bulky things like the kind Mexican farmers wear—but my wife is now well past aesthetics. We start in on the big sell. "Oh, honey—what beautiful shoes! They look *cool!*" (a word our daughter's recently begun using, though God only knows how she defines it). "I bet you could run like the wind in those! Hey! They're the same kind Alex has" (the little boy next door). "He got them last week, remember?! And they'll match all your dresses . . . " (Black goes with everything, right?).

Looking tentative, Shilly-Shally stands in the sandals, peers in the little foot-mirror, then, saints be praised, begins to jump kangaroo-style.

"How much are they?" I whisper anxiously to my wife.

"I don't care if it's seventy bucks!" she hisses.

When we get home the three of us rush in, all excited to tell the brothers. Then of course we invite in the neighbors, slaughter the fatted calf, set out food and drink, hire musicians. The war is over.

So I decide not to say anything when I notice how the soles of Alex's sandals—the little boy next door, remember?—are beginning to flap apart and obviously won't last the month.

There's plenty to get you down in life with kids; it would be naively dangerous to think otherwise. I wish I could say I've never lost my temper, wallowed in self-pity, snapped at people, etc. I've done all this and more, have acted just as childishly as my child does. You probably will too, if you haven't already. We all fail as parents from time to time. And what we hate most about such failures, I think, is simply having to face the fact that we're capable of such things. But that, as Stuart Smalley says, is all right.

In fact, it's more than all right; such lapses are an essential and natural part of the overall process. They remind our kids that we're just as human as they are, that no one is free from error, that adults too have limits. And children, whose lives are shaped by adult power, very much need to be reminded of such things. Besides, our mistakes with our kids, if they're not truly damaging, help us to maintain our compassion and empathy for the struggles of childhood, inspiring us, through a certain amount of shame, to do better. And we do.

All the problems I've mentioned so far can in fact be overcome by hard work, loving patience, a willingness to learn, and an active sense of humor.

Not everything, though, can be attacked so frontally.

The hardest thing of all, at least for us, is what my wife and I refer to as "the siren call"—which at times has seemed almost capable of destroying us.

An adult home with kids can get to feeling very strange, almost unnatural (which is odd when you consider how profoundly natural parenting is, with all the force of evolution behind it). But there are times, as I've said, when your house feels like a prison. You get lonely; your brain begins to go soft; you feel so out of it! The neighborhood streets are empty except for occasional children, very old people, cats and squirrels. Sometimes it's as if you've been marooned. From time to time I'll glance out the living-room windows and happen to see some adult walking down the street—and suddenly feel strong unbidden emotions rushing through me. *I should be out there,* an inner voice says, *out in the world. That should be me.*

For a moment then I can't shake off the passions I usually manage to keep quiet: pride, ambition, my love of physical activity, my career, even the echoes of my male upbringing with its emphasis on action, reward, and respect—and I look at myself and my life with something like disgust. *What am I doing here?* I wail silently to myself; *I've turned into a goddamn housekeeper!*

But even this isn't the truly difficult moment. For one thing, I recognize such outbursts for exactly what they are: frustration, selfishness, impatience, all the shallower emotions growing restless beneath the primacy of love, which rightly holds sway over them. As quick and hot as such feelings burn, they pass away—because I know what my presence in this house means to my children, to laying the foundations of their lives. But my sudden vehement protest leads me, sooner or later, to the other moment, the truly difficult one—difficult because it's not mere indignation but a profound call, a power trying to seduce me not with weak and childish selfishness but with the deeper reality of myself and the world.

Just as the sirens called Odysseus when his ship sailed past their rocky islet, the world itself suddenly sings to me with over-powering sweetness, right in my ear, as if a divine temptress standing next to me. I'm bending over the wash machine in our little basement, lifting soggy laundry out, when I suddenly pic-ture Mt. Kilimanjaro above the savannah, clouds sweeping from its dark summit, just as we saw it that long-ago afternoon—and then see stilt houses over shining mud at twilight, a fishing vil-lage on the South China Sea—and then Paris, the Pont Neuf and the Orangerie—all places I've been, in a life we had to give up, at least for a time. Then I imagine myself with a real office of my own (we don't have the room just now), with hours and hours before me for the thrilling labor of writing or music, the life of art I crave—and then with even greater suddenness the Call itself comes, searing through me like a summons from some Rilkean angel. For a moment I feel an indescribable pang. To be stuck here like a janitor or cleaning woman, in this basement with its half-dirt floor, in this little house, this little town, day after day, when I should be out in the world living my life to its uttermost! . . .

I hang my head for a moment. Then I notice water from the wet clothes dripping onto my tennis shoes. So I push the sodden load into the dryer, take a deep breath, feel my heart begin to slow.

Not yet, I whisper to myself. *Not yet. Love is more important.*

CHAPTER FIVE

Your New Stress Chart

A CERTAIN AMOUNT OF STRESS, of course, is inseparable from life as we know it. But the man spending time at home with kids will find his stress patterns have changed significantly.

One night, in an attempt to help my exhausted wife get some rest, I slept on a futon in the den so I could get up with Shilly-Shally, who was still a terrible sleeper. Things had been crazy, so I got to bed way too late. But Shilly-Shally had been playing earlier with the fold-up lamp/digital clock we keep in the living room—dear little gadget—and had somehow managed to set the alarm for two in the morning. When that hideous beeping began I sat bolt upright, emerging violently from the deepest possible alpha state without the slightest idea where I was. Groping for the alarm beside my bed, I slowly realized I wasn't even in my bedroom. So, fighting disorientation as if all the fogs of Newfoundland, I stumbled through the darkness over toys and furniture till I reached the little shrieking object on the book case—but then had to figure out how to open it and unfold the lamp part, so I could turn it on so I could find the alarm so I could turn it off.

The next night the same thing happened again.

I offer this little experience as an example of the unforeseeable stresses life with kids inevitably presents. The following chart, in turn, may alert you to the variety of stress you'll be facing.

STRESS CHART FOR MEN AT HOME

(0 points represents no stress at all; 100 points signifies complete mental and physical breakdown.)

Forget it. *Nothing* in your life happens at this low a stress level.	10 points and below
You wake up, realize it's morning	10 points
Your eight-year-old cuts his own hair	15 points
Your eight-year-old cuts his own hair; neighbor kid tells him it looks cool	17 points
Your fifteen-year-old cuts his own hair—all of it	19 points
You serve ramen noodles for lunch; your three-year-old makes noodle necklace	20 points
Your three-year-old wants to learn how to play "Monopoly"	23 points

You have company for dinner	24 points
You have company for dinner and your child spills crackers	26 points
You have company for dinner and your child spills milk and applesauce	28 points
You have company for dinner and your child spills milk and applesauce on your company	30 points
Your child's favorite picture book is *Everyone Poops*	33 points
Your three-year-old loudly disagrees with you	34 points
Your three-year-old loudly disagrees with you at the mall	36 points
Your three-year-old loudly disagrees with you during sermon on "Harmonious Family Living"	39 points
Your child is painfully shy	40 points
Your child is not shy at all	43 points
Toast in DVD player; rented DVD in toilet	44 points
Oatmeal in toaster	45 points
Oatmeal in toaster overnight; small fire in the morning	47 points
Younger teenage son gets in fight with three-year-old	48 points
Older teenage son gets in fight with younger teenage son	49 points
Three-year-old beating on both sons	50 points

You accompany child to toy store	52 points
You accompany bull to china shop	53 points
You accompany child to china shop	55 points
Your kids play Spider Man in china shop	57 points
You experience a minor illness	58 points
You experience a major illness	63 points
Your kid wakes up feeling grumpy	65 points
Trying to show child how to eat liver, you actually *taste* some	67 points
You're a childless couple and you move to Baghdad	70 points
You're a couple with children and you move down the block	75 points
While intoxicated, you agree to take kids to video arcade the next day. You forget; they remember	78 points
You promise three-year-old you'll watch a video with her; she chooses *David the Gnome*	80 points
You promise three-year-old you'll watch a video with her; she chooses *Barney*	83 points
Three-year-old has doctor's appointment	84 points
Three-year-old has doctor's appointment and must get a shot	87 points
Three-year-old must get a shot but nurses are all out of *Finding Nemo* band-aids	89 points

Every member of family gets flu	90 points
Every member of family gets flu and throws up	91 points
Every member of family gets flu and someone throws up in dishwasher	93 points
You can't afford a mini-van	94 points
Divorce	95 points
Divorce and you get kids	97 points
Death of spouse	98 points
Death of spouse but you don't notice because it's car-pool day	99 points
DVD player won't work	100 points

CHAPTER SIX

Lost Children

"The best way to make children good is to
make them happy."
—Oscar Wilde

SHILLY-SHALLY PLAYS A GAME with me that reveals, I think, some of the deepest fears and desires children know.

We call the game "Koe-chai" or "King and Koe-chai." You could say she invented it since it was all her idea, but in fact it just seemed to well up within her. We played our most recent version when my mom, having come to visit over Thanksgiving, took us all out to eat on the evening of the big day. (Not having to do dishes certainly put me in the spirit of thankfulness.) Naturally, Shilly-Shally talked more loudly, fidgeted more energetically, complained more bitterly, shaped her food more creatively, commented on other diners more pointedly, and finished far earlier than any child in the history of restaurants. So, as usual, I ate fast and took my restive three-year-old outside while everyone else finished their rather expensive meals. Standing on the sidewalk under the restaurant awning, day slowly dying around us, she started up the game.

"You be a king," she told me, shivering a bit in the late-November air, "and I'm a little girl who's lost, and you find me."

With that she sat on the step and put on the forlorn look she sometimes gets: eyes big with sadness, head bowed slightly, hands folded in her lap, knees and feet drawn together—the very picture of a Pitiful Pearl doll. The street was deserted. But if a casting director for *Annie* had happened by, Shilly-Shally would've won the lead on the spot. She loves to assume this expression as she acts out her endless versions of what you might call "Comfort-the-poor-little-weeping-one."

I walked off a few steps and then came back along the sidewalk, strutting like that stumpy mustachioed guy in the tux on the Monopoly cards. Suddenly I stopped in pretend surprise. "Little girl!" I gasped, with deep sympathy and kindest eyes. "Why are you out on this cold night all alone?" I knew my part, you see, and had begun to pay attention to what she was so passionately but wordlessly saying.

"Well," she answered quietly, looking up so I'd be sure to get the full effect of her sorrowing fawn-eyes, "my mother left me forever and I'm all alone."

(When I told my wife about this later, she winced. It's very difficult for her to leave Shilly-Shally every day. And though she understands the Electra complex—the tendency of daughters to bond more readily with their fathers—that knowledge doesn't bring her much comfort.)

Then Shilly-Shally looked down sadly at the sidewalk, quiet and utterly still, just waiting, a behavior so unusual I wondered if she'd gotten some bad turkey and felt sick to her stomach. But that wasn't it, of course. The drama had captured her completely; for the moment, she really was the winter orphan.

And here I realized in full what was actually going on. Sometimes we don't listen to our children simply because we're in that habitual fog of thinking about other things, or even the habitual fog of thinking about the practical things we have to do for them at the moment.

If you're open to it, spending time with a young child is profound, engaging, and fulfilling. But it's not adult brain-food. I'd been thinking about my work, about the grown-up conversation I was missing back in the restaurant, about how to keep warm in the cold of deepening twilight. And I was gauging just how I could entertain my charge with the minimum amount of mental and physical effort on my part—a state of mind which, I hate to admit, I slip into far too often. The words *left me forever and I'm all alone* cut through my fog like a bright light. In that instant I realized she was speaking to me straight from her little heart, calling out from her depths, whether she knew it or not.

When they're given some theatrical or representative way to express themselves, children are remarkably open to their own deepest feelings. Puppets or other character toys, stories, games, and, in this case, dramatic play—all of these can bring out the most heartfelt emotions and concerns. Shilly-Shally knew instinctively that she had to reach past her ordinary self for this important bit of playing. So she became the Lost Girl, and by doing so opened up a world of fantasy from which to look at the real one in which she must live.

It may be objected here that so young a child doesn't really understand the loss of parents or being orphaned, particularly if she's never been separated from her mother and father. And it's true that Shilly-Shally still has a hard time grasping what "preschool starts again in two weeks" really means; a concept like "forever" is completely over her head. But children don't have to understand abstractions in order to feel anxious about separation from parents. In our experience, a child's first strong reaction to learning about death takes the form of an overwhelming fear of that separation. And even a three-year-old has already learned the hard lesson that bad things can actually happen. Perhaps in overhearing some of her parents' arguments and frustrations Shilly-Shally has even glimpsed the meaning of "divorce," that frightful reality shadowing American childhood today. I certainly worry about the general effects of divorce, and I know something further about it: When a family falls apart completely, a spouse leaves a spouse—but a parent abandons a child.

How often are children actually abandoned? Infanticide was, apparently, far more prevalent in the past than most of us realize; babies with deformities or abnormalities were often left to die, and sometimes simply because they were female. In other cases, famines or similar pressures led to infant abandonment as a desperate form of birth control. And sometimes children were disposed of simply because they weren't wanted. Nor were such practices restricted to "primitive" cultures; according to *The Well Baby Book,*

> "During the Middle Ages [in Christian Europe] the killing of infants—especially females—was not infrequent, especially among poor people. During hard times children were often sold into slavery or abandoned and left to die. As late as the mid-1700's in Europe . . . abandonment and infanticide were still practiced . . . "

But are we in the modern world so utterly different? Most of us can recall news stories in which infants have been found in dumpsters, public bathrooms, or the like. Besides, abandonment can take less obvious forms. Various sources report that something like 40 to 50% of marriages in the United States end in divorce, and *The National Catholic Reporter* quotes Sylvia Ann Hewlett from her *When the Bough Breaks*: "Half of all divorced fathers fail to see their children in the wake of divorce, and two-thirds fail to pay child support."

But we don't need statistics to know that many children are also suffering from another great social ill, another form of loss of parents—children whose parents are, either by necessity or choice, rarely at home, or not emotionally available for their kids even while they're in the same room with them. I think of a *New Yorker* cartoon I saw, one in which humor vies with bitter revelation: A boy has just opened a birthday present, holding a toy car as his father stands over him, hands in his pockets. The boy is grateful. "Tell your assistant," he says, "it's perfect."

And of course there are the horror stories. My local paper recently reported how a mother in Tennessee left her one- and two-year-old boys strapped in car seats for up to ten hours while she drank and played video games with friends until falling asleep, waking at 1 p.m. to find the outside temperature almost 90 degrees and her sons dead in the car. Such stories have become all too common in the national media. This parent didn't intend to abandon her children, but in effect that's what she did. And for every case of this kind that ends in tragedy, how many more occur in which children are "merely" injured or hurt and manage to survive?

How much of all this was my three-year-old aware of? None, I hope. But the suffering of so many children around us brought a poignancy to our little game. As we stood on the sidewalk, a icy gust suddenly shook the windows along the street.

"My mother left me forever and I'm all alone . . . "

Now I knew what she was saying to me. Young children often speak to adults almost as dreams do, indirectly, through image, suggestion and symbol. Sometimes when Shilly-Shally and I play this same game, she uses a slightly different version, saying "My mother went to Florida and left me all alone." But what strikes my adult sensibilities as humorous is still deeply serious to her. Standing there on the sidewalk I reminded myself how it must feel for her to have to share her parents with two older brothers, and then share them with Grandma during the Thanksgiving visit. Where need is absolute, fear will always be present.

You can see this universal fear quite plainly in folktales. The best known example in Western culture is probably the Grimm Brothers' "Hansel and Gretel." It's sometimes forgotten that this story begins with impoverished parents agreeing to abandon their children deep in the forest and so "be quit of them." Other cultures have similar tales. Around the turn of the century, Knud Rasmussen collected Inuit stories in which thunder and lightning and the all-important sea-goddess Sedna each began as abandoned children who were then magically transformed into vengeful powers. For the Arctic peoples, fear of having to abandon children during the famines that often beset them, and the inevitable guilt such desperate measures created, seem to have led to the conception of the goddess on whom life depended. In other words, the abandonment of children was seen, in some way, as a crime against life itself, including the lives of individual adults and of society as a whole, just as Sedna the sea-goddess could grant or withhold the precious sea animals everyone depended on for food.

This connection between the welfare of children and the welfare of society is a reality for us too. We don't face the kinds of catastrophes that make child abandonment necessary, and yet children in our society are sometimes abandoned. And abandonment of children, in whatever form, seems to contribute directly to crime, poverty, unemployment, psychological crises, and general malaise. In spite of this, we don't seem to take the connection very seriously overall.

Edward Curtis recorded a similar story from the Gros Ventre, a Plains Indian tribe, which he calls "The Deserted Children." In this story, two children are left behind when the adults break camp, children who later acquire the ability to kill people and animals simply by looking at them. This is of course a powerful metaphor for the righteous anger abandoned children may feel, and for the guilt adults must face if they've commited such crimes. And it's echoed with uncanny similarity in Flannery O'Connor's short story "A Circle in the Fire," where three adolescent boys, traveling on their own, are looked on suspiciously and ultimately rejected by the adults they encounter. The boys then set fire to nearby woods. O'Connor presents the violence of their arson as an almost prophetic manifestation of the wrath and desperation of children abandoned in more contemporary ways.

Stories like these—just like Shilly-Shally's game—sprung up because such feelings are profound and universal in both children and adults. And such stories speak to the horrible damage wreaked both on individuals and society when the bond between child and parent breaks down, when parents betray the aching need so deep within every child.

Bringing all this to mind, I saw clearly what my character and spoken lines should be in Shilly-Shally's little psychodrama. I knew I had the opportunity to help transform her fear into the perfect story: the kind with a happy ending.

"Oh, little girl!" I said passionately, "what a terrible thing! Left you all alone?! You must come home with me. At once. Will you come home with me and be my little girl?"

She nodded bravely, still stony-faced.

"You see," I continued, "I'm a great king, and the queen my wife and I have dreamed about having a little girl. An old witch"—(here she shot me that "Make-it-a-*good*-witch!" look)— "a *good* old witch, a kindly old witch—told us that someday a little girl would come into our lives, and be ours, and we would be hers. So we have our palace all ready for her."

She looked up at me. "You made a room for her?"

"Oh yes!" I said, and described her own room to her as if she'd never seen it.

"And you made toys for her?"

"Yes, lots of toys!" I said, and described her own toys. Then I ticked off all the wonderful things she'd find in her new home:

soft bed, good food ("Do you have Wheatables for her?" she want-ed to know), shelves full of books, Disney videos. And right next door two little princes to play with.

We went on and on, cataloging her life, laying it out for her to see, reinfusing it with wonder and preciousness. And I kept say-ing that we'd waited for a little girl to love, and here she was, and we'd be her family, the queen and I and our two fine sons.

I paused for a moment. Cold winds now flapped steadily in the awning above us as night settled over the city. "So—will you come and live with us, little one?" I asked her gently.

"Yeah, sure!" she said, smiling and jumping up. "As soon as the queen's done with her turkey, and your fine sons."

I smiled down at her. "Oh, by the way, little girl," I said, "what's your name?"

"Koe-chai," she answered without hesitation, making the name up on the spot. But only the name was original; the char-acter she played was as ancient as humanity's deepest fears and fondest hopes, a presence in our oldest stories.

I took her hand and pulled her into my arms. "Oh Koe-chai!" I declared, "we'll love you forever!"

She held me as tightly as her little arms could. "Oh king!" she murmured.

CHAPTER SEVEN

Your Child

*"The interaction between an adult and a child is like a
dance. The child leads and the adult follows . . . "*
—psychologist Lem Vygotsky

*"When a child is at the age of 1-2 then that's when he
starts getting into alot of trouble.
He is learning."*
—Felicia Johnson, 9th grader

IT'S THAT RAREST OF OCCASIONS: For a time, at least,
Shilly-Shally is content to sit on our bedroom floor and play while
I work at the computer. This doesn't mean, of course, that I can
really concentrate. For one thing, she interrupts me at least every two minutes. For another, she's in one of her "opera" moods,
singing as she plays, setting her endless animal-character dia-
logues to loud and almost tuneless melody. If you've seen *Three
Amigos,* you'll understand when I say she's turned into the Singing Bush. Wearing a baby-blanket cloak and a tight red swimsuit
over her white pajamas, she belts out the following as a halting,
half-breathless chant—at about 45 decibels:

"MOTHER KANGAROO, I HAVE TO GO TO THE BATH-
ROOM!

WELL, BABY KANGAROO, WHEN YOU GOTTA GO, YOU
GOTTA GO."

My neighbors, incidentally, consider this behavior unbeliev-
ably precious and listen in rapture from their front porch when
Shilly-Shally does her recitative from ours. I, on the other hand,
find myself wondering if the young Pavarotti's father ever went
after his son with duct tape.

But at least I can do a little writing—and I couldn't find a better backdrop for this particular topic than my daughter's cater-
wauling. "Most of us have an image of what motherhood entails,"
Dr. Alvin Poussaint says, "but few of us recognize the different
models for fatherhood and their significance in the rearing of
children." Part of this general ignorance, it seems to me, is the
simple fact that many men just don't know enough about kids,
which, when you think about it, is like rams not knowing lambs.
So Shilly-Shally's endless bleating is an appropriate reminder of
the nature of the beast. My wife dreamed the other night that our
daughter had a tail, and that wasn't just coincidence.

Most guys, of course, have some vague general notion of how
kids act, or at least can recognize them on sight. *Why* kids are the
way they are is another matter. But a good parent needs to learn
how to read children, since what goes on inside a child is, ultimately, even more important than how that child behaves.

But first, a few reminders of what we're dealing with here.
Consider the following:

When our son Seth was about five, we went to Thanksgiving dinner at Grandma and Grandpa's. My wife's parents
are fairly conservative, and a number of other adult relatives were in attendance. I don't think the group appreciat-
ed the educational value of Seth's pointing to each in turn
and saying, "*He* has a penis…*she* has a vagina…*she* has a

vagina...*he* has a penis..." Afterwards, someone said to my wife, "I can't believe you taught him those words!" But I was actually kind of proud—he'd matched gender and organ perfectly right down the line.

• • • • •

My wife buys ten dresses for Shilly-Shally at the consignment store (at $50 total, a terrific deal!). Shilly-Shally's in hog heaven, changing like a traffic light. Before the afternoon's out she's worn each of the ten at least twice. For the next month she changes her dress every time she eats, naps, or goes to the bathroom—and sometimes just for fun. Think she hangs up the discards?

• • • • •

My wife and I were once out doing yardwork when our very young sons went in the house to use the bathroom. By the time we realized they were taking too long, they'd torn open a bag of Fritos, scattered half of them across the living room, and smeared bean dip all over the seat and arm of the couch. When we came in they were happily stuffing themselves with a wonderful new snack: couch-dipped corn chips.

And these, of course, aren't the half of it.

The first thing, though, is to think about kids in a general way. I don't mean that you have to formally study child psychology. But your basic assumptions about the nature of children will profoundly influence how you treat them, whether you're aware of it or not. If you begin to learn what makes kids tick—and if you come to believe that every child is unique and precious—you'll definitely be on your way to becoming a good father.

I think there are five qualities all children share, essential characteristics that parents need to keep constantly in mind.

The first is that, despite initial impressions, kids are *not* simple. Many people don't realize just how *complicated* these half-crazed creatures really are. Science, in fact, is only now discovering how much really goes on in those little hearts and minds. Research shows that infants prefer complicated visual patterns to simpler ones, recognize their parents' voices, are beginning language-acquisition behaviors, and "are pre-wired to make friends with any adult who cares for them." Kornei Chukovsky's wonderful book *From Two to Five* focuses on the profound language abilities ordinary children demonstrate. A two-and-a-half-year-old, he tells us, called out on first seeing a steamship, "Mommie, Mommie, the locomotive is taking a bath!" A young boy, naked, described himself as "barefoot all over!" Another said, "I sing so much that the room gets big, beautiful . . . "

Children, we've learned, are also deep thinkers. The philosopher Gareth Matthews recounts a talk he had with his four-year-old daughter. When she asked how their cat got fleas, he said the fleas came from another cat; her immediate question was how that cat got fleas. He answered, "From another cat," etc.—till finally the child protested, "But Daddy . . . it can't go on and on like that forever; the only thing that goes on and on like that forever is numbers!" (This is a simplified form of Aristotle's famous "Prime Mover" argument for the existence of God. Not bad for a four-year-old.)

But is there any practical value in knowing how complex kids can be? Yes, of course, every day. Last week I had to run into the dining room to stop a loud altercation between Shilly-Shally and our older son. After hearing heated accusations from both sides, I felt sure Shilly-Shally was to blame. She'd been sitting on the floor, her brother said, smashing a pea into the carpet. When he told her to stop, she wouldn't. Case closed.

But a little more investigation turned up new facts. It seems that during pre-school that day, Shilly-Shally's teacher had told them the story of "The Princess and the Pea." Remember? In which only a true princess can feel a pea through a tower of mattresses? To make the story memorable, the teacher had placed a pea on the floor and then let the children lay their hands on it, each on top of the others', to represent the mattresses.

Shilly-Shally was not only innocent; in fact, my true princess had been independently investigating something she learned in school—which, of course, is even more brain-strengthening than assigned homework! The wise teacher had used a dry pea; I, on the other hand, now had a patch of green slime driven deep into the pile of my dining-room rug. I sighed and went after the cleanser. But if I hadn't suspected there was more to my daughter's behavior than met the eye, I would have treated her unfairly—when she actually deserved praise for pursuing "independent learning." (We did have a brief but direct talk about peas and carpets.)

I pause above the computer keys, my head pounding. For the moment Shilly-Shally's tired of singing, but she's still feeling musical. So she's gotten out the pair of tap shoes her mother bought her at a garage sale, three sizes too large, and is now clattering out a jackhammer rhythm on our wooden floor. (You'd imagine such behaviors would make her mother think twice about buying this kind of thing, no matter how great a deal it was.) When I ask if she can dance just a bit more quietly, she gives me that stricken look, the one that says, *But, Daddy—don't you like my dancing?!* What better point, I tell myself, at which to discuss a second quality all children share: vulnerability.

Yes, kids are vulnerable. But not in a simple way. Consider, for example, the moral nature of the average child. The English philosopher John Locke believed children are filled with "native depravity"; the French philosopher Rousseau believed they have "innate nobility." Every parent witnesses both kinds of behavior, of course. So are children, by nature, precious angels or selfish monsters?

They're certainly capable of some pretty crappy behavior. Last Christmas we went to a party at our department-head's house; once Shilly-Shally had finished her punch and cookies and wasn't being entertained, she decided she didn't want to be there. My wife and I took turns talking to and pacifying her, but it was only a matter of time. On the front porch, the boss's wife bent down to say a sweet goodnight to our sulking four-year-old: "Thank you for coming! I hope Santa Claus is good to you!" Shilly-Shally looked her square in the eye and gave her a Bronx cheer.

On another but equally memorable occasion we were in a Japanese restaurant in Manhattan. My impatient daughter wanted me to separate her wooden chopsticks; when I did, she got mad ("They're *broken!*"). To vent her displeasure, she then snapped one of them in half; part of it went flipping off through the air and dropped onto a Japanese woman dining peacefully at the next table. It landed on her head; you could see she'd felt something, but not enough to reach up and search for it. So I had to go over, bowing like one of those little dinosaur-looking oil wells, and pluck the offending object out of the hair of a total stranger.

I mention these things because some childless people seem to have a naive view of children in this regard. They're not always little sweethearts. But I don't conclude from such incidents that kids are fundamentally selfish or mean—far from it. Shilly-Shally is constantly performing spontaneous acts of goodness and love, just as her brothers did (and still do). And in both of the cases above, she responded well to the consequences we meted out for her negative actions, and learned from them. The natural behavior of children, in short, is mixed.

Besides, so much of what we consider "misbehavior" is more or less just kids being kids. A little girl, for example, will want to wear her mother's shoes, just like on those cute commercials. But the cute commercials don't show you all the ramifications of this particular phenomenon. For a time, Shilly-Shally was in and out of her mother's closet all day long, strewing shoes around the house till it looked like there'd been an explosion at Famous Footwear. I'd find pumps behind the couch with stuffed animals sleeping in them, sensible heels propped up as lean-to's for her Star Wars figures, deck shoes and sandals buried in her toy bin. Every day I struggled to get all of my dear Imelda's borrowed shoes back into the closet by dinner time, feeling like a cowpoke chasing strays. By the time I'd get up to our room with my arms full, though, Shilly-Shally had usually disassembled the wire shoe racks themselves. Seriously.

So was she "being naughty?" Hardly. Shilly-Shally, in fact, worked her little rear off with all those shoes, at the very serious job of playing (which in our house has always been considered a kid's "job"). Children learn by doing, and much of what they do they're driven to do. Chukovsky writes about a child who, scolded for fighting, replied, "Oh, Mommie, what can I do when the fight just crawls out of me!" (Hell, I've used that excuse myself.)

So, are kids naturally bad or naturally good? Neither. Although children are instinctively "innocent," they're also instinctively self-centered. In order to characterize their moral natures, we have to look deeper. A child's feelings and needs are complicated, as is the world of social behavior itself (which, come to think of it, is exactly how things stand for adults too). In a word, kids aren't so much good or bad as they are vulnerable. And furthermore, they naturally *want* to be good (though they're not as naturally attuned to the work being good usually entails).

I don't mean to suggest that all children are fragile flowers; their inner strength can be quite surprising. What I know from experience, though, is that children have enormous capacity for good—as well as for being hurt.

When my older son was eight or nine he became fascinated with the King Arthur stories, learning more and more about the characters and incidents of the great cycle. One day I thoughtlessly mentioned something about Lancelot's rescue of Guinevere, and when he gave me a puzzled look suddenly realized—such moments always come too suddenly—that there was a great gap in his knowledge. "Lancelot fought—*Arthur*, Dad?" He had trouble even saying the words.

"Yes," I said quietly, knowing honesty was probably best.

"But *why*?!"

"Because Lancelot . . . and Guinevere . . . " (I struggled for the softest phrase) " . . . had an affair."

His eyes filled with tears, and I could see that life, in the person of his own father, had just handed him his first heartbreak.

His was a somewhat unusual reaction, of course; this is the same boy who, at age four, burst into tears when he saw a crucifix. But in his intensity and sensitivity he wasn't fundamentally different from any other child, only different by degree. Shilly-Shally doesn't seem to have an excess of this kind of sensitivity, is in fact the pirate to his prelate, a confident, hard-running, and often monarchial child. Still, it's in her, just as it's in every kid. The second-grade girl next door gave Shilly-Shally two bridal-veil blossoms for "hiding good" when they played hide-and-seek. My daughter displayed these flowers proudly in a vase on the dining room table, and for three days kept telling us how she'd won them. Such praise meant the world to her—precisely because, in her intense natural longing to love herself and be loved by others, she's utterly vulnerable. When she accidentally dropped a neighbor's little dog and it had to be taken to the vet's, she wept inconsolably, in an anguish beyond words, shutting herself in her room; my wife and I were horrified to think how such a trauma might affect her at such a young age. (Fortunately, despite its initial convulsions, the dog was fine, and eventually Shilly-Shally was too.)

Children are vulnerable—which means that the first thing they should learn is the language of love and affection. And such "instruction" should never end. But parents sometimes ignore this reality, or overlook it, or simply under-appreciate it. I was very moved by an article in the *New York Times* about a summer camp for children located in the Adirondacks. I'm certainly not condemning summer camps; under the right conditions, they're profoundly enriching experiences for kids, and they can be huge fun. But much of what I read in the article troubled me deeply.

This particular camp runs eight-week programs for six-through eleven-year-olds. The article focused on that weekend halfway through when parents come to visit, "a particularly delicate moment" after which the campers "must be wrenched from [their parents] again." Before their parents arrive, the kids are revved-up, to say the least, even chanting "Mommy! Daddy!" at their evening meal. After the visitation weekend, "[s]everal girls just could not separate from their parents one more time and decided to return home . . . " One girl, who'd suffered from "profound homesickness" at first, was doing wonderfully at the camp, but once her parents arrived she wept endlessly and then left with them.

The reporter emphasized that, although most of the kids cried when their parents left, most then "walked calmly back to their bunks"; some, however, had a harder time. A nine-year-old "shrieked as counselors tried to separate" her from her mother; the family was swept into the gym so as not to "upset the other children." Later "the mother emerged sobbing, and left . . . [T]he child . . . was flailing in [the head counselor's] arms. It took a couple of hours, including dinner and, especially, candy, to quiet her completely." In fact, the article says, "candy worked for everyone," quoting another nine-year-old who cried profusely but came round once she was "energized by sugar."

So it's just summer camp, just part of growing up, right? I don't think so. Six-year-olds going two months without their mothers and fathers? Intense homesickness and weeping? Candy as a palliative? Adults forcibly separating children from their parents? For every child who returned home that weekend, how many stayed by simply numbing themselves because of the rewards they got for staying, or because their parents insisted, or because they were afraid to look like "babies"?

Get used to it, kid.

A few of the girls in camp, most likely the older ones, had no problems at all separating from their parents; of the many who did, most were able to adapt to the circumstances. But even with their wonderful adaptability, the deeper reality of children is that they can be profoundly hurt. And one of the tragedies that can befall them comes when we adults, through abuse, neglect, or even just "going with the flow," teach them too early to adapt to circumstances that really aren't healthy.

For good or ill, a parent is the sun in the sky of a child's life. I love the story I read about Michael Finnegan, administration counsel for former governor George Pataki of New York, who gave up his job after five years of such extended hours that, as a reporter says, "his three children [gave] him none too subtle hints that it was time to spend more time at home." As Finnegan himself explains, "My son, the youngest, the 5-year-old, during the whole budget business refused to change his clothes. When I finally got home, he was in his 13th day of wearing the same pair of shorts." Can't get much more forthright than that. Along similar lines, Dr. Alan Sroufe points out that children with attachment problems reveal the depth of their parent-need even when their parents misinterpret it:

> Parents often think these . . . kids don't love them. They think the kid's rejecting them. The mothers . . . think, he doesn't like me, he's just ornery, and so forth. Are you kidding? He doesn't like you? You are the center of the universe!

And whatever our parents have been to us, of course, we carry all our lives. How astounding it is that even in old age, when our own parents are dead, we find ourselves still acting out this central relationship!

A third crucial fact about children sounds obvious but has enormous importance: They're "developing."

We all realize kids grow fast, and amazed parents are forever comparing notes on this. But we don't always realize just how *much* growing goes on, mentally and physically, and how this developmental reality affects the child's behavior. Dr. Warren Bentzen points out that parents regularly punish children for behaviors that are natural rather than immoral or selfish. He recounts the story of a father who, when his infant son grabbed his shirt, tore the child's hand away and yelled at him. The baby, of course, was simply exploring through its natural "grasp reflex." As Gretchen McCord of Cornell points out, "children learn best through action . . . by acting upon their world at their own pace."

A classic example of such ignorance is when parents get into a power struggle with a toddler reaching for things on the coffee table. "Don't touch that plant!" the father will shout; "Leave the magazines alone!" the mother warns. Time and again my wife and I have seen children spanked or hit for doing what to them is the most natural thing in the world: exploring by using their hands. This natural behavior is then used as justification for striking the child—after all, "He has to learn." But why not just put the plants and magazines out of reach till the kid's old enough to actually understand what we're asking of him?

And there are plenty of unrealistic demands placed on older children too. Kids should be held to a high standard; that's good for them. Challenge encourages growth. But "high standards" are useless or even worse unless they're appropriate. And since it isn't always easy to tell what's appropriate for a particular child, you have to stay attentive to your kid's reactions. One day our younger son, four at the time, brought home a sheaf of his pre-school papers. One of his drawings stopped me cold. We'd recently moved, he'd just started pre-school, and he'd been very difficult for the previous few months, crying more than usual, even throwing fits. His drawing showed a human figure, with those elongated, balloon-like limbs pre-schoolers sometimes draw. But within the arms, legs, torso and head, he'd written the word "NO" over and over in his childish print. The figure was virtually bursting with NO's.

My wife and I immediately talked about it. One thing was painfully clear: We were pushing him harder than he could bear. So we put a new management plan into action: We cut way back on saying "no," went out of our way to be positive with him, showed more patience when he was upset, showered him with love and attention. Within a month he came home with another picture. Amazingly enough, this time the figure was filled with NO's on one side, YES's on the other.

He'd learned something about the balance of freedom and responsibility, and his behavior had changed; the crying and the fits were over. But this progress had come only after *we'd* accepted where he was and what he was feeling, only after we'd assured him through love and understanding.

As a parent you can only help a kid move on in life by helping her master the stage she's currently in. Forcing kids to eat certain foods, for example, is of little value. Chinese Taoists divide everything that exists into Yin and Yang. For much of childhood, every kid has a similar philosophy but with alternative categories: Yum and Yuck. You're determined your monkey will finish that Santa Fe squash casserole you slaved over? Back off. Let her get more practice dealing with Yum and Yuck before you start pressing her to become a gourmet.

And sometimes we simply forget how much there is for children to learn. "Over-learning," for example, is one way young children handle all the information they need to digest. One day when I saw Shilly-Shally heading straight for a big splotch of bird-droppings in our driveway, I stopped her and talked to her about it: told her how to watch out for bird-droppings, how not to step in them, etc.—very technical. (It was a practical necessity, of course, since to kids younger than five or six, ALL goop-like substances are toys provided gratis by Mother Nature.)

Our discussion also meant, however, that for the next three months, every time we walked somewhere, she would solemnly and in great detail lecture *me* about not stepping in bird doo. "We don't step in the bird doo do we Dad that bird doo is YUCK I don't want to step in that yucky bird doo see that bird doo there Daddy? [Pause for breath]. We don't want to step in that bird doo . . ."

And about half the time she actually avoids stepping in it.

The point, though, is that this is what it takes for her to truly internalize new knowledge. And there's a lot she needs to know.

Accepting your child's developmental reality inevitably means more work for you. But being patient with children is central to parenting. Still, things can get a little nutsy. One day Shilly-Shally came running and asked if I'd buckle her sandals so she could go out to play. These sandals (purchased by her mother in some mood of vengeance against me) feature straps with tiny holes through which you must push little metal posts about as thick as sewing needles. So I'm hunched at Shilly-Shally's feet (like a worshipper kowtowing to a goddess, appropriately enough), trying to push those damn little posts into the tiny leather eyelets. But she's in a hurry and is being, as her mother likes to say, "more than wiggly." I calmly ask her to hold still, pointing out that her sandals aren't fully buckled yet. But she shouts that they are, pushes me away, gets up and runs off. The screen door slams.

Within seconds it slams again and she's back in the house, crying piteously and flapping at the feet like an eighteen-wheeler that's just blown a couple of retreads. She sticks one foot out in front of me and says accusingly—using my own words, mind you—"The strap isn't buckled all the way!"

We certainly did "discuss" the pushing and her impolite tone of voice—she knew better. But her inability to accept her own mistake, and her happy-animal impatience to go out and play, and her frustration (unspoken) at having to rely on me for something as basic as buckling her shoes—these were *not* appropriate topics for discipline. The whole incident, in fact, was a learning experience for her, in which actual circumstances were pushing her in the right direction—motivating her, for example, to learn how to buckle her own sandals—and even, perhaps, to listen to her old man when he says things she doesn't want to hear. Emotional control was another growth area here; I could see her, in Lorena Monda's words, "practicing emotion, just as she had practiced crawling, walking, and making her first sounds." And every child's natural "point of reference," as Gretchen McCord reminds us, "is intensely personal and . . . egocentric."

Surely a mature adult can keep his cool while a kid is doing such important work (at least most of the time). Surely a loving parent can provide guidance when necessary, lay down the law if need be, but also give the kid plenty of room to grow. Our children desperately need our help; as McCord so simply and powerfully puts it, " . . . their struggle is real." But maybe poet Eve Merriam sums it up best: "It takes a lot of slow to grow."

I pause in my writing as Shilly-Shally starts belting out "Happy Birthday"—to herself, of course—and find myself thinking about another essential quality of all children, one that's not always mentioned in child-care books: They can be downright mysterious! I suppose it's because human beings are so intricate, and because each kid is unique, and because sometimes there's just no accounting for personality. But one thing's certain: When it comes to kids, labels and generalizations may at times be helpful, but they'll only go so far.

Why did my three-year-old son love to take his clothes off in the backyard and stand with his hands on his hips urinating in great golden arcs beneath the summer sun? Why did my other son, at age seven, start wearing the same black sweatshirt to school every day, pulling the hood up and tightening the draw-string so he looked like a disgruntled little monk? Why did my daughter, as a three-year-old, give me the evil eye when she saw me in her room one day, then drag her potty thirty yards out into the crowded dining room for "privacy" while she used it? Why did my younger son boast about becoming world dictator and destroying the solar system by sending nuclear missiles into the sun? And why, for God's sake, did he eat his sandwiches by chewing a big path straight down the middle, leaving a piece of sandwich in either hand?

Who knows?

On the floor next to me, Shilly-Shally is now singing an old Doc Watson song, the only two lines she knows, as if nothing in the world could make her happier:

> *Muskrat, oh muskrat,*
> *what makes you smell so bad?...*

—which constitutes a perfect introduction to my final point about kids: that they're deeply, instinctively, endlessly, naturally joyous.

Adults often forget—or don't want to remember—that children are still wild. We surround them with civilization and domesticity, we coach them and prod them to follow the rules. And learning to control their animal impulses certainly is a crucial part of their destinies. But they're still animals. In my house we see a constant little reminder of this; we call it the Migration.

Shilly-Shally loves stuffed animals and has a whole zoo's worth, many inherited from her older brothers (who are now beginning to think of cuddling in somewhat different terms). She must have fifty or more—and we just don't have space in her bedroom to leave them all out. So we stuff as many as possible into a big tea-chest next to her bed, imposing adult order on the menagerie. But she keeps opening the chest and pulling them out, one by one, whatever penguin, panda or clicky-hoofed horse that, at the moment, she can't live without. She hauls a new one down-stairs almost every day, smothers it with love and affection, then drops it somewhere—usually within ten minutes and usually on its head. Of course she instantly forgets all about it. That is, unless I try to put it back in the tea chest, which invariably sends her into acute separation anxiety. Ultimately she allows me to put the dear creature no farther away than the basket in her little play-closet off the dining room. This basket, of course, is soon overflowing, as, day by day, animals trek from their summer pastures in her bedroom down to the living room and dining room where every-one can trip over them.

So when she's not looking I'll sneak an armload of stuffed an-imals upstairs and pack them away. But in a day, or a week, their journey begins again. Like the caribou of northern Canada or the wildebeest of the Serengetti, the sweeping herds go their rounds—and it's an Animal, a dear Animal, who orchestrates this endless migration, who identifies so deeply with lions, parrots, dolphins, and bears that she can't stand to be separated from them.

And just when I'm ready to make some rule about *leaving the animals in the tea-chest*, I'll see the rapture on her face as she hugs her kangaroo, or Guilty Dog, or rocks Hilda Hippo—and I'm abashed. Suddenly *she's* the authority and I'm the student, learning again about animal joy and how to give myself to the chaos of love. At times like these I realize that my parental task is analogous to mopping a dance floor.

The essential joyousness of children takes other forms too, which we sometimes don't recognize. For one thing, children are the most forward-looking creatures on Earth. I don't mean by this that they can make long-term plans, anticipate results, or postpone gratification—quite the opposite. Kids seem genet-ically incapable, for example, of picking up clothes or toys or closing doors, drawers, or toilet seats. No—by "forward-look-ing" I mean the way they focus so intensely and exclusively on the prospects for their own pleasure over the course of the next five minutes or so. But this seeming selfishness and greed are actually, I think, one of the most beautiful and powerful forces in the known universe.

Because children's relentless desires pretty much all come down to one thing: an unconscious but almost irrepressible drive to grow, to become, to experience and taste life. This hunger in the depths of every child isn't always compatible with the seemingly-instinctive desire of adults for order and soothing quiet. But it's this force that makes the child, and, eventually, drives the adult to make the world. And to me there's only one word for it—joy.

This great spontaneous joy, however, can be numbed or extinguished; a child can be taught to grow dull. What you must do as a parent is help her keep that fierce joy alive as she grows.

There are lots of ways to do it, but most come down to a few principles, which the following may illustrate.

Like her brothers before her, Shilly-Shally has distinct and detailed preferences for how her bedtime hour should go. "Let's play that Hannibal game," she'll say before getting into bed after stories. Hannibal is the cat in David Weisner's wonderful picture book *Hurricane*; Shilly-Shally loves to pretend she's the poor feline left out in the approaching storm but then brought in, toweled off, and tucked in before it hits. Her version is to lie the wrong way on her bed, without covers or her favorite stuffed animal, then meow piteously. "Now settle down, Hannibal," I'm supposed to say, without looking; "You're warm under your covers and you have your stuffed animal—and your pink blanket—and you're all tucked in." But another sorrowful yowl from the cat-girl alerts me that none of this is true! And her little fake shivers confirm it. "Oh, Hannibal!" I say, "this isn't right! Let's turn you around! Here's your pink blanket—your stuffed animal—let me tuck you in . . . "

It'd be easy to think of this compulsive ritual as just her "wanting things her own way." But that isn't true. The hurricane in the picture book scared her quite a bit; she talked about it for days. Children aren't stupid, and they know real fears. But they aren't all that capable of taking rational comfort. I'd told her many times that "here in upstate New York we don't get hurricanes," and I could see her trying to grasp that. But the facts hadn't helped her; after all, who needs a hurricane to be afraid when you already get plenty of good old-fashioned sky-booming thunderstorms? And to a child, what's thunder but the world bellowing its power? As H.P. Lovecraft said, fear is the oldest emotion—and children must "practice this emotion" too.

What *does* help is the nighttime sacrament we perform together, a ceremony in which she actually feels warmth, comfort, and safety. Kids are direct, concrete, present-oriented and physical; five minutes of lying in their mother's or father's arms is worth more to them than all the reassuring information on the planet.

This is at the heart of what we must give our children in order to keep their joy alive. One night when my wife and I were out on a date (an occurrence about as frequent as the return of Halley's Comet), our older son read Shilly-Shally her bedtime stories. When we got home she was still awake—and had plenty to beef about. "He read me my book sitting over *there!*" she barked, pointing to a spot about three feet from where I usually sit, her tone indicating the distaste you'd feel if someone at a dinner party drank soup straight from the tureen. When my wife asked if she could sit with Shilly-Shally, "to give Dad a break," our daughter answered, "Sure! You could . . . We could . . . No! Dad is the perfect one!"

Am I proud of this? As proud as my permanently numbed posterior will allow me to be, since I inevitably get pins and needles after about ten minutes on her bedroom floor. But I know why the ritual is important to her, and I'm deeply grateful that, by giving her such things, her mother, her brothers and I can help liberate the natural joy she was born with until it grows to support her whole life.

Maybe the most important trick is simply to keep looking at our children, really see them. There are times in our lives, unfortunately, when those we love most become invisible to us, or nearly so. A parent has to work hard against that tendency. I think I felt this most keenly when I read the following haiku by Chiyo, a Japanese woman poet of the 1700's:

> The dragonfly hunter —
> today where has he gotten to,
> I wonder . . .

On first reading, this seems a perfectly normal moment in parenting: *Now where did that kid go?* When you learn, however, that Chiyo wrote the poem after the death of her young son, its depths are revealed. How easy it is to take a child for granted, to be so caught up in adult concerns that the scurrying and chattering of the child mean no more to you than the dandelions growing out in the fields. And yet, if you were somehow to lose that child . . .

Add to this that we're often blind to our own childhoods, having abandoned such memories to the demands of the present. Children come into our lives, in part, to give us back this buried truth about ourselves. The poet Rilke speaks with great passion of the kingdom of childhood every adult possesses:

> And even if you were in some prison the walls of which let none of the sounds of the world come to your senses — would you not then still have your childhood, that precious, kingly possession, that treasure-house of memories?

I don't mean to be sentimental about this. Children can be, at times, the loudest, blindest, greediest little imps on earth; they really don't have all that much in common with the peaceful lambs of the pasture we sometimes compare them to. And for some adults, looking back to those early years is very painful, an exercise in sorrow, even in horror. But childhood *itself* is richly peaceful even in its wildness, and quiet, and slow, and charged with endless magic, a kind of Paradise within time that sets before us the profound wonder of things, the miraculousness of the world, and the power and tenderness of loving all that is.

Most children live, half-consciously, in the midst of this wonder. The irony is that it's often the child himself, with his pressing needs and demands, who keeps the adult from seeing childhood as it really is.

Adults tend to see childhood in practical terms, as a time of need, of growth, of demands on our schedules and our psyches for the benefit of the young—a time of food-fixing, shoe-tying, teaching manners, how to throw a ball, don't forget your coat, how's she doing in school? But childhood is something else too, something parents seem to glimpse only rarely.

Just after we moved here I began jogging in the mornings on a forest trail near our home. The trail has lots of little slopes, turns, and obstacles, is booby-trapped with roots and protruding rocks. Every step of the way I have to concentrate on where I put my feet. The crowded trunks and massed leafy branches keep off-trail visibility to a minimum.

But when autumn came and the leaves began to fall, I noticed something. Just beyond the thick trunks and bare branches I glimpsed an open space. In time I realized I'd discovered a hidden meadow. Completely surrounded by forest, it'd been there all along, all year, beautiful, quiet and small, almost right next to me—but I never knew. Then one day I saw how it was filled with milkweeds, how their dry pods had cracked open in the cool autumn air, the whole meadow brilliant with downy, shimmering filaments. Day after day the sun shines tenderly there on tall grasses, on dancing bits of milkweed fluff, the great trees shadow the grassy edges, dragonflies drone past, the last songbirds trill, butterflies wander. All is alive and good, calm and rich, the way it should be.

Childhood isn't just a passage to adolescence and adulthood; it's unique to itself. And the heart of childhood is a quiet and even subtler thing, easily overlooked by well-meaning adults who don't know how to empty themselves. It waits just beyond our range of sight, hidden in thick foliage, a place apart from our struggles. And we can enter it again, for a time—but only, of course, if we manage to actually see it. Which usually requires a native guide.

Well, so much for all that. At my feet, Shilly-Shally is now singing a sad but raucous kid-version of the blues. As her little voice roars out the impromptu lyric, she fixes her eyes accusingly on me:

"OH I'M SO HUNGRY I CAN'T PLAY ANY MORE, I WISH SOMEONE WOULD MAKE ME A PEANUT-BUTTER SANDWICH, BUT MY DAD JUST KEEPS WORKING . . . "

So my few moments of being a focused, meditative adult are now over, and her singing career is soon to be abandoned too, temporarily, for her even more intense eating career. As she and I walk down the stairs joking and laughing, I think about the amazing balance of chaotic noise and wondrous silence in the heart of every child—in the heart of my child, here, today, this astonishing creature wearing mismatched clothes, a dirty bandaid on her knee, ever an obnoxious song on her lips, who at the moment is giggling and imperiously listing just what I'll be making her for lunch.

But suddenly I'm inspired. Once I put the ramen on to boil, there'll be just enough time for us to dance the Hokey-Pokey once through, right there on the kitchen floor—which I mopped just yesterday.

And she *loves* the Hokey-Pokey.

CHAPTER EIGHT

Your Kid's Development: The Important Stuff

"If they don't walk and talk before they are two,
we worry, we fret, and we frown —
but from that point on it's all we can do
to make them shut up and sit down.
—Unknown

"I am 26 times a grandma. They can run you bow-legged
in their silly seasons."
—film version of Arthur Miller's *The Crucible*

THE EXPERTS TELL US INCREDIBLY IMPORTANT THINGS about how our kids grow and learn. Piaget studied the development of abstract thinking; Kohlberg analyzed moral stages; Vygotsky looked at language, thought, and learning. We hear about psychological growth, fine and large motor control, emotional strategies, identity and gender formation, etc.

A good parent cares about this information—of course. But he also wants to know when his kid will tie her shoes, butter her bread, stop pulling the cat's tail, and be able to watch *Charlie Brown's Summer Vacation* without weeping profusely when Snoopy and Woodstock are separated in the forest.

Parenting, after all, is a very *practical* undertaking—and the experts, it seems, don't always discuss the purely practical stuff. The following are generalized schedules of your child's progress in some of the areas you'll really want to know about but usually only hear about from other beleaguered parents.

FOOD:

— Adorable infant at breast. Easy for you; wife feeling "drained." She watches cable half the night while nursing, falls asleep when you're talking to her at dinner.

— First solids. Dinner and clean-up now take three hours; kid gets gas and/or allergies.

— Kid begins eating variety of foods. Spoon-feeding, you learn, is like basketball with moving basket. Your kitchen "psychedelicized" by thrown food of various colors.

— Kid begins to eat on her own; 1% in mouth, 99% on body. You and wife discuss putting tile and central drain in kitchen for hose clean-up like at zoos.

— Kid develops food preferences (Translation: Won't eat what you fixed).

— Kid now into finger foods; you begin finding half-eaten crackers and brown apple slices under couch cushions or in toy bin. Sometimes ants find them first. Worse yet, kid sometimes rediscovers these hidden treasures and, squirrel-like, consumes them.

— Sooner or later, kid stuffs some type of edible material into DVD player.

— Kid starts to like "fun foods"—pancakes with faces, neon-colored juice, wiggly stuff, etc. You enroll at local clown college for meal ideas.

— Kid fixes on about five favorite foods; eats them day after day. If favorites not available, tantrum follows.

— War breaks out over "healthy" vs. "unhealthy" foods. (This conflict only ends when child leaves house as young adult for a life of Reese's pieces, Pop Tarts, pizza and beer.)

— Kid learning to fix own food; 99% mess, 1% clean-up.

— You begin buying kid "treats" at gas stations and convenience stores—dangerous precedent that negatively impacts your checking account and earns you dirty looks from wife and dentist.

— On entering cereal aisle in grocery store, kid goes into hyperactive trance. Manufacturers continue to load as much sugar and gimmick as possible into each box; your kid passionately interested in this process. Jumps for joy on hearing Lucky Charms has added a new color of dyed marshmallow.

— To your disgust, kid develops taste for gimmick candies: gummi worms, pixie dust, circus peanuts, Pop Rocks. Worst thing is realizing you used to love all this crap too.

— Worn down by battle over nutrition, you find yourself ratio-
  nalizing that hot dogs, with their wide variety of animal parts,
  pretty much cover all the food groups.

— Kid starts school. Though probably not one of your career ambitions, for the next sixteen years you *will* be a professional
  sack-lunch maker.

B A T H R O O M :

— Adorable infant can be bathed in sink. Spits up in water—or
  worse. You develop new appreciation for antibiotic and abrasive cleansers.

— Kid in diapers. Your entire life tied to excretory rhythms of a
  small mammal.

— Kid now bathed in expensive baby-sized plastic tub. Bathtime a
  wonderful moment of sharing between parent and child—until child defecates in expensive little tub and must be whisked
  out.

— You scrub expensive little tub with steel wool in backyard;
  minimum 30 minutes.

— Kid learns to crawl, regularly visits bathroom. Telltale signs:
  toilet paper unrolled, towels pulled off racks, shower curtain
  ripped off rings, toilet brush removed from its place of shame.
  You refuse to imagine what followed that removal.

— More exploratory bathroom visits. Toilet seat falls on kid's fingers. Kid screams.

— Kid pushes down bathroom trash-can pedal, opens lid. Lid
  then falls on kid's fingers. Kid screams—but not before drag-

ging trash out and scattering it across floor. You enter bathroom. You scream.

— Kid now bathed in regular bathtub. You develop lower-back
trouble and housemaid's knee.

— Bathtime a wonderful moment of sharing between parent and
child—until child defecates in regular bathtub and must be
whisked out.

— You scrub regular tub with industrial-strength cleanser you
bought on black market from de-frocked Amway salesman.

— Potty-training. Bathroom becomes command center of a war
zone. For weeks you spend half your waking hours there. You
get to the point where words like "poo-poo" and "pee-pee"
roll right off your tongue.

— When kid actually *goes* in expensive kid-sized potty, wild celebrations ensue. You're shocked to realize how slight an excuse
you need to drink heavily.

— Kid now goes to bathroom alone. This means that when he
feels urge, he drops trou wherever he is, runs to bathroom
with pants at ankles, then must be cleaned up—and that's if
his aim was good. Your day regularly punctuated with these
wonderful moments of sharing between parent and child.

— Kid becomes serious bath-time player. Bath-toy collection
grows to flotilla size. You purchase expensive water-vac for
after-bath clean up of flooded bathroom and hall.

— You take that photograph of kid naked in tub which delights
you but mortifies child for rest of life.

— Hair-washing war begins. Kid who'll dive headfirst into any available mud puddle simply can't endure a few drops of water in eyes.

— You may end up buying a strange bit of soft-plastic headgear — basically a wide brim with a hole for the crown of the head — to keep kid happy when you wash his hair. (Believe me, they're available in stores.) At bathtime your kid looks like a college fellow from the Roaring 20's with the top punched out of his boater. The humor of this is something of a consolation to you.

— To encourage kid to brush teeth, you buy him fancy toothbrush with popular movie character on it. This act of bribery doesn't bother you in the least.

— Your wife puts soft-soap dispenser and paper-drinking-cup dispenser in bathroom; kid apparently unable to use bar soap or lean over and suck from faucet like you do.

— As kid matures, spends less and less time in bathroom. This will change radically, of course, with puberty. Enjoy privacy and availability while you can!

TOYS:

— Adorable infant. Whole world is toy. Makes no distinction, though, between "playing" and "eating." Your kid is a sucking machine.

— Adorable infant's favorite toys? Mom's earrings, Grandpa's glasses, Uncle Herman's beard, your ears.

— Adorable infant learns to roll over; now mobile, so can suck on more stuff.

— Learns to crawl; can suck on even more stuff.

— Toddler ignores store-bought toys, preferring empty cereal boxes, dust-balls, and water in toilet.

— Kid becomes aware of stuffed animals; soon prefers them to people.

— Kid gets first "gender-appropriate" toys, usually from anxious conservative grandparents: Barbies with huge breasts or male action-figures swollen as if by steroids.

— Kid develops sense of ownership concerning toys—which means she throws a fit if anyone else touches them—except, of course, when it's time to pick them up and put them away.

— Kid develops passionate yearning for any toy other kids in neighborhood have or want.

— Kid hypnotized by TV advertising. Develops craving for both big expensive toys and an endless supply of crappy little ones (as found in gum machines, cereal boxes, Happy Meals, etc.).

— Excited grandmother brings kid antique wooden truck she found in antique store; he chucks it across room.

— Kid becomes full-blown toy faddist. Develops powerful ability to ignore the many toys she already has while yearning for those she doesn't. Discusses new toys in rapturous detail with neighborhood friends. Asks twice a day how long it is till Christmas—and not for religious reasons.

— Kid now interested in toys that come in series. Your initial toy investment soars since you're required to buy each new addition to her various "collections."

— You begin to resist kid's impulse-buying and hyper-consum-erism, thereby becoming selfish tyrant determined to deprive kid of what millions of other kids (with *"nice* fathers!") are already getting.

— Kid loses or breaks one of her toys, screams as if heart broken. You hope this will ease toy mania some, teach her how to do without; has opposite effect.

— You begin harboring a poorly-disguised hatred for neigh-bor-parents who buy their kids the latest toys—to say nothing of the distant toy manufacturers and advertisers who control your child like a marionette, and before whom you're so helpless that your endless contributions to their hefty salaries might as well be taken from you at gunpoint.

— Having suppressed memories of your own intense toy-horn-iness in childhood, you often complain about the younger generation's lack of imagination when it comes to play; find yourself starting many sentences with "When *I* was a kid . . . "

— Kid learns truth about Santa Claus; now focuses his adoration on the mall itself.

— Kid asks for allowance. Delighted when you say yes—shocked when you say how much. Bitterly retorts, "I can't meet my expenditures on *that!*"

— Kid starts a serious "Toys I Need" file on his PC.

— Kid's birthday comes; many presents. Kid is happy. But when he gets up next morning, he asks for an advance on his allowance so he can buy something. You sigh, remind yourself that, for a kid, this is the first day of the new fiscal year.

— You're shocked, at a dinner party, to meet adults who don't know all about I-Dogs, Bratz, Furbies, Super-Soakers, Spongebob, iZ, Tickle Me Elmo, Bob the Builder, Thomas the Tank Engine, and the Dora the Explorer Talking Kitchen. What, do these people live in a cave?

BEHAVIOR:

— Adorable infant clings to you—then spits up.

— Adorable infant smiles at you—but it's just gas.

— Adorable infant really does smile at you—it's not gas! Then spits up.

— Adorable infant begins to play peek-a-boo, tickle, and other games. Games end when kid spits up.

— Kid crawls, walks, and begins tearing house apart. You smile, resist impulse to tie her to leg of kitchen table.

— Kid learns the word "No;" practices with great emphasis and frequency.

— Kid discovers that great passion of childhood: toys. Grabs each one she sees. Store managers and other children not pleased with this tendency.

— You buy kid toys—she's happy.

— Kid takes her friend's toy. You pull it away and give it back to friend. Your kid screams.

— Friend takes your kid's toy. Friend's mother does nothing. Your kid screams and keeps screaming.

— Your kid's selfishness grows from mere impulse to studied strategy. Grabbing becomes highly proficient. Many social conflicts result.

— You invite playmate over for your kid. For two hours they never look at each other, but, working in tandem, manage to destroy house.

— Kid starts playing make-believe games. You always get to be monster.

— Kid starts playing make-believe with friend. They fight over who gets to be what. Both scream. You introduce the "time-out" concept.

— After making mess, kid tells you the Easter Bunny did it. You gently introduce concept of "telling the truth." You also worry that your kid would blame so blameless a figure as the Easter Bunny.

— Next day kid tells another stretcher. When you remind her about lying, she angrily insists you've never mentioned it before.

— Kid learns to say things like "Oh God!" and "Don't even think about it!" and "You're a dirty dirt-face!"

— You try to teach Golden Rule. "How would you feel if Jennifer did that to *you*?" "I wouldn't care at all!" kid wails.

— Kid learns that getting in trouble just isn't worth it—then forgets and gets in trouble.

— Kid lives to play with friends—then fights with them constantly.

— Kid learns to say "I hate such-and-such!" and "That's stupid!" When you ask, in shock, where she learned such phrases, she answers "From you."

— For joke, you foolishly offer kid choice: Play with Dad or get Snickers. Without blinking she chooses candy bar.

— Kid begins to learn that sibling rivalry is a lifelong form of personal expression and creativity.

— Little by little and very gradually, kid learns that being nice feels good—and sometimes actually pays off.

CLOTHES:

— Adorable infant wears anything you put on her. You spend exorbitant amounts of money on breathtakingly cute ensembles that fit for about three weeks. She spits up on them.

— Toddler stage. Kid indifferent to clothing; you're still dressing her in attractive matching outfits. Child not averse, however, to rolling in mud, slime, sand, beach tar, wet clay, dirt, or, occasionally, dead animals; you struggle to keep expensive outfits stain-free. Your commitment to this goal, however, is largely imposed on you by your wife.

— Kid develops first fashion independence: "I wanna do it all by myself!" This unfortunately includes choice of garments.

— Kid comes downstairs wearing purple plaid pants, long-sleeved shirt with huge green and brown fruit designs, and orange socks with jack-o-lantern faces. (Actual example.) Point-of-view problems here: Kid longs for independence; you have some glancing concern about public opinion. War begins.

— You try to explain to three-year-old about "matching," which is equivalent to explaining the paradox of the Holy Trinity. Kid does *not* get it.

— War rages for a week or two. You finally throw up hands and say, "All right—wear whatever you want!" And you stick to this—till next time kid comes down stairs.

— Kid enters second phase of fashion independence. This invariably means passionate allegiance to a certain piece of gaudy or gimmicky clothing: an "Indian dress," a jumper with yarn-haired cats on it, super-hero underwear, or anything featuring characters from a Disney movie.

— Kid seriously addicted to this favorite piece of clothing. Must wear it every day; you find yourself protecting it even as kid wears it, constantly anxious that it not get too dirty for kid to sleep in.

— It gets dirty. You tell kid it must be washed. All hell breaks loose.

— You put it in wash machine by itself—but only after stealthily removing it from sleeping child. You're up half the night making sure it's dried and ready to wear.

— Kid wakes up, immediately screams "Where's my Indian dress/ superhero underwear/yarn-haired cat jumper?!" You run in with it, claim kid must have taken it off while sleep-walking. You feel absolutely no guilt about this.

— Neighbors and strangers in stores begin to comment on kid's Indian dress or yarn-haired cat jumper. Comments are generally pleasant and amused, but you detect subtle note of "Your daddy lets you wear *that*?"

— Kid's obsession with single piece of clothing finally ends. She's now ready to branch out into a *variety* of expensive, tacky, all-the-other-kids-have-it styles.

— Kid near despair unless you buy her current trendy clothes. Shouts bitterly that you're not "a good daddy!"

— Kid's love of Disney-character clothes extends to lunch boxes, notebooks, backpacks, shoes, pajamas, sunglasses, hats, key chains, pencils and sippy cups, not to mention underwear. You consider writing the Disney CEO for some kind of high-volume discount.

— Kid's devotion to clothes has not translated into caring for them. Main principle of clothes removal for children: Drop 'em—they'll be fine right there.

— Just when you think it can't get any worse, kid points to some playmate's $200 NBA-pro-endorsed tennis shoes, says "I want some of those." Whole new phase about to begin.

CHAPTER NINE

Men at Home: Action and Inaction

*"The extravagant gesture is the very stuff of creation. After
the one extravagant gesture of creation in the first place, the
universe has continued to deal exclusively in extravagances,
flinging intricacies and colossi down aeons of emptiness, heaping
profusions on profligacies with ever fresh vigor. The whole show
has been on fire since the word go!"*
—Annie Dillard

*"There is a mystical rite under the material act of cleaning and
tidying, for what is done with love is always more than itself and
partakes of the celestial orders."*
—May Sarton

THIS EVENING AFTER DINNER, Shilly-Shally and I have come
to play at a pocket-park a few miles from our house, a small clus-
ter of trees and playground equipment tucked next to a Little
League field. Shilly-Shally loves it. Going to the park is, for her,
what rum is for me; each brings an automatic fiery response we're
quite fond of. After monkeying over the balance beam and wood-

en playscape, my darling acrobat runs up to me with her predictable breathless request: *Swing me, Daddy!*

So I begin to push, feeling the weight of her little body against
my palms as the backward swoops return her to me again and
again, listening to her singsong commentary and squeals of delight. But it's been another chore-heavy/ stimulus-light kind of
day, and the repetition of swinging makes me even more bored
and tired than I already am. I love to play with my kids, but I'm
a grown-up—I have limits. Sometimes the dragging uneventful-
ness of this life gets me down.

Next to us, swinging one of her kids and watching the other
play in the dust, is a woman I can only describe as the Absolute
Mother. Most of us know this kind of person. Soft-spoken, endlessly patient, constantly solicitous, smiling without fail, she never raises her voice. She's the kind of woman you always see bending over to help her kids, or someone else's, in an almost peasant
posture, one that reveals what seems to be her basic orientation
to life. And you can see in her face how she takes every step with
them, watches every move, shares utterly in every small triumph
and defeat. This is a mother who never spanks a child, but not so
much because she thinks it's wrong as because she couldn't bear
to do it.

After finally tiring of the swings, Shilly-Shally manages to
scratch her leg while climbing the slide, then punctuates the quiet
twilight with unholy shrieks. The Absolute Mother hurries over,
anxiety in her eyes, looks at me with the deepest, most kind-heart-
ed concern and asks, "Is she okay?"

This is not a slyly over-bearing woman, as can sometimes be
the case. Shilly-Shally suddenly realizes she isn't dying, snaps her
mouth shut in mid-cry, and runs for the monkey bars—and the
relieved smile the Mother gives me is every bit as beatific as it
seems. She's not trying to one-up me, or show off her dedication
to parenting; she's not trying to teach a male how it's done; she's

not even trying to strike up an adult conversation, the way bored parents at playgrounds often do.

As the two of us stand there watching our kids, a group of young adults has gathered in the parking lot. These are people in their twenties. They drove here in convertible jeeps or small cars with rock-band stickers on the back windows. Now they're all putting on roller-blades, joking with each other and skating around to warm up.

I'm more than envious—I'm dying. Lack of time and money has prevented me from learning to roller-blade (among many other things), which I know will be ecstasy. So of course I have to witness *this*, stand here feeling bleary and overweight, tantalized by this free-wheeling group whose independence is so complete they hardly see it themselves. They move through life with a fluidity of schedule and an ease of responsibility I haven't known for decades, can give themselves fully to school or job and still have plenty of time for serious recreation and socializing. Desire for that kind of freedom—especially the freedom to do my chosen work in life—never leaves me, seems always boiling just under my skin. After a while they take off as a group, gathering speed on the neighborhood street like a pack of wolves starting a thirty-mile run.

It comes to me then that this is where I am in life: somewhere between the Young Wolves and the Absolute Mother. The Young Wolves answer to themselves, are out doing things, satisfying their own desires; the Absolute Mother leads a restricted life, her central dedication to domestic harmony taking the place of adult work or play.

And I want both, which puts me smack in the middle, suspended over my own life. Which, for most guys, is, yes—a big deal.

The Mother's little boy is now swinging again; so is my mercurial Shilly-Shally. I'm back to push pause push pause push pause push. "Look, Daddy!" my girl suddenly calls from the height of her arc above me. "A great blue heron!" I lift my head just in time to see the heron gliding on its strong wings over the houses across the street. A pang of envy cuts through me—where I should behold beauty and be grateful for it, I can only rue an elusive freedom. Then I see my daughter smiling with contagious delight as she swoops toward me and away. "Isn't this perfect weather?" the Absolute Mother murmurs.

I'm right in the middle. And right in the middle, it seems, is where a lot of parents are today, women as well as men. Society often seems to give adults with children two choices: Either give yourself completely to parenting and drop out of the world of action and career, or pursue a career and hardly parent at all. These two choices have nothing inherently to do with being female or male, of course, but for a number of reasons they tend to split along those lines.

This doesn't mean, of course, that the Absolute Mother is a typical female. She is, instead, a particular kind of person, most of whom, at this point in time, may happen to be women. And there's plenty about her parenting style that should be praised to the skies. She weaves a sweet cocoon of love and tenderness, and, perhaps, servitude, around her children. She's deeply *good,* and loving, and empathetic, and she gives unselfishly, continuously. Her version of parental love should be a model for all of us, particularly in a culture that hasn't always, it seems to me, made the full commitment to its children that it should.

But what happens to her when her kids are grown and gone? Will she be left empty too? Those who live the other life, the life of action, develop *themselves* as they do so, become independent and self-sustaining. Is she doing that, or has she let her self be eaten up by this role? Will there be anything left when the role comes to an end?

I'm only glimpsing a fraction of this woman's life, and I could be dead wrong about her. She may be a soft-spoken welder taking the kids out after work, or a concert pianist postponing her career, or a hard-driving executive who knows how to shift gears for her family. But I don't think so. She seems to have given up the life of action and self-fulfillment for the sake of her children, or to have found all her natural inclinations satisfied by life at home.

And this, of course, is exactly the ideal we've imposed on generations of women in our culture, raising its image over our heads, praising it and praying to it, "M is for the many things she gave me . . . ", etc. I still remember the painting of the Virgin Mary that hung in our house when I was a boy; she wore exactly that same expression of unquestioning devotion to others, and, looking down in rapture, to the Child on her lap. The Absolute Mother here at the park may not be as saintly as she seems, but I sense that such devotion comes very naturally to her. And what she has to give is precious; I remember as a child how my whole self warmed to that tender, utterly loving gaze from the Mother of God on our living-room wall.

The roller-bladers, of course, embody the other extreme, and I deeply value that way of living too. The totally active adult, the do-er and shaker, the person out there eating up the world whether at work or play—this excites me, won't leave me alone. Of course there are millions of women who feel exactly the same about this, and as human culture slowly swings toward true equality of the genders there'll be even more. I'm married to one of those "other" women, a person of such dynamic energy and passionate skills that she works a sixty-hour week, is the finest mother I've ever known, stays in impeccable physical condition, and would, if you asked her, be ready to leave for Paris in fifteen minutes. And I've never in my life met a woman more feminine than my wife.

She and I react to Annie Dillard's words, quoted at the opening of this chapter, as if they were scripture. Dillard's fiery sentences remind us that the universe is above all a place of Action, that creation continues, life is constantly amazing, constantly moving forward—and my wife and I long for as much of this action and experience as our own lives will allow. And yet, raising children, for all its "activity" and hard work, is often the opposite of the active life we seek. Because of the nature of family, it's more often, in contrast to the pop song, what you *didn't* do for love.

One night last week we snuck off to see a movie, a welcome break and a long-overdue chance to be together. But by the time we left the theater we both felt frustrated and defeated. Why? For one thing, the movie was set in Kenya; we watched the landscapes with breathless awe and deep yearning. We've been to Kenya, and we want to go back; we can't accept the notion that the active life we knew as younger adults is gone forever. It was painful to see those green hills and yellow-grass savannas only on celluloid, when we can still remember, as if in our own bodies, the smells, the heat, the overwhelming beauty of elephants, lions, giraffes, the white sun, the scatterings of dry acacias.

And as if that wasn't enough, we happened to see the name of one of my wife's high-school boyfriends in the credits, a guy who's having great success creating special effects for films and TV. The contrast between his active, artistic life and our worka-day, domestic one was tough to take. We felt sluggish and stuck, as if helplessly watching the world go by.

So women can feel it just as keenly as men do. At this moment in history, though, the orientation to action seems more general-ly characteristic of men. There are plenty of lazy or unambitious men, of course, and the only "career" some guys have is putting up with the dead-end job they let themselves stay stuck in. But since the male in our culture is expected to be active, physical, and adventurous, men often pursue the active role (and are often selfish about it). This reality, of course, can certainly complicate their dedication to parenting.

A lot of guys are ambivalent about being fathers, it seems, precisely because they don't think they can handle the inactivi-ty and house-bound nature of the job—and because they haven't been taught all along that they *should* be able to.

In fact, men have often been told the opposite, and this has taken, I think, some pretty ugly forms. "Curiosity," a poem by Alastair Reid, contrasts the vital curiosity of "cats" with the stodgy predictability of "dogs," praising the cats' restless yearning to know and experience. But this is presented as applying only to males, as the following lines reveal:

> *Dogs say cats love too much, are irresponsible,*
> *are changeable, marry too many wives,*
> *desert their children, chill all dinner tables*
> *with tales of their nine lives.*
> *Well, they are lucky. Let them be*
> *nine-lived and contradictory . . .*
> *A cat minority of one*
> *is all that can be counted on*
> *to tell the truth . . .*

Is this the "truth" an active, curious, passionate male should learn — that it's fine for him to abandon wife and children in the pursuit of adventure and self-fulfillment, including the sexual?

Even men who understand family loyalty, though, are sometimes reluctant to become domestic, fearful they'll have to choose between being committed fathers and being themselves. But this just isn't true! If parenting required me to be anything like the Absolute Mother, I'd have hit the road long ago. It makes its demands, of course, but it doesn't require *that*.

Imagining the roller-bladers off swarming down the streets somewhere, I remind myself where life is taking these free and active world-eaters. In the excited smiles some of the young men and women were exchanging, I saw my own young-adult years and remembered how my ferocious desire to live and experience things also expressed itself, predictably, in sexual-romantic desire. In time it led me to the woman I'm spending my life with, then led the two of us to having children.

Although lots of movies and TV shows build a great false wall between romance and pregnancy, the two are inexorably linked in human desire. For most of us, the passion for experience and the passion for children, though they may seem diametrically opposed, are just different forms of the same thing. The life of action and the quiet, patient life of parenting are actually the same force in different phases, at different seasons.

So it doesn't really make sense to split adults between the two extremes. This has already happened, to some extent, for women; I've witnessed firsthand the largely unspoken tension that sometimes exists, for example, between "career women" and "housewives." And now, with so many women leading lives of action, we've created an army of nannies, baby-sitters, and day-care workers as substitutes for what all women were once expected to be. I don't mean to imply that this is automatically unhealthy; many people need that kind of support, and many are happy to provide it. But specialization can easily turn into over-specialization, our lives can become fragmented and compartmentalized, and we can lose touch with the roots of who we are—and this *is* bad for us. All of us.

Human beings, most would agree, are meant to live broad and varied lives, to take care of the basics even as they reach for higher achievement and excitement. But this goes both ways. We can learn as much about ourselves among dirty pots and pans as we can in factories or boardrooms or lecture halls, or on hiking trails or kayak runs. For all its drudgery, domestic life keeps us grounded and balanced. Adults with children, it seems to me, should take care of those children themselves, even while they pursue careers and personal fulfillment, at least as much as possible.

The last thing we need is for our most active and ambitious adults to opt out of real parenting. Then we have to leave some of our kids to those care-givers whose love and devotion and hard work are preciously important, but who can't always model for children what it means to lead a fruitful homelife and still be energetically engaged in the wider world.

Achieving this balance, of course, is difficult. And it's a hell of a lot of work. But for most of us it's the only healthy option; most people don't really want to be Absolute Mothers *or* lonely single adrenalin-junkies living for action—or workaholics consumed by career. The main point, guys, to repeat: You don't have to be one or the other. You can be both.

But first you have to believe it's *possible* to be both, and value that possibility, or it won't happen—since it's not going to be any walk in the park. (Figuratively, I mean; you'll be at the park plenty.)

And if men in general became truly committed fathers, their unique approach to parenting would help unsettle some of the old notions, lending precious energy and impatience to the whole mix. I love my children, and I'll give up a lot in order to care for them, and for however long it takes. But I can't stop chomping at the bit, and that imperious desire is helping me work out the balance in my life, both for my family and myself. I'm inventing my own tricks of the trade, and some of them are great, if I do say so myself.

Still pushing Shilly-Shally as the sun begins to set, I find myself remembering a book I once read. It featured a prominent writer's arduous search for the snow leopard of the Himalayas, an elusive creature who also became symbolic of the writer's search for himself and for spiritual fulfillment. I read these chapters with the deepest interest and excitement; his treks through the mountains, his contacts with Tibetan Buddhist monks, his experiences with local people—all this was breathless adventure, the kind that made my mouth water. But he also wrote—with admirable honesty, I must say—about leaving his young son behind in the States so he could make this journey of many months, and about the pain this brought to his child.

The whole thing has haunted me ever since. Such separations for professional reasons aren't automatically traumatic for a child, but this one seemed to be. *Why*, I cried out silently again and again, *why would you leave your son in order to find yourself? Can't you see that your child's desperate need for you is part of who you are? That your relationship with him is who you are? That what the two of you are together is part of your essential self, your deep spiritual being? Why go to the Himalayas when the first place to look is into that boy's eyes?*

Besides, being a parent doesn't mean *giving up* the life of action—just postponing it. The Himalayas aren't going anywhere; they'll still be there when your son's old enough to look after himself. But that's not true of his childhood.

The writer never saw a snow leopard. I can't help but admire the love of action that drove him to look, and the titanic effort he put into his search. And I know that my own envy sharpened my criticism of him, since I'm often impatient with my fathering role these days, and have to remind myself forcefully why I've postponed my own career for my kids. But I still think his search was backwards.

Darkness has begun to gather under the close-standing trees of the park. It's time to take Shilly-Shally home. She throws the obligatory fit, of course, swears she could stay forever in this pleasant little chain-link cage. I work her through it. The Absolute Mother, kneeling before a child as she ties his shoe, smiles sweetly up at us, says goodbye, maybe they'll see us here again. I drive home very slowly. With Shilly-Shally's mom at work till nine or ten tonight, I've had a little too much one-on-one with this angel of mine (and not nearly enough with the other). I'm fatigued, but not with the good fatigue of strenuous effort; this is the grogginess of standing around, counting the hours.

I give Shilly-Shally a bath, a snack, read her some picture books, tell her a story, tuck her in. As we lie there together, me on the floor with a couple of old pillows under my head, she suddenly asks, "Daddy, you're not mad at me, are you?"

I look up. She's leaning over the side of her bed, peering down into my eyes with that heart-wrenching expression of sadness and fear—and this is my reminder that I've momentarily lost sight of what I mean to her, of why I take care of her, of how important every minute I spend with her really is—a reminder that I've temporarily lost track of myself.

It's not that I've done anything wrong. I don't expect myself to be a perfect parent. And fatigue, after all, is fatigue. But being a parent will always mean giving some things up, paying a certain price. And in life we get what we pay for. (They know about that in Tibet—they call it karma.)

Besides, what's the alternative—letting my child languish and wither while I'm off chasing my dreams? Or teaching her a daily and heart-chilling unease as I stew or fantasize about my own postponed adventures?

I've learned as a father that fatigue doesn't so much lead me to regret—as to forgetfulness. On a long day like today, I often lose sight of my deeper realities. So what have I forgotten this time? It comes to me as I look into my daughter's beautiful blue eyes: that right here before me is one of the extravagant gestures of creation Annie Dillard speaks of—that this little girl in fish pajamas clutching a stuffed armadillo is a complex and astounding creature—is, in fact, one of the intricate bedazzlements of the universe.

So I shake myself, put all the crap behind me, smile at her from the bottom of my heart. It's time to be Dad. I sit up. And as I give our family's standard reply to her question, her face lights up with relief and shining happiness:

"I'm not mad *at* you," I say, "—but I'm mad *about* you! . . ."

CHAPTER TEN

Home Management: Some Do's and Don'ts

"A real man will know that he has to overcome anything that gets in the way of him caring for his family…that he's a better man with one arm than other men are with two."
— Easy Rawlins, detective character created by Walter Mosley

"A house is not home unless it contains food and fire for the mind as well as the body."
—Margaret Fuller

OKAY, PHILOSOPHIZING ABOUT CHILDREN IS IMPORTANT. But the most pressing concern for the inexperienced father is probably just how to deal with kids day to day—what the experts call *animal husbandry*. (There are surprising parallels, in fact, between parenting and zookeeping; in each case you must deal with the complex psycho-behavioral needs of the "residents" as well as with simpler things like feeding time and poop clean-up.)

So what about the practical stuff?

Well, there's a lot of it, and not even a big thick book could cover it all. So I can only offer some principles and suggestions. (I've thrown in a few points about housekeeping too, for good measure.)

But let me make one little disclaimer. Yes, caring for children is a kind of science, comprised of learnable skills. But if you think your new expertise will bring a general orderliness to your family life, you, my deluded friend, are sadly mistaken. If a b-ball player hits 60 or 70% from the floor, he or she is doing great; if a parent can keep things running smoothly even 50% of the time, he or she is magnificent beyond words.

A handout I picked up at Shilly-Shally's pre-school included a terrific little parenting idea. What do you do when you're running late and your kid suddenly throws a fit, demanding your help with something? According to the expert from Cornell, " . . . [T]ry writing a note to yourself and reading it aloud: 'Tonight when we all get home, I will help you learn to tie your shoe.'"

Wow, I thought. Sweet move.

The opportunity to test this strategy soon presented itself. I'd just gotten home from teaching a three-hour class; it was 7 p.m. and I was famished. But Shilly-Shally wanted me to sit down on her pink hobby-horse blanket and help her dress her stuffed animals in shirts and socks. I tried to put her off, but that only brought howls of protest. *The IOU trick!* I exclaimed to myself. So I wrote it in big letters, read it out to her dramatically: RIGHT AFTER DINNER I WILL PLAY STUFFED ANIMALS WITH SHILLY-SHALLY. SIGNED: DAD.

She looked at me in surprise, cocking her head and narrowing her eyes. As she was taking it all in, I saw a certain thoughtfulness in her expression. *She's growing up!* I told myself, smiling down at her.

"But, Dad . . . " she said, her objection trailing off into, what? Patience? Maturity? A new sense of *my* needs?

"Yes, sweetheart?" I asked tenderly.

"NO-O-O-O!! I WANT MY DADDY TO PLAY STUFFED ANIMALS *RIGHT NOW!!!!* . . . " The noises following this statement were too horrible to relate.

You can't fool all the people all the time; hell, you can't even fool one of them when you really need to. So much for slick tricks. Sometimes they work, sometimes they don't. But I'll bet they know that even in the Department of Child Development at Cornell.

In any case, I hope you'll take *my* suggestions with a grain of salt.

Let's start with the DON'TS. My recommendations are in no particular order, nor are they exhaustive. But they're the only weapons I can give you. And, son—you're going into battle.

DON'TS

1. Don't assume that all the parenting you witness is the way it should be.

And don't assume that all *mothers* actually know what they're doing, either. I've seen things that would curl your hair. People should have to take tests before they can be parents; it's at least 500 times more difficult, and more important, than driving a car. Model your parenting on what you think is right, not just on "the way it's done."

2. That finger-painted masterpiece your child taped to the refrigerator two months ago—don't just heartlessly toss it in the trash!

Bury the sucker. If your kid sees it there among the egg shells and coffee grounds, you're sure to hear that broken-hearted cry, "Daddy, you threw away my PICTURE?!" This of course means that, however badly it may now smell, it's up on the fridge for at least another six months.

3. Don't let your child control you.

Sally and Jim, a childless couple we know, once went to play tennis with some friends who had a young son. The couple brought Ben along and provided him with all the tennis equipment and toys he could possibly want. Then they put Ben on one court and the four adults began playing on the next. But Ben kept wandering onto the adults' court. The mother told everyone that Ben wanted to play on *that* court—could they all just move down one? When they did, Ben kept interrupting, then wanted *that* court, his mother said. Et cetera. Once Ben had driven them to the last court—and then decided *that* was the one he *really* wanted—the mother and father said they were sorry but Ben wasn't having a good time and they'd have to leave. This was just silly. (These parents probably wouldn't catch the humor in Harry Truman's statement that " . . . the best way to give advice to your children is to find out what they want and then advise them to do it".) Adult inconsistency is, in fact, one of the best ways to spoil a kid. Ben shouldn't have been there in the first place—duh. But once they began capitulating to him, they'd created a monster. It's not such a long way from *What can I do for you?* to *Your wish is my command*—and then to *Thy will be done.* The ultimate loser is the child himself, who's been given a control over adults he doesn't know how to use, which only makes him anxious and unhappy, fueling further unreasonable demands and continuing the cycle.

4. On the other hand, don't suppress your child.

Why do kids love Bugs Bunny, Curious George, the trickster in folktales, all of Disney's formulaic little id-characters (chittering Abu in *Alladin*, Mushu the jive-talking dragon in *Mulan*, and of course the almost psychopathic Stitch in *Lilo and Stitch*)? Because that's what kids really are. And denying them that will only make them worse. In the kid-level psycho-dramas of these stories and movies, the little wild one often becomes the Accomplisher; this is what kids long for. Accept them as they are. Only then can you help them become who they're supposed to be.

5. Don't automatically deny certain things to kids.

Last Christmas when we were wrapping presents, Shilly-Shally wanted to play with the wrapping materials, including the scissors and glue. I immediately refused; kids aren't supposed to mess with stuff like that, right? But my wife pointed out that I needed a conceptual shift; what harm could Shilly-Shally do? My wife was right. Shilly-Shally had a great time, and, while she was working on her fine motor skills, did no more damage than to paste and cut up a couple square feet of cheap Christmas paper. My refusal had been based on nothing more than a thoughtless formula. As writer Joyce Maynard says, "The word *no* carries a lot more meaning when spoken by a parent who also knows how to say *yes*."

6. And don't laugh when a child makes an honest learning mistake. Without errors there can be no progress.

One day Shilly-Shally and I were looking through a book on birds, marvelling at the sulfur-breasted toucan, the yellow-shafted flicker, the red-headed duck—and I'm proud to say I didn't even giggle when she told me with a serious look that she herself had once spotted "a three-headed albatross." (Maybe it was near the nuclear-power plant.)

7. Kids understand a lot more than we give them credit for, but don't burden them with heavy abstractions they just can't grasp.

I made the mistake of sharing with my older son, then four, the idea that "God is everywhere." For a month he walked around addressing inanimate objects, including his own knee, with "God? You in there?"

8. Don't assume that every time your kid acts up he's just being ornery.

Consider for a moment how many things can afflict the normal kid in the course of a day. He might have a stomachache, a headache, a rash, a scrape, a cut, a bruise, a goose egg, sunburn, windburn, fever, or chills; he might be cutting teeth or be constipated or carsick or have gas pains or a cold or allergies. He might feel dizzy, hungry, tired, mad, sad, scared, or embarassed about something. He may be suffering from pre-nap exhaustion or post-nap grogginess. He may be getting measles, roseola, mumps, pink eye, flu, sinusitis, chicken pox, or an ear infection (or, if you feed him nothing but the cereal and frozen waffles he wants, scurvy). And take another look at this list. It's not only incomplete, it's also just the regular stuff, the kind of mundane disasters that come up all the time. All these things *will* happen, and your kid *will* act out because of them—and you need to be sympathetic even if you have to discipline.

9. Don't ever touch your child in anger.

Don't grab, push, or even take hold of him roughly. And for God's sakes, don't spank! Recent studies suggest that about 90% of American parents spank in some form or other—so I'm obviously expressing a minority opinion here (although the poll also showed that only half the parents *agreed* that a "good hard spanking" is sometimes necessary, and some experts believe the rate of spanking is dropping). The vast majority of child-care experts, however, are against it.

I'd never claim that all spanking inevitably warps children. But I know one thing: It isn't necessary. Spanking, it seems to me, teaches kids about power, pain and fear; it doesn't help them learn or understand, and, by making them defensive, it often actually reduces their ability to criticize their own actions.

There are many alternatives that, in the long run, are more effective in producing independent and intrinsically moral children. Not spanking means more work for the parent; you have to come up with non-violent strategies and then patiently apply them. But if you don't spank you never have to answer to the charge, "Why can't I hit him, Daddy? You hit *me*!" Our simple rule: In this family, nobody ever hits anybody.

If you think spanking is necessary, consider my kids and the thousands, maybe millions, like them. My sons are thoroughly human and quite capable of "lively" behavior. But they're also good-hearted, successful, active, fun-loving, moral young men—and we've never laid a finger on them.

10. Don't yell at your kids.

No more high-volume parenting! The more you scream, the less it means. If you know what you're doing, there's no need to raise your voice. I've yelled at my kids before, believe me. But doing so was a mistake, my own failure to keep my cool, and it invariably did more harm than good. Besides, the habit of yelling keeps you yourself from developing truly effective ways of dealing with your children.

11. Don't nag your kids.

I recently read an advice column in which a California mother complained that her son kept using the word "yeah." The columnist's reply amazed me:

> "Nag him . . . to exclude this non-word from his vocabulary. If you are within hearing distance of him, each time he says 'Yeah,' call out 'Yes!' loud and clear. Finally, he'll stop saying it just to get his mother 'off his case' . . ."

To me this is ludicrous! The columnist's self-righteousness about "yeah" (somewhat undercut by her inability to use adverbs) is exactly the wrong attitude toward such natural behavior. Barking out "Yes!" might be appropriate for an animal trainer, but not for a parent. The son will, in all likelihood, respond with resentment to such hostile and seemingly arbitrary reminders; he may quit saying "yeah," but only around Mom. So what exactly has been accomplished?

The basic principles of good discipline are simple: First, shower your kid with love. Then, decide what behavior is *truly* important and teach your child how and why to live up to it—but only when the child is actually ready to understand. If the kid has trouble complying, set logical consequences—not punishments—and carry through with them consistently. Under these circumstances, the kid will eventually come around.

12. If you have a long roadtrip to make, don't fall victim to the fatal assumption that your kids can just "play in the car."

The reality is much darker. A friend of ours described a family trip from Texas to Indiana, with her young daughter, as "a seventeen-hour puppet show." Just think about that for a moment.

13. Don't project your own fears and insecurities onto your kid.

So you grew up embarassed about being skinny, or fat, or klutzy, or shy, or poor, or whatever. Okay, you have to deal with that. But come to terms with it on your own, and don't make it an automatic issue in your child's life. I've seen this kind of thing again and again—at Little League, to cite the most famous example, where underachieving or "I coulda been a contender!" fathers (and mothers, often enough) regularly pressure their kids way too hard for athletic success.

And since we all tend to do this kind of thing unconsciously, each of us must strive to examine our own demons and face them, without mindlessly passing them on to torment our children.

14. Don't push very young children for academic achievement.

No less an expert than Captain Kangaroo, the *New York Times* says, warns against parents' " . . . obsession with reading and writing skills . . . [T]urn instead to the emotional issues between parents and children." Pressuring kids at such ages is counter-productive; it's much more effective to surround that child with unconditional love, model good literacy habits, read and tell stories to the child constantly, and watch for academic readiness, only then stepping in to help the child develop—at her own pace. And you're hearing this from a writer and former English teacher who's married to a university reading specialist, and whose children have graduated with nearly perfect GPA's from Cornell, NYU, and Berkeley respectively.

The same applies, of course, to sports, acting, music, or any other demanding pursuit.

15. Some guy-to-guy advice here: Housekeeping is important—but you don't have to become a lean, mean, cleaning machine.

Don't assume, for example, that you have to vacuum the whole floor constantly (though your Commander-in-Chief may well think you do). Through "selective maintenance" you'll be able to cut back on your vacuuming time and still keep up appearances. A few stand-out pieces of lint or food residue can make all the difference between "Looks okay" and "Must be vacuumed *now!*" So, as any dictator will, you crack down on the ringleaders. A long white thread, for instance, can make your house look like a hovel; remove it by hand, and those few potato chip crumbs, and the stray bag-tie, and your place once more becomes the great American home, with that nice "lived-in" look.

This method can save you maybe 20% on vacuuming time. But don't feel guilty about taking a short-cut—you'll still end up slow-dancing with that machine far more often than you did with Jennifer Thompson at your sophomore Sweetheart Dance.

16. And don't let yourself get too fixated on household chores in general.

Picking up toys is a good example. A perennially messy house is a drag on the whole family; keeping things in some kind of order is good for everyone. But at times I've sunk to a kind of *competitiveness*: How many toys can I put away without Shilly-Shally catching me?! I'll even get to the point of following her around to clean up in her wake.

Shake off this lunacy. It'll drive you to Balloon Land—and you'll never win anyway. No adult can keep up with the mess-making abilities of a healthy child; it'd be easier to stop an avalanche with a blow-drier. So work hard and do what you can when you can, and then let that be enough.

17. Don't assume, in fact, that housekeeping overall is a discrete, neatly scheduled series of tasks.

Nothing could be further from the truth. Houses with kids in them get dirty endlessly; waves against the shore aren't more relentless. You'll *never* be able to finally sink into a chair knowing you're finished. Accept this.

18. Resist the temptation to use soccer techniques for clean-up when your kid's around.

That is, don't kick her stuffed animal from the hallway into her bedroom. She'll view this as assault and battery. (When she's gone, though—World Cup time.)

19. Don't assume that any outing with a child is going to be simple and easy.

My wife once protested when I actually took the car to go sledding with Shilly-Shally—at a park only four blocks away. But I knew how bad things could get, how likely my daughter was to get cold (under the five layers of clothing I'd wrestled her into), how inevitable it was that she'd insist on coming home, blubbering, her nose running, the wind whipping along the street, our little sledding trip having turned into something like Scott's trek from the South Pole. I took the car. And thank God I did, since all my fears quickly became reality.

Planning for this kind of activity is like piloting a fighter jet: You go prepared to bail out.

20. Don't assume that the way you manage little things isn't important.

Sure, you can learn to plan the big stuff so it doesn't blow up in your face, so the hiking expedition or the trip to the doctor's won't turn into a disaster. But there's a deeper kind of disaster too, a quiet kind that can spread over years. It happens when a parent and a child are constantly at odds over how things are done in the home.

If the child's feelings and capabilities aren't taken into consideration, daily life can become nothing more than an adult pushing a kid around—*Go here, Do this, Not now, Hurry up*, and *If you don't like it, tough*—whether these things are ever spoken aloud or not.

This kind of stress can drive a child to anxiety, insecurity, and a sense of powerlessness. She may react with outbursts, or with numb silence, or in some cases with a dogged rebelliousness that exists only for its own sake. And this can lead the parent to even stronger displays of power. Such a power struggle generally leads to serious emotional disconnection between parent and child, and then we've got one more kid growing up to be an insecure, power-hungry, inflexible adult—who in turn may push her own kids around.

Even the little things—having lunch, naptime, rules, conversations, etc.—must flow to some degree with the child's natural rhythms. This doesn't mean you stop teaching her. But you bend her, you don't break her—and you bend softly.

21. Don't drag kids to adult events and expect anything less than Armageddon.

An experienced parent develops a reliable sense of which activities will be appropriate. Baseball games, for example, are *not* practical outings for most children seven or under, who simply get bored and usually find a way to assuage that boredom by getting in trouble (there are some die-hard-fan-type exceptions to this). Even some older kids aren't ready for nine innings of what is, after all, a pretty slow and technical game. And if you think they'll let you watch in peace, think again. Not all the peanuts and hot dogs in the world can buy you that.

Some friends of mine, vacationing in India, overheard a little boy complaining to his parents as they all stood before the magnificent Taj Mahal. "It's too white!" the kid kept whining. "It's giving me a headache!" Imagine going halfway around the world to learn that your kid's reaction to world-class architecture can only be soothed by Tylenol. These parents learned about karma the hard way; they were certainly paying for their sins.

22. Don't assume that "simple" things are simple for kids.

A guy we know just did his student-teaching in a local kindergarten. On his second day, the regular teacher asked him to teach a game to a small group of children. He chose tic-tac-toe; after all, how hard could it be?

"It was the worst hour and a half of my life," he later told us. Among the problems he encountered:

— At first, none of the kids could grasp the "You be X, I'll be O" concept.

— Once they did, they started fighting over who got to be X's and who got to be O's.

— Then some kids couldn't make X's or O's.

— Then they began to play—but kept forgetting whether they were X's or O's.

— In the middle of the game, some kids switched from X's to O's, or vice versa, to help their friends—or because they just forgot.

— Most of the kids couldn't understand the "three in a row" concept.

— Once they got that, he taught them the "three down" concept. Then the "three across" concept. But that made them think "three down" was wrong.

— "You can even," he told them, "do three diagonally, like this." The kids all just looked at him. Then they started fighting again about who got to be X's and who got to be O's.

— At this point the teacher sent him a brand new group.

— Out of the entire class, only one child stayed with him the whole hour and a half, and in the end even *she* didn't get it.

"Want to play this some more tomorrow?" he asked her.
"I don't think so," she said.

23. Don't ignore received wisdom about kids.

Men are perfectly willing to accept traditional ways of doing things in *some* areas. When you throw a football, you keep your elbow down; in basketball, you set the pick. So why do we resist the hard-won precepts of child management?

I used to scoff at my wife's rules of thumb, the one about birthday parties, for example: "Invite the same number of kids as your child's age, plus one." *How compulsive!*, I thought. *The more the merrier!* So I had to learn the hard way that throwing a birthday party isn't as much like running a pirate ship as I'd assumed.

Ever been to a kid's birthday party with more than ten participants? Young children have a very flexible notion of ownership; in other words, if they want it, they take it. So you bring a big group of kids together, with a pile of presents sitting out in plain sight—and you expect everyone to be happy when all this loot goes to just *one* kid? That by itself is simply too much for children; no FBI sting operation could provide as much temptation. And of course you've already got the normal chaos and mayhem that inevitably result when kids come together in groups.

My neighbor just rolls her eyes when she recalls how her husband invited eighteen kids to their son's sixth birthday party. "They were *killing* each other!" she says breathlessly. "One kid was calling the others 'babies,' and three of them were crying, and fights kept breaking out—one kid spilled a soda in his lap—another kept saying he peed his pants—then someone turned on the hose . . . "

Believe me, guys, if you get this one wrong it'll cost you more than any poorly thrown pass ever will. So show a little respect for those who've gone before and have generously shared the benefits of their experience. Even if it's "just" your wife.

24. Don't let adult reactions keep you from appreciating your child's accomplishments.

You collapse on the couch as your two-year-old's watching *Mister Rogers*, then drift into half-sleep—are suddenly wakened by a horrible, pungent smell—open your eyes to see your darling beaming at you with pride and delight, holding her newly filled potty.

You know what to do. And it can't be any harder than forcing yourself to compliment your boss on his golf game.

But enough of the negatives; on to the positives!

DO'S

1. Let your kids know you love them — both by *telling* and *showing* them.

The foundation for good child management is kids who really feel loved; nothing's more important than that! And please note: Knowing you're loved is one thing, but *feeling* loved is much more. For children, feeling is everything.

The power of love in a family, however, is often obscured because that love isn't fully expressed. Some adults feel uneasy with such emotion, and some don't realize how much this means to their kids, partially because kids don't always express themselves either. And some adults don't realize that their kids need to feel loved *all the time*, day after day, year in and year out.

When our sons were younger, my wife and I used to write little messages on the napkins we packed with their school lunches. The boys got a big kick out of this, we could tell, though they didn't say all that much about it. Every day we sent new ones, each with some picture, joke, or endearment. One day a friend of ours called. Her son, a tough little guy and good friend of our younger son, had been working quietly in his room one night when she came in. She was surprised to see him writing with a ballpoint on a napkin — and then saw that he'd written a note to himself in his shaky, little-boy print:

Dear Kyle,

I love you.

Mom

When she asked what he was doing, he said he wanted messages in his lunch like his friend got. ("Thanks, you two!" she told us on the phone; "At least now I *realize* I'm a failure as a parent!")

Nor is this hunger confined to younger children. Another friend of ours told us how he wrote to his daughter every day when she first went off to college. He figured the letters would help her get through that difficult transition (and he knew they'd help him!). Although she never mentioned it when she called or wrote back, he continued with his plan.

Then he and his wife went to visit her. Imagine his feelings when they entered her dorm room and saw that she'd taped each of his letters to her wall, arranging them in a line that stretched all the way around the room. Although she couldn't or wouldn't bring herself to express her feelings, it was clear that she'd taken the love those letters represented and wrapped it around her like a blanket.

2. A basic principle of effective child-management: First make your kid happy, *then* worry about discipline.

Parents constantly put the cart before the horse on this one, focusing on control, on authority, "He's going to mind me!"—which is, if you'll pardon my pig-Latin, totally bass-ackwards. If you don't *feed* that horse, hitching it up to the cart won't do much good. Happy kids are usually willing to learn.

In addition, there are two crucial things we must always teach our children: HOW to do the right thing, and WHY. Then we should let them try it by themselves. This "guided independence" approach produces self-motivated kids who, despite the inevitable mistakes they make, actually learn to think on their own.

3. Play with your kids—immeasurable benefits to them, immeasurable benefits to you.

In fact, when you're with your kids make a game out of whatever you can.

One of a parent's ultimate weapons, in fact, is the "project." "I know you're upset, honey, but why don't you and I get your coloring books out?" or "...cut paper snowflakes?" or "...play with blocks?" or "...cook something for lunch?" (The "and I" part, by the way, is critical here; just telling a kid to "go play" isn't going to work in most cases.) Not only can you avoid the outburst, but you're also contributing in the most profound way to your child's social and educational development—and building love between you. When I tuck Shilly-Shally in after an evening of glitter, glue, and construction paper, her whole head is sparkling like the inside of the Seven Dwarves' jewel mine—but then, so are her eyes.

4. Read to your kids constantly, tell them stories, talk to them.

In other words, surround them with the joys of language in all its forms, and make the sharing of language a fundamental part of your family relationships. After almost 30 years of teaching and 32 of fatherhood, I know that a good parent can guarantee school success for his child—and much more. The attitudes and skills that lead to academic achievement are formed in childhood; when adults and children constantly play with language, kids learn magnificently.

5. Memorize the locations, both in your home and the world at large, of all the snack foods your kid loves.

From generation to generation, Bedouins in the desert learn by heart just where each far-flung well and spring is; your need is just as great. For Shilly-Shally, it's Wheatables, Ritz Bits, pretzels, Munch-em's, animal crackers, Goldfish, Snorkels, and of course that food of the gods—Pringles "Right" Potato Chips. I've had to fix in my brain just which grocery store carries which kind, what snack bar or vending machine is likely to fail us or save us, and I carry this map always in my head. The secretary where I work sometimes has Triscuits; a local bakery gives free cookies; the drug store down the block doesn't have the *crunchy* cheese puffs my connoiseur daughter requires.

Keep in mind that, at times, getting a snack to a hungry kid can save your butt. A true hunter knows the land, and the land yields its abundance.

6. When your kid's bored or fussy or ready to blow a fuse over something, use the ancient parental technique of distraction.

Throw those sticks in that puddle, my mom would say, *and play ships.* It worked—and we never had a clue.

7. Set high standards for behavior.

Your kids are up to it, and they deserve no less. At the same time, understand that they're going to mess up regularly. That's how they get to be grown-ups; there's no other way.

8. Set high standards for behavior, yes—but on occasion, when the kid does something negative but not earth-shaking—just let it go.

My tendency is always to hold them strictly to account; maybe that's a guy thing. And overall, of course, such consistency is necessary. But sometimes everybody's just too tired for a confrontation to be productive. There are those moments when discretion's the better part of discipline. So just chill.

9. Develop house-cleaning "moves."

You've struggled to master the sliding bunt or the fade-away jumper; you've spent hours on the guitar learning that blues lick. But domestic life has its own athleticism, and you'll need a repetoire of moves as surely as a boxer does.

Here are a couple of old standards. (Tell me you haven't seen *women* do these a million times!):

— "the housewife scoop": Coming through the living room, telling one kid to turn off the TV and another to set the table, she suddenly stoops and sweeps a toy or piece of litter or hunk of discarded sandwich off the floor with graceful automaticity—and without breaking stride—looking for all the world like a rodeo rider plucking her kerchief from the ground at full gallop.

— "the dinner-table spring": Watch during dinner as the mother, with an almost kangaroo-like instinct, keeps popping up out of her chair at brief intervals to fetch those all-important things like condiments, more water, clean napkins, etc. (The trick here isn't so much the bouncing up as the willful suppression of intense concentration on your own food.)

10. Buy some Ray Charles, or Stevie Ray, or Chili Peppers, or high-energy swing, whatever—and crank it up when you clean house.

Nothing like good tunes to help you get your vacuum on.

11. Slow down; pace yourself.

You can't muscle your way past the rhythms of childhood. I don't mean that you should "kick back"—but it doesn't do any good to "kick against."

12. Get organized.

When you're home with kids, you have to be a bear for details—if only because it takes much less energy to get organized than it does to fight the endless stress of chaos.

Some people are born organized. But some aren't, and the majority of the latter group, it seems, are male. When my wife does laundry, for instance, she actually *folds* dresses downstairs—that she's going to *hang* in the closet upstairs. I've never been afflicted in that way; I'm the kind who shuffles down the street with my hands in my pockets, whistling and wondering what's going to happen next. So I had to *learn* to be organized. It wasn't easy. But it was worth the effort.

Some people, through lack of organization, let their whole domestic life become "routine panic"—and yet it doesn't have to be this way. Make the necessary changes. Your own sanity hangs in the balance, not to mention your kids'.

13. Be flexible.

A guy I know, wanting to be a great husband after his wife's surgery, tried to feed their four-year-old at dinner time. A logical enough approach. But the kid wasn't hungry. So at 9:00 that night, as the husband's trekking upstairs loaded down with folded laundry and toys, he's also trying to hustle the little boy to bed. The boy refuses, citing that inalienable political right of childhood: He's hungry.

Crying kid and frustrated father are getting louder and louder; the wife has gotten out of bed to see what the commotion is. When she appears in the hallway her husband looks at her with intense exasperation, his face contorted in that "WHAT THE HELL DO I DO NOW?" expression. He's ready to force the kid into bed.

No. Forget your plans and your schedule and feed the kid. He's hungry—all his cells are clamoring for nourishment—you think he's going to fall asleep under those crazed-animal conditions?

For all his wonderful willingness to work, this frustrated husband is still clinging to the luxury of a non-parental mindset. Once you've got kids, there's no more point A to point B; a parent learns instead to be satisfied with merely covering the basics.

How would a guy react if his wife said, "Tennis would be a lot more fun if you'd just hit the ball *to* me"? His answer, of course: Then it wouldn't be tennis. If life with kids always worked out as it should, we wouldn't have major "guilt-and-gift" holidays like Mother's Day and Father's Day. And the cheap perfume and soap-on-a-rope sellers would be out of business.

14. That male reluctance to go down on your knees and use carpet cleanser: Get over it.

For years my wife's pointed reminders on this topic had no more effect on me than those of Dame Van Winkle on poor Rip. Then I stayed home for a while. In time, even a *guy* gets sick of looking at those stains on the couch or carpet. You realize you don't have to live surrounded by ancient pancake syrup, dehydrated yoghurt, crusted-over ketchup, petrified silly-putty, and a variety of dessicated body fluids.

Some guys even get to the point where they carry that spray-bottle around in a holster.

15. Of particular importance to fathers—who often don't have much experience with kids—is the checklist.

Kids freaking out? Go over your list:

Are they hungry?
Thirsty?
Tired?
Hot/cold?
Need their pants changed or have to go?
Sick or getting sick?

Kids are physical creatures; the checklist simply catalogs some of their basic and endlessly-repeated physical needs. And until you've gone over the list, you don't have the right to throw your hands toward the sky and scream "NOW WHAT?" Nine times out of ten the problem will be on the list.

My wife taught me this the first week I stayed home with our sons. When she got back from work one evening, both of the boys were fit to be tied—grumpy, growling little saber-tooths roaming the house in search of trouble. "They're in such terrible moods!" she observed with alarm as she took off her coat. "I know!" I complained helplessly. "I can't figure it out! They were fine until about an hour ago. Kids!"

With professional aplomb, she sat down and starting going through the checklist. "Let's see," she said. "Could they be cold?"

"Nope," I answered, "they're both wearing sweaters."

"Are they tired?"

"We all took a good rest about two o'clock."

"Think they might be coming down with something?"

"I don't know. They aren't flushed or hot to the touch or anything. Nobody puked."

"Hmmm. What did they have for lunch?"

My quick-moving thoughts suddenly slowed to a very specific point.

"Lunch?" I echoed weakly.

To this day, whenever they need support for the contention that their father mistreats them, my sons refer accusingly to that now-legendary time I forgot to give them lunch. Life with children, just like zoo management, has one basic rule: The most important thing you do each day is feed the animals.

If only I'd used the checklist!

16. Understand that transitions can be difficult for young children, even simple ones like "Now it's time to take a bath."

In a young child's brain the past hardly exists, and the future isn't quite real. So bedtime, bathtime, mealtime, we-have-to-go-home-now, etc., are like fences over which the child has to climb. Many avoidable child-parent confrontations occur at such vulnerable points.

If you can learn to *help* your child get through these moments, rather than just blow a fuse, you'll both be happier. And there are lots of ways to do it.

17. Stay positive—which is one of the single most important things a parent can do.

Sometimes being positive means finding humor in that which drives you crazy. Sometimes it means looking the other way when your kid insists on pouring her own milk or making her own peanut-butter sandwich. Sometimes it means forcing yourself to smile for no reason. Sometimes it's giving yourself little rewards, or stepping back from a tense situation to find a broader perspective. Sometimes it means swearing under your breath instead of out loud. One particularly powerful form is, as the saying goes, to "catch your kids being good" and then let them know about it.

But what it *always* means is pushing yourself past relatively insignificant frustrations and inconveniences to find faith in things as they are—a profound human skill requiring effort, imagination, and a kind of spiritual determination. Work at being positive; it can actually make the difference between happiness and misery for your family.

18. In *Discipline Is Not a Dirty Word*, Jennifer Brickmayer sums child management up in the simplest way possible: "Work *with* children instead of *against* them" (emphasis mine).

I recently read an account by Greg Gilland of a tense moment he witnessed between a father and son. The boy, a Little League second baseman, had lost his concentration in the afternoon sunshine and began playing out on the basepath, making shadow puppets with his hands (the kind of behavior I've heard sports-minded Texas dads scornfully refer to as "daisy picking"). The boy didn't see his father, a big, heavy-set man, coming towards him across the infield.

We can imagine how Greg felt watching this unfold; we all fear being witness to that terrible moment when an angry parent hurts a child.

The man slowed his pace as he got closer to the boy, who was still lost in his shadow games. Then " . . . he raised his arm high above Tommy's head . . . and . . . began to open and close his hand in the air . . . "

He was playing shadow-puppets with his son.

Tommy looked up in surprise and delight, then smiled at his dad, who smiled back, patted him fondly, then had his shadow-dog remind the boy about "playing heads-up ball." Mission accomplished.

The parenting rule here? There's more than one way to wake up a second baseman. A good parent can turn potentially negative moments into wonderful ones—if he works *with*, not *against*.

19. Find time to share with your child—just the two of you (even if you have other kids).

Some of this you can plan; some you just have to grab as it comes along. But make this happen, make it a priority; of all the work you do, this is among the most important, and the most lasting in its effects.

20. Celebrate holidays, birthdays, family traditions.

Women tend to understand this; many men, it seems, don't. But such celebrations define who you are as a family, and provide formal outlets for the expression of—and *development* of!—deep family emotions and allegiances.

And in fact, it can be incredibly fun to make up new family traditions as you go.

21. Develop slick tricks, nifty little strategies for everyday use.

For example:

Your child's watching *Scooby Doo* with the volume at about 43. Your ears ache, Shaggy's lame observations are ricocheting through your skull, you desperately want to turn it down—but the last thing you need is to simply substitute kid-volume for TV-volume. Trust me—if you just punch it right down to where you want it, your kid will inevitably protest, "Now I can't hear it!" So slide on over and hit the remote till you can't hear anything at all; drop it to about 5. Then ask, smiling and feigning innocence, "How's that?" Kid will of course scream bloody murder—"I CAN'T HEAR!!" So you just raise the volume, slowly, to where you want it, say, about 20—and kid's satisfied. Do the math. Cool move.

22. Develop "regimens" or protocols for dealing with certain predictably challenging situations.

Be professional; every venture with a kid will go more smoothly if you have an experience-based response.

Example: You're on vacation. What are the first ten things you do upon entering a hotel room with your three-year-old?

1. Give kid empty ice bucket. Novelty will buy you about three minutes. Move quickly to #2.

2. Unplug phone. Don't think it necessary? Within five minutes she'll be ringing every number in the hotel.

3. Want rock music at sixty decibels? Cover or camouflage power button on that radio welded to the bedside table.

4. Don't mind 500% mark-up on peanuts, candy bars, and soda? Use duct tape to seal the mini-bar.

5. Clear away all hotel freebies and general supplies: drinking glasses, sewing kits, shower caps, laundry bags, shampoo, soap, stationery, guidebooks, etc. Curse the friendly staff for laying this stuff out so you have the chore of cramming it all onto that little shelf at the top of the closet. Give kid the laminated menu for over-priced hotel restaurant; may buy you two more minutes. Move quickly to #6.

6. Put the TV remote somewhere at least 5 feet above the floor. The spot in the room that's most inconvenient for you will probably be best.

7. Remove all writing utensils, especially from the area of the drawer with the Bible in it. (And keep in mind—even God Himself can't protect that Bible.)

8. Put your suitcases on the floor—certainly not on those convenient suitcase stands! Your lower back may not like it, but a child and a suitcase stand are an accident waiting to happen. Besides, being flattened by Mom and Dad's big Samsonite tends to make a kid peevish.

9. You can't move most hotel beds; therefore, to keep kid from jumping back and forth between the two beds and breaking her neck, bribe her with a snack. (Please tell me you were professional enough to bring your own! If not, avail yourself of mini-bar and let wife know you'll be taking out another loan.)

10. Quickly set up your child's travel crib, whose forty-pound bulk you've hauled in from the car. 37 easy steps. (And you're probably wise enough, after all this advice, to know where it should go—right? Remember the bed-jumping problem?)

23. Remember: Anything you plan to do with kids will always take significantly longer than you estimate.

It's an act of arrogant pride to assume otherwise. And pride, as we all know, comes before a fall. I know—I've fallen.

24. Learn how to communicate clearly with your children—and realize this isn't always easy!

Beverly Cleary's *Ramona* features a kindergartner who, on the first day of school, is directed by her teacher to a chair (there's a shortage of desks) and told to "Sit here for the present." When she gets home that afternoon the little girl is boiling mad—she'd never gotten the gift her teacher promised!

One day at our local beach, Shilly-Shally told her mother she had to go "whiz" (yes, I know—the phrasing is my fault. What can I say? She's been raised by a male jock). My wife replied with a phrase that, I imagine, has been used by mothers since Paleolithic times: "Just go in the lake, honey." So Shilly-Shally dutifully walked out, stopped in about two inches of water, pulled her one-piece to her ankles, and blithely urinated in full view of an extensive crowd of locals and tourists, who all clearly enjoyed the performance. My wife was mortified. But Shilly-Shally was only doing what she'd been told.

25. "Acknowledge a child's bumps or bruises . . . " (*Life's Little Instruction Book*.)

The reality is that the nearly invisible thorn-prick on your child's thumb is a big deal to him; the fastest way to get his mind off it is to acknowledge it briefly and then move him on to something else. (I learned this from many failed attempts to get my kids to scoff in manly tones at their own microscopic cuts and scratches.)

26. Strike a balance when it comes to stimulating your child: as much input and inspiration as possible, but never so much as to overwhelm.

Sometimes guys overstimulate kids; I know I've been guilty of this, partly out of my own home-bound desperation for stimulus and partly out of my half-canine instinct for endless play. Learn to read her behavior for signs of what she can handle at the moment. Nobody likes a kid meltdown!

Naturally, the older a child gets, the more she can take on.

27. Be careful, too, about how much guilt you teach your child to feel.

As a natural reaction to our own misdoings, guilt is important and helpful, and can lead us to self-respect—which produces
more self-esteem, not less. But it's easy to overdo this, and overwhelming guilt is profoundly harmful to a child. When your kid
does something wrong, deal with it. Then drop it, love the kid up,
and move on.

**28. No matter what happens, sit down regularly with your
spouse and talk about how things are going.**

This is as necessary for a parent as having air to breathe. You
may have to go to amazing lengths just to get a chance to con-
verse—but go to those lengths. Husband and wife must always
be able to compare notes, track progress, re-assess, support each
other, and share all the humor, frustration and delight that come
with parenting.

And who knows? Such discussions, under rare conditions of
privacy, have been known to lead to other, more thrilling, and less
verbal exchanges.

**29. Set up some kind of support system in addition to your
spouse, a network of open-minded and sympathetic friends or
relatives.**

Finding this kind of support can be more problematic for men
than for women. But it's just as important for a man, and maybe
even more so, since men aren't "supposed" to be with kids regularly and may be less likely to talk about the experience even
when they have a greater need to do just that.

If you let yourself become a domestic hermit, you're bound
to get a serious case of psychological cabin fever—and burn-
out's not far behind. Besides, we all need to vent a little, and your
friends may have the kind of helpful hints that can save your rear
on occasion. Find friends, male or female, whom you can talk to,
listen to, and share with. Your own parents or siblings may be
wonderful in this regard.

30. Finally, celebrate your child.

The first step is to wake yourself from the stupor of daily living and realize what he or she really means to you, reminding yourself what you felt when you first held that infant in your arms—that transcendent moment which should inform every day of your parenting life. When the Prodigal Son returned, his father suddenly learned again the truth he'd once known, and so called for a feast, sparing no expense; he felt in that moment the same overpowering joy he'd known when his son was born.

The second step is to regularly and passionately express this joy. From time to time, Shilly-Shally comes begging to drink her apple juice from one of our good goblets, which we keep with our wedding china in the dining-room hutch. The rich blue glass, the elegant stems and flowing lines of the goblets in their rows—this must look like palace riches to her. Of course it's all expensive and fragile, shut away in the big hutch as much for protection as display, our little family treasure. Most kids, I imagine, aren't even allowed to touch such things.

But what are a family's true treasures? When she asks for a goblet, we say *Yes! Of course! Let's get one down for you!* . . . We take her by the hand, open the big glass doors. Then with all the seriousness of a royal cupbearer she carries the goblet to the kitchen sink; we wash out the dust, pour in the apple juice. *See how beautiful the golden juice looks through the glass?* we say, and she gazes at it with bright eyes, holding it all by herself, nodding and smiling. Then she drinks with a royal happiness (which is only appropriate, since, as she never tires of reminding us, she *is* the Queen).

Someday she may drop a goblet and break it; we've certainly had to clean up whole bathtubs' worth of spilled apple juice. But would that be so terrible? What if there somehow came a time, under some bizarre circumstances, when we had to choose between her and the goblets? Wouldn't we gladly smash every one of them to bits if it meant her safety, her happiness, her contin-

ued presence in our lives? Wouldn't we spend our last dime—
sledge-hammer the car—happily set fire to our house and watch
with passionate gratitude as it burned to the ground?

The goblet is more than just a physical privilege, more than
parental indulgence of a child's whim. When she takes it so rev-
erently into her little hands, we're giving her something much
deeper. Our children are the center of our lives, of who we are;
our love for them is supreme. The sparkling cup is like the life
we give her, her access to the heart of the family, a symbol of her
absolute participation in our love. This precious, glittering thing
is an outward sign of her place in our union, of our ecstasy at her
coming to us out of the mystery of the world. By giving her the
goblet—just as we gave goblets brimming with apple juice to her
brothers when they were little—we make it clear that, no matter
how young she is, nothing stands between her and the undying
essence of our family life. *You belong*, we're telling her, *with all of
us, at the very Center* . . .

Toast! Shilly-Shally commands at dinner time, her eyes sparkling like the goblet in her hands. So over sandwiches, tortilla
chips, and macaroni and cheese, we all raise our glasses.

What finer thing could we possibly find to celebrate?

CHAPTER ELEVEN

The Male As Domestic Wanna-Be

"A successful marriage requires falling in love many times,
always with the same person."
—Mignon McLaughlin

WE HEAR A GREAT DEAL about women in management reaching a "glass ceiling" that keeps them from the highest positions. But we don't hear much about a similar problem for men on the homefront. There's a "plastic-wrap ceiling" too, which often keeps hard-working males from winning their wives' full acceptance and respect in domestic matters. Men need to anticipate this, and women to understand it, so both can work beyond the natural tensions toward more effective parenting and true partnership.

Such tensions can damage marriages, sometimes seriously. But even in happier couples, the failure of husband and wife to really work together at home can create hard feelings that rob a

relationship of some of its vitality. More and more men are becoming involved in domestic life, but there's a danger here, a
predictable kind of obstruction to the development of the new
male. And it waits in ambush for the unwary. So listen up, guys,
and be warned: In your wife's eyes, you may never be quite good
enough in the domestic sphere.

This may sound frustrating. But it doesn't have to be. In fact, it
can be a tremendous opportunity for growth in your relationship,
enriching you both—that is, if each can recognize and accept it.

First some explanation.

When I say "you may never be quite good enough," I mean
that it probably won't be easy for your wife to accept you as an
equal when it comes to running a household. And she certainly
won't at first! She may be deliriously happy with the new qualities you've found in yourself, she may brag about you to her
friends, your whole family may be happier and healthier, more
connected, more organized, more productive. And you may rise
to dizzying heights, doing laundry with ease, preparing complicated meals, healing your children's physical and psychic ills with
professional self-assurance. If your heart is in it, you'll come close
to perfection over time. You may in fact become 96 or 97% effective when it comes to house and kids. But I'm here to tell you it's
pointless to go for the top. You'll never make those final few percentage points—and she may keep reminding you of this, either
out loud or in those oh-so-endearing non-verbal ways.

And she's not the only one who's likely to withhold this last
bit of recognition: Your "constituents" too may regularly threaten
to vote you out of office. I make my sons great school lunches
every day, but they love to complain, especially to their mother, about my shortcomings as a lunch-maker. To them, getting a
sandwich with mustard instead of mayonnaise is a heart-rending
catastrophe. And pre-packaged foods, which I see as one of history's great contributions to school-lunch making, don't thrill them
at all. They like the royal treatment, and the Queen never fails to

deliver it. Once in a while she makes the lunches, and I'm sure to hear a mournful and explicit comparison from my children the next day. Last week I overheard a father talking to his kids at the mall, and from one phrase saw plainly how much men share in this regard: " . . . Listen, you guys—I just can't do this like your mother does . . . " I can't help thinking of the anecdote I related in an earlier chapter: my daughter calling out right in front of me, "Mom, would you come here and do this better than Dad?"

But stick with me here, because the picture isn't as bleak as it may look. At first your family's reluctance to fully recognize your new expertise (much less praise you for it), coupled with your own continuing minor errors, will frustrate you. It's like basketball, when you drive the paint and slip past two defenders only to blow the lay-up—and then some testo-moronic teammate starts ragging you for forcing the play. After transforming yourself into a Schwarzenegger of homelife, you'll be shocked when your wife criticizes some piddly little screw-up. So you accidentally dropped a white terrycloth robe into the wash machine with a load of darks, thereby covering every piece of dark clothing the family owns with a layer of white lint—so what's the *big deal*? You'll be stunned at how she overreacts (even while you secretly yearn for one of those lint brushes they advertise on late-night TV). *Why is she acting like this?* you'll fume; *Why can't she admit that I know what I'm doing—or at least give me credit for trying?*

To begin with, you have to face one truth here: Part of what really bugs you is the fact that, in spite of your best efforts, you keep making those few inexplicable mistakes. I know it got to me, and it still does sometimes. *I've come so far!* you'll tell yourself, *So why can't I just take it to the hoop?* This combination of pressures— your wife begrudging her trust and your own frustration at not being able to will yourself perfect—can drive you crazy. You'll ponder and pray and mull these things over in the deeps of yourself, till your heart gets to boiling like a crock-pot at three in the afternoon.

But in time you may realize that things are actually better this way—and she of course needs to realize the same thing. There are a number of reasons why 100% domestic capability will always elude most men—and some very good reasons why this isn't so bad.

First, a disclaimer: There are a few guys out there who *will* make it—all the way—MVP's in the NBA of home management. You may already know the kind of man who's progressed to the point where a triple-star chef couldn't argue with his omelet, whose bath towels are folded with machine-like consistency, whose grocery coupons are all regularly clipped and whose bathtub never has a ring. A small minority of men already are, or will become, something like male domestic deities. Well, actually, there's a better term for what they are. I saw a t-shirt with a message that, to me, sums it up: IS THERE A HYPHEN IN ANAL-RETENTIVE?

But for most guys this will never happen. And the main reason is simple: lack of long-term training. Males in our society haven't been raised, traditionally, to even *think* about domestic issues, much less *deal* with them. And even though our ideas about gender seem to be changing overall, we still have a long way to go. Are boys in the United States today, as a group, learning how to wash dishes, clean house, change diapers, cook, shop for groceries? Some are; many are not. And this is boyhood in the twenty-first century; those of us who are now adults were certainly not exposed to the kinds of expectations and experiences our sisters knew.

As I sweated over my floor-scrubbing one Saturday morning, my wife gave the tiles a critical glance and then told me airily, "Don't worry—you're still in your formative years as a cleaner." She thought this was a very cute remark. I felt a little differently; I guess twenty years of housecleaning under her strict tutelage hasn't been enough. (And this must be why *I'm* not allowed to walk on a wet floor *she's* just cleaned, but she can dance the Macarena on mine.) Still, I have to admit—she's right.

Can training make that much difference? You bet—especially when we're talking about becoming an expert, climbing right up to that 100%. A comparison may help here. Like many guys, I imagine, I have an ongoing fantasy you might call my "Undiscovered Sport" dream. It goes like this: I possess, without even knowing it, world-class ability in a certain sport, but it's a sport I've never played. The first time I even attempt it, I'll blow people away; fans will talk about Gretzsky, Jordan, Ruth. Soon I'll dominate the professional ranks, and the sportswriters will go ape. Maybe my sport is buz-kashi, that central Asian form of polo where horsemen fight over the sewn-up body of a goat. Maybe I'm actually the greatest buz-kashi player since Tamurlaine. I'll dip from the saddle, gracefully snag the carcass . . . well, you get the picture.

Then reality comes chiming in. What makes a super-champion? Is it natural ability, the profound innate gift? Yeah, sure, but we all know it's also training. The greats are, generally speaking, the ones who first swung a tennis racket, kicked a soccer ball, or picked up paintbrush or trumpet when they were still in diapers. They didn't play a lot of buz-khashi in the Colorado Springs housing development where I grew up. Why can't you, American male, ever be 100% domestically efficient? Because you didn't imbibe it with your mother's milk, practice it at your father's knee, live it and breathe it from the beginning. Remember how your high-school coach kept screaming, "You gotta eat, sleep, and dream basketball!" (football, track, whatever)? One of my coaches lectured us about a player who actually took his basketball to bed with him, cradling it like a teddy bear. We considered such behavior amazing, but not unthinkable. Now imagine the same story about a guy with a hand-held vacuum. Kind of loses its force, doesn't it? Face it, man: You'll never be Michael Jordan— and you'll never be a domestic superstar either. No matter how good you get, you'll never quite possess the ineffable grace and super-efficiency that come when one's youth and one's professional training were the same thing. (One of the great secrets here is that not all women are actually that good either—but that's another story entirely.)

But lack of profound training isn't the only reason you won't go all the way. Reason Number Two is also simple: You'll never be able to care quite enough.

An essential part of becoming a real man is learning to truly care about what goes on in your own family. So I don't mean to restate the tired old stereotype that women care more about family than men do. But there are differences between male and female in this regard. It seems to me—*seems*, I say—that women in general have a stronger "nesting instinct." Men also have one—just not to that same dizzying intensity. My wife rhapsodizes about buying a house with an intensity I can't fully share; I yearn for one too, but it doesn't occupy my thoughts as it does hers. She goes at interior decorating with an energy I can't muster (though I have to muster some, since I'm usually the one moving the furniture). She suffers more when our kids get hurt, is more offended when they don't like dinner (even if I made it), and cleans house with a dedication that shades into out-and-out enjoyment. I just can't match her in these things.

It's 11:00 at night and I'm exhausted. There's one more dirty dish on the counter, and we can't leave it out since we've been having trouble with ants. There are clean dishes in the dishwasher—so to deposit the dirty dish there I'd have to empty the whole freaking thing. God forgive me, but at times in my weariness I've washed that one dish without dish soap.

I tremble as I write this. When she reads these words, she's going to rear back in shock and fix one of those looks on me, that expression somewhere between "How *could* you!" and "Men are DISGUSTING!"—you know the one. So I hasten to add that I no longer do this. Although she may be exaggerating when she insists this practice will lead to bubonic plague, I see now that she's right. The point, though, is that the level of concern she brings to the issue just doesn't come naturally to me.

(Why, by the way, should you always use soap? Let me put it in male terms. Remember when you went camping that time and ate your meals with your Swiss army knife, and, for the first time in your life, washed your own dishes? Remember how you just swished them in the stream till the big chunks came off? Remember how you got the trots for three days? That's why.)

And while I'm at it, I may as well confess another transgression. You know how when you've wiped off the dining room table after dinner, and the washrag has a few crumbs in it—just a few, I mean, not enough for the ducks in the park or anything—and there's nobody around, so you go ahead and chuck the rag into the kitchen sink from ten feet out rather than carry it over the same boring way you always do?

Yep. Done it. On the same principle, I suppose, as when you jog back to the dugout after an inning in the field and chuck the ball against the chain-link fence. You sure as hell don't *carry* it in and set it down.

I love my family, I work hard, and I want my house basically clean. I'll do the right thing. But I'll never be quite as intense as my wife. Believe me, if *she* ever forgets to put the toilet seat down, the time-space continuum is going to tear wide open.

But I can hear some of you sincere young guys raising objections. You say you'll care every bit as much as she does?

You boys actually *experienced* this yet, in the real world?

The other day my wife glanced into a kitchen cupboard and remarked with disgust, "Want to hear something men are ignorant about?" (This was, I quickly realized, a rhetorical question; the *No* died in my throat.)

"How to nest pans or bowls when you put them away," she continued sternly. "You men just stack them—you don't care if they fit together or just pile up. Men have no concept when it comes to nesting." Then she gave one of those "I Have Spoken" nods and left the room. (I don't think she had the slightest notion of the layers of meaning in that word "nesting".)

Now I'm sorry, but the very existence of the term "nesting" in this context is something I want nothing to do with. And she spoke of being able to "nest" bowls as a valuable, even indispensable skill, one with almost athletic features! I know myself well enough to know I can't operate at that level. I've searched my heart from top to bottom, and I just don't give a rat's ass. I suspect no healthy male does. Hear me, comrades: Don't try to go there. That way lies madness and the loss of your soul.

A third reason you'll never reach the top has to do with gender-related approaches to problem solving. Men and women often do things the same way, but just as often approach them from different points of view. If you've paid any attention, you know that male and female, whatever their similarities, will always be significantly different. The average guy could be subjected to sex-change surgery, dressed in a skirt and heels, etc.—but he'll still be able, at any given moment, to put away two specialty burgers, two super-size fries, large coke, large shake, hot apple pie, and a bag of cookies. And there never will be, I think, a man equal to my wife's delight at buying high-tone clothes at low-tone prices. These are only tendencies, of course, but they seem to be generally applicable to many of us.

Such differences, naturally, are reflected in domestic strategies. My wife, for example, has a strong aversion to throwing things in the house. Not only would she never do it herself, she doesn't want anybody else to either (which is just so . . . so *Puritan* of her!). My perspective is different. I think it's perfectly acceptable to call out my son's name and launch that spray-can of furniture polish toward him (provided, of course, that it's a lob and not a line-drive; after all—safety first). No harm can come of this, even if he misses; at the least he'll get in a little practice, and maybe the accident will even provide us all with a good laugh. My wife, however, finds such reasoning inane. To her, even the possibility of the can clattering to the floor produces anxiety and results in stern warnings of the "You'll put your eye out" variety.

I heard John Stossel assert on *20/20* one night that there's nothing wrong with leaving beds unmade if a family just doesn't have time in the morning. As reactionary as John can be, he had a point. But my wife scornfully disagreed, insisting that such a barbaric practice would leave the beds " . . . all covered with dust." I wasn't quite sure where she was coming from on this—we live nowhere near the Sahara. But it was clear she had a mental framework from which to approach the question, a framework I was ignorant of. (I've since learned, by the way, about dust mites and their role in allergies; God, I hate how she's *right* all the time!)

When my brother Mike and I were young, we invented a dazzlingly efficient new way to make our beds, which we named "hillbilly style." It consisted of dumping your pillow, blanket and sheet in a big pile in the middle of the bed. Just that; nothing else. We could have lived our lives out this way—but Mom didn't agree. Though she never gave specific reasons, her strong reaction made it clear that such a strategy was unthinkable—from her perspective. We didn't have the same perspective, so we never really understood. But, as she reminded us, she was Mom, and we weren't. Hillbilly style quickly passed onto the refuse heap of bedding history.

There's an inevitable conclusion to all this. Even though many domestic solutions will work for both men and women, some won't, and there's bound to be something of a gulf between the sexes on this point. All the more reason that your wife may never fully trust you. She *knows* what you're capable of, and she doesn't like it. To me, having lunch without dishes is an accomplishment, even a triumph; I can't help feeling this way. To her it's an abomination; she rolls her eyes in that charming manner I've grown so fond of. Husbands and wives should always make a serious effort to accept their differences—but not with the false idea that such differences will ever completely disappear.

Another reason you won't reach the highest levels of domestic performance is the simple fact that, when it comes to house and kids, your wife was there first.

Before you even thought about being domestically involved, she was carving out an empire for herself. She worked hard, and she did it on her own. Like the Little Red Hen, she planted the wheat, tended it, then baked the bread. And it's not that you're now asking for a freshly buttered slice; it's much worse. Now you want to help grow the wheat and make the bread! But how can she be the Little Red Hen if you do? You've co-opted her role. She's struggled to establish her own way of doing things, and she feels she's achieved a perfect system (and may have developed an enjoyable sense of martyrdom along the way). She's transcended her own mother and made a new woman of herself. So no matter how close a domestic partnership you have, she'll still tend to see you as something of an outsider, even a claim-jumper. After all, she's probably the one who trained *you*.

All this can be summed up in a single word: turf. A young guy I know told me that his live-in fiancee, even though he does all the cooking, is still the domestic "boss," telling him where and how to put the dishes away, etc.—"And," he adds, "it's *my* house and *my* dishes!" A professor I work with, in his fifties, says his wife "guides" him through dusting a shelf by offering "seven minutes of instruction, then four minutes of criticism." The other side of this, of course, is how so many women accept similar dominance and criticism from their husbands when it comes to driving, doing yardwork, talking about sports, or the like. My friend Anne says that when she's driving with her husband, "He treats me like an idiot—and I *act* the idiot!" Consider further how men openly mock the general female ignorance about subjects like football.

These discourteous and insulting exchanges between the sexes seem to be almost automatic. It's hard for me to keep a straight face when my wife tells people I used to play "quarterblock" (I was a fullback—I don't think they have "quarterblocks" even in Australia.) But it can't be any harder than it is for her to bite her tongue at the many forms my ignorance takes—what David Bly refers to as "cupboard blindness," for example, a sorry male inability to find things in the kitchen that any wife will be able to give you an earful about.

How did we ever get to this sad state of affairs? Simple: by dividing labor so strictly according to gender. The situation can become intensely territorial. But the problem isn't so much that we're mistreating each other—though we are—as that we don't really see how we're caught up in this, haven't fully grasped the whole unhealthy dynamic.

Dividing all tasks as "male" or "female" will, at any given moment, make half of us defensive idiots and the other half arrogant taskmasters. "Turf behavior" often pits as enemies husbands and wives who honestly love each other and want to work together. It can leave spouses feeling humiliated and resentful (though these feelings are rarely expressed openly). Men lord it over women in one area, women retaliate in another, and so on—the cycle continues. So the car is your turf, the kitchen is hers; you criticize her sense of direction, she mocks your cooking; you both feel insecure and insulted and so become even more critical when it's your turn to be cock-of-the-rock. Instead of helping each other learn, you both simply turn up the pressure. The result? No one's productive, no one's well-rounded, no one's compassionate, and there's a lot of resentment boiling just beneath the surface.

A certain amount of struggling over turf is natural in any marriage, particularly at first. (And of course many of us will be acting out the turf behavior modeled for us over decades by our own parents.) But such "relationship adjustments" can easily get out of hand. The good news is that serious battling just isn't necessary. Husband and wife must take down the fences. A man has no right to stay out of the picture at home when it comes to the pressing complexities of housework and childcare—he can't just be a big selfish rock in the middle of the road that the rest of his family is forced to go around. By the same token, a woman has to give in too—not in the usual overwhelming way many women have been giving in all along, but in a new and subtler form. A wife has no right to talk from both sides of her mouth, complaining about uninvolved husbands but then resisting her own husband's sincere attempts to become involved.

Men have to get off their duffs at home; women have to make room for them—by cheerfully sharing power, by letting men make their own mistakes, by truly believing in the whole process. It's bound to bring some uncomfortable changes, but those changes can be worked through.

I don't mean for a second to overlook the enormous selfishness in a lot of men. But some women don't really want domestic partners; they want "go-fers," grown-up domestic assistants. "My way or the highway," however, isn't a workable system. After all, there's a big difference between a "domestic" male and a "domesticated" one. And some men, in selfishness or reluctance to work, will latch on to their wives' reluctance as the perfect excuse to leave things just the way they are.

My rule of thumb is that, since men need to change most, they should at first adapt to their wives' ways of doing things. That's the way it always is when you're a rookie. But if husband and wife are both open and willing to work, this should gradually evolve to the point where the man is on his own. Only with total responsibility and independence will he be forced to fully develop his skills and attitudes, to sink or swim.

But I think we can all be realistic about this too. Sometimes a little division of labor is exactly the right strategy, especially when it follows the natural abilities of the respective spouses. An example of this is how my wife and I handle our checkbook. As a true math-spaz, I'm no longer allowed even to subtract individual check amounts to get the balance. I can enter the check but subtraction is taboo. And this doesn't bother me. (I mean, I feel stupid, but I accept the wisdom of the system.) For a long time I worked hard to get the numbers right, but I still screwed up regular. So balancing the checkbook is her job now. This doesn't mean, of course, that I'm off scot-free. In fact, it imposes *more* responsibility on me, since I've had to find a counter-duty in order to maintain our balance of labor. *My* labor-specialization is taking care of any purely physical errands that come up, hauling groceries, picking up kids late at night, that kind of thing. I feel very comfortable with the dumb ox stuff.

But we still do all we can to make sure neither of us completely identifies with a separate "turf" — which, after all, usually has more to do with a couple's attitudes than with the nature of the tasks themselves.

A man should understand all these things from the beginning. If he doesn't, he'll waste a lot of emotional energy wondering why his wife hasn't jumped up to hand him the keys to the kingdom. And he won't see that this whole business is one more case of *vive la difference*, that precious and delectable contrast between the sexes which has been endangered at times in our struggles toward gender equity. Men and women should be equal, but they'll never be identical—and none of us, I think, really wants that.

My sister Katie and I were talking once about fashion trends that defy traditional gender roles, buzz haircuts for women, earrings for men, etc. Katie dismissed all the particulars, then summed the whole situation up in an off-hand but profound way. "What people look like or wear," she said, "is always going to change. But there's a line between women and men, and there always will be. It doesn't really matter where the line is—because there'll *always* be a line."

The same is true for domestic behavior. We *can't* be exactly the same, and we don't *want* to be the same, though sometimes we think we do. (This desire to be "the same," I've noticed, usually takes the form of wanting *You* to be more like *Me*.) It's *good* to be

somewhat different, and to be somewhat distant from each other—because those are precisely the conditions required for that
great and satisfying coming together we call love.

One night my family was peacefully eating dinner when my
wife somehow got onto the subject of Being Hard To Live With. Naturally, I was the focus of her rather pointed musings.

"*I'm* hard to live with?" I asked, a spoonful of mashed potatoes poised in my hand. "*Me?*"

"Yes," she said in a definite tone. "You're always...forgetting
things."

This, I hasten to confess, is completely true—though, as my
stock but heartfelt response goes, I'm working on it. Of course
it's annoying to one spouse when the other regularly spaces out
important practical stuff. But was this single shortcoming really
enough to put me into the "Hard To Live With" category? Probably not; she seemed to be searching her memory for more sub-
stantiation. I'm proud to say she had to think a bit.

"And you . . . you make noises . . . "

With the wisdom of experience I didn't challenge this; she'd
only produce graphic examples (which would later be taken up,
at my expense, by our children). But she seemed a bit short on
evidence of my general obnoxiousness, so I took the opportunity
to move from defense to offense.

"I don't know, honey—you have your ways too."

She looked stricken. "*You* have to put up with *me?*" she
gasped.

"Well . . . " I had a few examples at my fingertips too, but in
such instances I find it far wiser not to enumerate.

But then a thought struck her, and she laughed—that beautiful sound which always reminds me why I love to live with
her. Her laughter is as clean and cooling as the rain.

"I suppose," she said smiling, "that what you really have to
put up with—is me not putting up with you!"

And in some ways that said it perfectly. Males tend to be more easy-going about things around the house, which is both good and bad. But then, so is the opposite approach. She was right about our respective roles, about the equality in our relationship: an equality in being Hard To Live With, but also in having the affection and strength to Put Up With The Other.

Yet she'd also managed, of course, in her clever way, to leave unspoken accusations hanging in the air. The phrase " . . . me not putting up with you" suggested a long list of my faults. This wasn't lost on me. Then I saw my chance.

I'd happened to glance at her plate. She'd been eating an orange. As God is my witness, she'd *arranged* the peels as she pulled them off. The thinner ones were lying in concentric curves on her empty plate, like commas curled up together to sleep. The thicker ones were stacked symmetrically next to them. It looked something like a little German lumberyard.

"Well," I said, in a quiet but knowing tone, "all we have to do is look at your plate to see how easy *you* are to live with." Then, with a purely thespian timing, I got up and carried my dishes to the kitchen—listening, I must admit, for that sound I love.

And it came. She laughed and laughed. All over the city, it seemed, sweet rain was falling, waking leaves and blossoms, driving dust away, filling the air with fragrance, enriching the light. Sometimes I think she's God's way of keeping me grateful.

I came back in—ostensibly to point out that, for basic purposes of civilized behavior, it's enough merely to get your orange peels *onto* your plate. But what I really wanted was to be close to her, to share her laughter. Besides, I knew damn well I hadn't "won" any argument. This is my wife we're talking about. For her the merely sufficient is *always* insufficient. Though she laughed with ease and grace, deep in her heart she doesn't really believe symmetrical orange-peel stacking is all that bad.

There's far more to laughter than mere humor, especially for husbands and wives. We laughed because it was funny, of course, but also because that moment reminded us that the differences between us are obvious, real and inevitable. We'd caught ourselves being utterly human and suddenly found a way to celebrate that. And the laughter taught us, again, even more: that these differences, with which we sometimes annoy each other, are in fact desirable.

Spouses should realize how the very qualities that first attracted them to each other often turn into points of conflict as their relationship becomes more organized. Yes, relationships always try to organize themselves, which is a good and necessary thing. But a partnership can only be organized up to a certain point. Sexual-romantic relationships are a kind of fire. The wildness and emotional risks of first falling in love must stay at the heart of a marriage. And this means simply beholding who the other really is and passionately wanting that person. We often try to re-create the other in our own image, or in ways convenient to ourselves. But how foolish this is! Not only will it never work, but in a healthy relationship we learn that we don't really want it to. One of the keys to successful marriage is the realization that we don't always want what we seem to want. And the more we laugh about our differences, the more we understand that.

They say a comedy traditionally ends with a wedding. All I can say is that my wedding was the beginning of a kind of comedy—a beautiful, human story full of weakness and strength, generosity and selfishness, but illuminated throughout by the divine gift of laughter. When a husband and wife laugh together, that laughter can bring both acceptance of the other and honesty about the self. This kind of laughter is often a form of realism about natural human failings and shortcomings—as well as a statement of confidence that such realities can't undermine the serious passion and mutual respect at the heart of the relationship.

Later, as I was scraping the plates before loading the dishwasher, I could hardly bring myself to destroy the intricate arrangement of those orange peels.

God, I love the girl!

CHAPTER TWELVE

Men and Women: Domestic Differences

"'Inherent differences between men and women, we have come to appreciate, remain cause for celebration, but not for denigration of the members of either sex or for artificial constraints on an individual's opportunity."
—Justice Ruth Bader Ginsburg

LONG AGO, according to an ancient Greek story, human beings were so powerful they threatened to storm Mount Olympus and attack the gods. But these humans were not like we are today. Each had four legs, four arms, and two heads; they were faster and stronger than any animal, and far more intelligent than modern people. Overall, they were monstrous in their perfection.

Fearing these super-beings, the gods turned to Zeus, their king, who then called for his terrible thunderbolts and hurled them down at the Earth. His lightning split the humans in half, making two weaker and more manageable creatures out of each powerful one. The new beings are what we now call "male" and "female," each with only two arms, two legs and a single head.

And ever since that time, men and women have been trying to get back together, to be one again, however temporarily.

But this wonderful story leaves out a crucial detail. Maybe Zeus's aim was off just a bit—because we don't seem to have been split right down the middle. The two halves of humanity are never exactly the same. Men and women don't simply leap together into easy harmonious wholes. We're more like puzzle pieces, just different enough, and similar enough, that coming together is—well, interesting. Consider the following conversations, each of them real:

ME: That Janet and Dave! Now *there's* a different kind of couple!

MY WIFE: What do you mean?

ME: Well, I was talking with her the day after she and I took the kids to the beach. So she tells me she said to Dave that night, "You should have been at the beach today. There were some real babes." Then she says "Dave is quite a girl-watcher, you know . . . "

MY WIFE: What's so strange about that?

ME: (surprised) Well, I mean . . . he ogles other women . . . and she's just blasé about it!

MY WIFE: (definitively) I think that's good. It's healthy.

ME: Well, I don't know . . .

MY WIFE: Besides, *you're* a girlwatcher.

ME: Me?!

MY WIFE: Yes. It's just natural.

ME: Oh sure, everybody looks *some*times . . . Women do too. But you don't just stare, or talk about it like that. You wouldn't tell a friend "Tim's a girlwatcher . . . " — would you?

MY WIFE: That's because you don't do it. (Pause) I don't see you do it. (She pauses again — then is suddenly fiery.) And I better not catch you doing it either!

Anyone notice how we went from *It's natural* to *Just try it, buddy!* in about seven sentences?

But men, in fact, are just as illogical as women — only on different topics. Before you congratulate yourself on being a rational male, consider how many times you've sounded like this:

MY WIFE: You're two hours late!

ME: Oh. We were just having a few beers.

MY WIFE: So why didn't you call? You knew I'd be worried!

ME: Well, I thought about it — I really did. But then I figured I'd be leaving any minute. Besides — I didn't want to worry you.

MY WIFE: *Worry* me!? How could letting me know where you are worry me?!

ME: Well, if I called, that would make it a big deal. And it wasn't a big deal. We were just having a few beers — and I figured I'd be leaving any minute. And I lost track of time . . .

From a male perspective, the illogical nature of this explanation is understandable in terms of the man's deeper feelings and basic orientation. But of course the same is just as true, in both conversations, for women.

All of us, in other words, must deal with the fascinating oddities of gender. I think the jury is still out on which differences are natural and which are learned, and if such distinctions can have any practical meaning. Whatever the case, though, the observed differences come into sharp focus when a man and woman share domestic life. The abyss between male and female can open up in the kitchen even more easily than in the bedroom.

My wife and I agree about all the important things at home— how to raise kids, manage money, keep house, etc. In fact, basic disagreement and marriage are more or less incompatible; sooner or later, something—or someone—has to "give." (I love the double-meaning of that word there.) But when it comes to pillow shams, we seem to have been permanently planted on opposite sides of the fence.

If you're a red-blooded male, you may not even know what I'm talking about; I used to think a "sham" was some kind of Irish hat. But if your wife is a red-blooded female, you may be quite familiar with them. As its name suggests, a sham is a completely unnecessary fake pillowcase that you put on a pillow that already has a pillowcase. To me, kind of like wearing two coats at once. Shams fall into that general category of "nice things for the house" (the same category which includes ornamental soap, tissue-box cozies, doilies, and a host of other objects whose only legitimate functions seem to be the creation of employment and giving your wife of sense of having "good taste"). And shams of course—usually have ruffles.

My wife is definitely not the cutesy-domestic type. Our decor is that popular Late-American style known as "Lived In," and the only serious color coordination in the house is when Shilly-Shally insists on matching her dress, socks, and underwear. Still, even my wife seems to have that profound female attraction to ruffles, which geneticists have now isolated on Chromosome 14 (exactly analogous to the male gene that forces men to put their feet up on coffee tables). In other words, she wants ruffled pillow shams and that's all there is to it. Every night as I take my pillow out of the sham, I feel foolish by association. But I know we'll never see eye to eye on this. And I just can't care as much about it as she does, so she wins.

Ask any married woman for a list of male domestic qualities that drive her nuts and she'll immediately start reeling them off (usually starting with the observation that men have no domestic qualities whatsoever). Men, by contrast, tend to be less specific in their grievances. When their wives talk to them about domestic matters, they're usually too busy trying to plug the appropriate vocabulary into sentences whose overall structure they're already painfully familiar with:

> "Don't you remember?" she says. "The _____ goes in the _____ drawer!" (He's thinking, *Socks in sock drawer? Naw—too easy . . .*)

So the male "list" usually comes down to a generalized "I wish she'd lighten up!"—or the repeated complaint I put into haiku form:

> *A woman will shout*
> *"All right! Do what you want!" This*
> *is not what she means.*

These gender differences can affect a couple's balance of power, of course. One night my teenage sons and I were arguing over who got to hold the TV remote—that trophy of manhood, scepter of the male in his castle—when I said something like "Look, guys, I'm the father. I have the power." (I stole that line from He-Man, of course.) "No way, Dad," my older son countered. "Mom has the *real* power—she doesn't even need the remote."

And this power is perhaps based on her all-too-female assumption about male stupidity—an assumption, I admit, that I
sometimes give her evidence for—but one that clearly goes to extremes when she says something to me like, "My friend Bertha
told me she has a serious drinking problem, and her husband's
at the state prison for grand larceny. But be sure not to say anything about it to her." If I protest that I don't need that bleedingly
obvious warning, she looks offended and tells me it was just a
"reminder." I may have the brain of a three-toed sloth, but I know
better than to put my foot in something like *that*.

So men and women have to be realistic about their differences. But that doesn't mean we can't live happily together. It does
mean that husbands should think about all this, and work with
their wives toward solutions. Things can get very tense; in some
marriages, such issues become destructive. As Robert Bly says,
"The sexes tend to shame each other."

But there's a way out.

One thing to keep in mind is that we live in complicated
times, especially when it comes to male-female stuff and the nature of family life. Stephen Jay Gould once wrote that " . . . the dynamics of immediate family . . . to later historians, will probably
define our . . . decade." There's a lot of tension and confusion in
the air; I sometimes wonder if men and women have ever been so
much at odds. While sexist stereotypes about women are slowly
giving way—a sea change that's long overdue, but which some
still resist—others are avidly substituting sexist stereotypes about
men. To a certain point this is natural; a lot of women are carrying resentment and anger that *should* be expressed, privately and
publicly. But there's a fine line between the open expression of
righteous anger and the tendency of such anger to become habitual and prejudiced.

An otherwise insightful article in an issue of *Redbook* asks
"Why do men fail so predictably?" in terms of having extra-mar-
ital affairs—a gross generalization at best! The author, a male,

then quotes a female family therapist who says that men who verbalize their problems are "much less likely to jump the pasture fence"—which, to me, unthinkingly depicts males as incontinent animals who can hardly contain their sexual urges—and on top of that makes marriage sound like prison. An ad in another magazine, this one for a women's writing conference, states that "In the modern world, the lives of women are emerging as the most interesting ones"—thereby blithely dismissing half the population!

And women as a group aren't always completely clear on what they want men to be, nor do all women agree about the wider questions. *Redbook* also reports on research from UCLA that shows American women attracted first and foremost to "masculinity" in their partners ("qualities like independence, assertiveness, and willingness to take a stand"), with a man's ability to be "caring, communicative, attentive" taking a back seat—in spite of how much we hear these days about the "sensitive male." This confusion is expressed perfectly, I think, in an article by a feminist mother concerned for her son: "I am very clear on what I don't want him to be, but I am hazy on what I do want him to be."

It's certainly true that, in general, men have a long way to go when it comes to domestic life. But it's naive to assume that all women automatically make good parents or know everything about running a house. Many have told me that, going into marriage, they were as ignorant as their husbands were. And women, of course, though generally light-years ahead of men in domestic awareness, still make mistakes. I once overheard a wonderful mother I know teaching her young son not to lie by warning that, if he did, the Easter Bunny wouldn't come.

There's even some serious doubt in our culture, it seems, about the nature of parenting itself. Some appear to be questioning its basic sanctity—which disturbs me very much. A book ad in a national magazine begins with "Psychoanalysis has given us permission to hate our mothers—but what about mothers who feel hate for their children?" The ad goes on to describe this feeling as "common."

So suddenly the inevitable emotional outbursts of parenting, the stress-inspired negative thoughts, the sudden blow-ups passing as quickly as they come, are a form of *hate*? And we're all supposed to accept this as *natural*? Besides, does anyone remember when we all "received permission" to hate our mothers?

Beneath all this, of course, is a new kind of glacial force—the profound awareness that men must treat women as equals, and must carry that respect into the shared running of a home. But in our current climate, striking a balance probably won't be easy for most of us.

Understanding often begins with details. Following are some of the male-female differences that make married life, at least in my house, so bumpy at times—but always adventurous. I suspect many of these are universal.

TIM'S RANDOM SAMPLING OF MALE-FEMALE DOMESTIC DIFFERENCES

1. Clues We Each Should Have Picked Up on When Dating in College:

ME: When she came to visit me at the dorm, she brought her own can of Ajax cleanser.

HER: I expressed surprise that, after she cleaned it, my bathroom sink was actually *white*.

2. Clothes Closet:

HER: Two or three hundred garments hung with such precision that they never wrinkle each other; eighty pairs of shoes lined up so neatly you'd think a company of soldiers was still standing in them.

ME: I just want a room with a bunch of hooks on the walls.

3. Care of Clothing:

ME: If it's dirty, I'll wear it one more day and then throw it in the direction of the hamper.

HER: After letting Shilly-Shally eat in her lap, she's disgusted to find her houserobe spattered with chocolate. So she vigorously scrubs out the stains before putting the robe in the wash. Our older son observes, "Mom scrubs her robe—so that a piece of clothing she can never be seen in—will be perfectly clean."

4. Trouble Over What to Wear:

HER: In her dresser drawer she keeps long lists of various outfit combinations (this blouse with that skirt and belt, etc.), which she consults religiously.

ME: If the holes aren't too big yet, I'll wear it.

5. Attitude Toward Tags on Back Pocket of Newly Purchased Jeans:

HER: Immediately cuts them off. "If I didn't," she explains (as if to a dolt), "then just *anyone* could read my jean size!"

ME: "What tags?"

6. Philosophy Concerning Toilet Seat:

HER: TOILET NOT IN USE? SEAT MUST BE DOWN! And this doesn't mean the seat women *need* to sit on—it means the other, superfluous one, the lid.

Her feelings on this point are mysterious and fierce. The Catholic Church split over papal succession, but that was eventually smoothed over; men and women, however, are still profoundly separated by the question of toilet-seat position.

ME: My concern? Noticing if the lid's down so I won't urinate all over it. The rest is details.

7. Laundry:

HER: As God is my witness, she actually folds in the laundry room (and I mean *folds*: 'tight-corners, no-wrinkles, bounce-a-quarter-off" folds)—a dress that she's taking upstairs to *hang* in Shilly-Shally's closet.

I'm repeating myself here? Yeah—I still can't fricking believe it.

ME: Sometimes there's not all that much visual difference between clothes I've folded and a pile of dirty clothes on the floor by the wash machine.

8. Attitude Toward Nifty Household Hints:

HER: These "Fast Facts" from a Heloise column, which my wife thought were terrific:
"Here are five handy uses for the versatile clothespin:
1. Keep some near your hamper to clip on stained garments.
2. Clip them on retractable cords to keep them in place.
3. Use to hold several playing cards together for tiny hands.
4. Take when shopping to hold coupons.
5. Use to hold drapes closed in a motel or hotel."
ME: Male list of clothespin uses:
1. Hang clothes.
2. Throw at people.

9. Attitude Toward Housecleaning:

HER: My wife suffers from "Dutch Woman's Disease," named for the woman in the story who scrubbed the steps off her porch, the faces off her children, and eventually went off to scour the moon featureless, which she's still working on. My Delicate Flower lectures about cleanliness with a papal fierceness that, in medieval times, would have launched a crusade or condemned a heretic. (Take a wild guess who plays the heretic here.)

ME: I'm just a guy. Sure, I like a little order in my life. Cleaning day means you pick the stuff off the floor and put it somewhere.

10. Doing Dishes:

HER: "Leaving dishes in the sink to soak is a form of procrastination!"

ME: "Oh yeah—I forgot those dishes I left to soak. But I bet all the food's come off by now—I won't even have to use the dishrag!"

11. Willingness to Change Vacuum Bag:

ME: Like most men, I find myself mysteriously reluctant to empty the vacuum bag. It may be swollen like a fat man in a tight shirt, ready to explode as in cartoons, may in fact be spitting dirt *out*—but I always figure there's a little more room.

HER: One bout of vacuuming means it's time. "Feel this!" she'll say sternly, then quote the instruction book with fundamentalist fervor: "It says to empty it when it's a third full! A *third full!*"

(She's less willing, of course, to actually empty it herself. Some girls don't like that kind of thing.)

12. Visual Acuity in Domestic Contexts:

ME: When we make up our bed together I always get impatient, keep saying "Okay, that's fine. That's fine." She ignores me.

HER: Finally—when the bedding looks like she used a t-square and a carpenter's level to position it—I ask if we're finished. "There's WAY too much blanket on my side," she says. "Pull yours over."

The instant I merely take hold of the comforter in order to pull it, she says, "There. That's fine."

13. Kitchen Appliances:

HER: Her skill with appliances is instinctive and driven by delight; she plays her Cuisinart like a Stradivarius. And she looks after these gadgets and machines as if caring for pedigreed dogs.

ME: Toaster, microwave, crock-pot—that's it. The first two because they're easy. The crock-pot because she can put something in it and I don't have to do anything—and there'll still be dinner.

14. Appliance Crises:

HER: She calmly deals with flaming toasters, volcanic juice-makers, and hopelessly mis-programmed microwaves. I suspect she memorizes the instruction books while I'm napping.

ME: When the wash-machine hose split, I panicked, grabbing paper towels, oven mitts, and pot-scrubbers in an idiotic attempt to soak up the water as fast as it was filling the basement. After ten minutes of this Niagara, it occurred to me that all I had to do was turn off the water.

Surprise—there was a turncock on the pipe right behind the washer. I then spent four hours mopping up the rest of the flood. Later my neighbor told me that her husband—a big-shot sportswriter—had done exactly the same thing.

15. Classification of Trash:

HER: Household trash is highly complex, with various types and appropriate methods of disposal. "Wet" trash isn't the same as "dry," and must be treated accordingly. And we must add "scheduled" trash too, since (as she told me while cutting up a pineapple) you try to prepare such foods on the night before the garbage collectors come. Otherwise a "trash crisis" may result. (Translation: the kitchen garbage will start to stink.) I'm sure that when they empty our barrels, the garbage guys appreciate the freshness of our pineapple scraps.

ME: If it smells, take it out. If not, wait till it overflows.

16. Attitude Toward Rags:

ME: A rag is a rag. What the hell.

HER: Just as medieval people believed in a Great Chain of Being, my wife believes in a Great Hierarchy of Rags. It's not so much a classification, in fact, as an ecosystem. Some rags are fit for the kitchen sink, others only good enough to wipe floors with. Some are for dusting, some for heavy bathroom work, and some are site-specific, to be used only in basement, garage, or to wipe off the washer and dryer. An individual rag's origin—i.e., was it formerly a towel, a cloth diaper, a washcloth?—usually determines its position on the hierarchy. AND YOU CAN NEVER USE A RAG FOR ANYTHING BUT ITS APPOINTED FUNCTION.

But her system isn't really even *this* simple—because the hierarchy of rags isn't static. Individual rags are constantly changing position, in a relentless downward movement. That which is high will sooner or later be brought low (and eventually thrown out). A bright cheery new dish towel, lord of the kitchen linen, will in time begin to wear. One day it must face an abrupt change in status. Naturally, I don't even notice this—but she looks at me like I'm daft, says things like "You can't use that on the *dishes!*"

"But I saw you drying plates with it last week!" I sputter.

She rolls her eyes. "That was then; this is now," she reminds me, holding the pathetic thing up to expose its disgracefully thinning fabric. "Now it's a *rag.*"

So it moves down the ladder. But not to utter humiliation—not yet. A rag is still a powerful laborer. This newly demoted soldier will be stationed at a more dangerous domestic post; he will work hard, but he will be cared for.

Some fateful day, of course, the Queen will declare him useless, force him into retirement—and shoot me another look because, again, I wasn't paying enough attention to do it myself.

But how am I supposed to notice the frayed edge of a rag when I'm happy wearing an old sweater that's unraveled up to my navel?

17. Definition of "Basic Shelter":

HER: The bare minimum: A five-bedroom house with spacious lawn—stylishly appointed living and dining room—rec room with Stainmaster carpet—three bathrooms, with matching shower curtain, rugs and toilet-seat covers—and approximately $20,000 worth of furniture, curtains, pictures, wall-hanging baskets, plant holders, statuettes, throw rugs, ornamental tissue boxes, vases, and, of course, pillow shams.

ME: One of those single-hamburger-cookers, a single-hot dog cooker, and a mattress in the back of a van. Oh, and beer.

18. Etiquette:

HER: A careful and complex system whereby people are considerate, never make body noises, and actually try to help each other out.

ME: The "jock etiquette" she objects to: I'm happy to throw her anything she wants; if I bump into her I always say "My bad."

19. Hospitality:

HER: If we've invited guests, she feels the need to make about three hundred specific preparations, which usually culminate in some kind of banquet and result in enough dirty dishes for the back of a restaurant.

ME: As a stay-at-home dad, I offer my female neighbors beer at 10 in the morning. The cool thing is, they're tempted—this is a whole new world for them. Who says men aren't contributing to American domestic life?

20. Urination Strategies:

HER: None needed except during pregnancy, when a woman must come up with excuses for her thrice-hourly trips to the bathroom.

ME: There are a number of aspects to this important behavior:

1. The ever-present danger of missing or splashing and thereby incurring spousal wrath.

2. Tricks like "rimming." (Once when I mentioned this to a guy, he said "Rimming? Never heard of it." I said, "You know—when you want to be quiet." "Oh," he said, nodding, "when you aim high on the bowl.")

3. Finding the "no-splash" zone: The water-air interface is usually your best bet, but don't be naive; a certain amount of splashing is unavoidable. (Of course you could always break with centuries of male tradition and actually clean up after yourself.)

4. The Superman stance: Hands on hips; just for fun. (A good man usually saves this for outdoors.)

5. Proper shaking: Difficult. Too much and you make a mess in the bathroom; too little and it's on yourself. Guys constantly seek the perfect wiggle.

21. Body Temperature:

HER: Always too cold.

ME: Always too hot.

(At times our conflict over car AC or bedroom windows has threatened to turn violent; she once actually attacked me with her blow-dryer.)

22. Sleep Habits:

ME: I sleep soundly and rarely wake. But I snore, turn over constantly, get up to go to the bathroom, and make what she calls "pupping" sounds (and others of a less delicate nature).

HER: A very light sleeper, easily awakened by the free-wheeling slumberfest beside her. She's like a smoke-alarm trying to sleep next to a fire.

What cruel trick has God played on men and women, we may ask, that love and sex draw us into the one bed but sleeping drives us out of it?

23. List of Stuff One Sex Does that the Other Can't Understand:

HER: Pretty much everything I do, besides the stuff she *tells* me to do.

ME: I just don't get some of her rules. To wit: Put the napkin in your lap while you eat (instead of leaving it conveniently on the table). Don't use your knife as a pusher (even when you're eating peas—and of course you aren't allowed to use the fingers God gave you to pick stuff up with!). Dry the wet dishes right away (you'll find them in the *drying* rack!). And when you set the table, turn the blade of the knife toward the plate—or away from it?

Damn.

24. Tendency to Talk About Things Incomprehensible to the Opposite Sex:

HER: She and her mother say of Shilly-Shally, in sighs that fairly plummet with envy and resignation, *She has naturally curly hair* . . .

ME: I say I'd kill to have my b-ball partner's vertical leap and she just looks at me funny.

25. Knowledge of Sports:

ME: I know, for example, the difference between a touchback and a safety.

HER: She overheard me talking football one day, picked up on "tight end" and "split end"—then accused me of analyzing other women sexually.

26. Level of Complexity of Domestic Systems:

ME: During a busy time in her life, I offered to take over the grocery shopping. "Sure!" she retorted, "you could do it. But we'd live in chaos for two months while you figured it out."

Not really, I thought. And not because I'm foolish enough to think shopping is easy. There'd be no chaos simply because I'd buy the same 20 items or so each week, in bulk, and no more. Lunch would be three choices: PB & J, macaroni and cheese, or ramen—and you make your own. I'd rotate five or six basic dinner menus—nothing fancy and nothing else. Within days I could reduce our whole grocery system to brainless simplicity, which is just where I feel comfortable, domestically speaking. The intricacies of silverware and dishware, those huge collections of kitchen gadgets they have in the stores? Forget it. I'd get each of us a Swiss army knife and let it go at that. (My wife, on the other hand, is capable of statements like "You know, we really need a nutpick.")

Like Thoreau in his little cabin at Walden Pond, I'd simplify, simplify, simplify. (Of course, Thoreau did sneak off regularly for dinner at Mom's.)

HER: The husband is usually at a disadvantage here simply because he has trouble even *perceiving* the domestic complexity his wife absolutely *revels* in. The organization of my wife's clothes drawers is a good example.

My sons and I have four categories: things that go on your feet, things that go on your legs, things that go on your upper torso, and things that go on your bits and pieces. But my wife's chest of drawers is, for me, a kind of wicked IQ test. Parts of her system are understandable, of course; I usually get her lingerie in the right place (Category: "things that, hopefully, come off"). And there does seem to be a basic "pants/shirts/sleepwear" breakdown. But I'm often confused. Is that heavy turtleneck a "sweater" or a "shirt"? How do you categorize a vest? Do panty hose go with "lingerie" or "socks"? (Surprise: Socks.) Day after day I stand above open drawers with her folded clothes in one hand, scratching my head with the other.

But the kicker came one day when we were in the room together. Opening a drawer, she discovered one of my garment-place-
ment errors. Without a word she pulled a pair of jeans from the
drawer in which they rested—among *other jeans*—and put them
in a different drawer. I was stunned. *Jeans*, I'm thinking, *made from
denim . . . long-legged pants . . . other jeans have these same characteristics . . . so why . . .* ?! Even at the risk of a lecture, I had to find out.

"Oh," she said offhandedly, carefully smoothing the pillow
shams, "that pair goes in the drawer with the old things."

Old!! Nobody ever said anything about *old*!

And suddenly I realized my error. I'd been caught off guard
by a sudden shift from *functional* to *chronological* organization. But
that wasn't the error; my failure lay in once more underestimating
her instinctive domestic complexity.

I should have known better.

These gender differences often show up in your children
too—even in a household like ours, which is about as "liberated"
as they come. When Shilly-Shally and I play with our Match Box
vehicles and such, I'm ready to crash, career, and attack, as my
sons and I used to do (back in upper grade school, my friends
and I thought the car chase in the movie *Bullitt* was the coolest
thing in the universe). But my daughter chooses two little metal
planes, names them "Birdie" and "Little Jet," then gives me one
and carefully explains a scenario whereby Little Jet cries because
she has no friends and Birdie comforts her. What we males saw
as action play has now become relationship play. "Don't worry, Little Jet," I find myself reluctantly saying, "They just don't
understand you . . . " As my younger son has observed, "I've discovered how to distinguish between male and female children: If
it takes longer to *organize* the game than to *play* it, it's a female."

Although my sons often cared for and hugged their dolls and
stuffed animals, they just as readily converted them into balls or
hand-grenades, once even hammering flat their Barbies' breasts

(to increase their aerodynamic qualities, no doubt). My sons are surprised when their mother mentions using a washcloth in the shower; the whole point of a shower, they insist, is the convenience of getting clean simply through contact with running water. As little boys they loved to throw dirt-clods at their action figures or play tsunami in the bathtub; Shilly-Shally, in contrast, turns a toilet-paper tube into a gentle and pleasant volcano decorated with pink hearts, three shy little flames of white paper peeking from its rim.

Non-sexist modeling does have some effect. When Shilly-Shally first stood at the toilet, she looked down at her crossroads in confusion, as if something was missing. She also cracked up my neighbor once by announcing, during a visit, that she had to "whiz." (On the other hand, I've had to learn a whole new vocabulary concerning "panties," "panty-hose," "leotards," "tights," etc.)

But a lot of this, it seems, is only skin-deep. My daughter's still the one who stops me during "The Three Little Pigs" to give her own long explanations of how each pig is dressed. The following incident, too, may indicate that she has her mother's instincts for domestic control.

Playing with his sister in her bedroom on a winter day, our younger son, eleven or twelve at the time, was sitting on the floor in a shaft of sunlight from the window. "Are you cold?" Shilly-Shally asked with sweet and maternal concern. "Do you want a blanket?"

"No, thanks," he answered, smiling. "The sun is keeping me warm."

Without a word she jumped up, crossed to the window, lowered the blinds with an angry whack against the sill, then threw her rocking-horse blanket over him. "And *don't* take that off!" she commanded.

Okay. The overall picture is very clear. To paraphrase Mari-
lyn Monroe, male-female differences are here to stay. And they're
bound to challenge husbands and wives. So what can we do?

The first thing is to realize that we can face up to gender
conflict without letting it utterly dominate our thinking. We can,
obviously, recognize the *similarities* between us as well as the differences. One great benefit of all that "battle of the sexes" comedy
we hear on TV is to reveal to men and women their *mutual* pecu-
liarities. Our differences, the stand-ups keep reminding us, are
part of what makes us so similar. And no matter how mysterious
gender differences may seem, no matter how much they bother
us, we're still drawn to each other by a magnetism as strong as
anything in the universe—and for far more than merely sexual
reasons.

Another crucial point is to realize that our behavior is often
determined more by our social roles than by gender itself. Once
they take on jobs formerly reserved only for the opposite sex,
males and females often begin to act in surprisingly similar ways.
Because my wife takes care of all our finances, she's a bit particular about giving me money; "You'll just spend it!" she'll say, in
tones reminiscent of sit-com fathers from the 50's. And because
I now do serious house-cleaning, *I'm* the one who most sharp-
ly reminds our kids about coming in with mud on their shoes.
We've even had conversations in which *she* complains about the
burdens of the working world and I bitch because she's too tired
after work to be "emotionally available" to me. Then we catch
ourselves and laugh, a little wiser about the humanity we share
beneath our differences.

A third point is more obvious: Each sex must learn to accept
the basic domestic style of the other. For a woman this means a
couple of things. First, she must accept both her husband's right
to be domestically involved—and his right to be himself. Second,
she needs to let him get in there and learn it on his own (at least
to some degree), without her constantly looking over his shoul-

der, or criticizing too much, or mocking, or taking over in disgust—all of which can simply drive the guy away, and is bound to dampen his enthusiasm.

And this means learning to live with Guy Style.

Guy Style does *not* mean that men can do whatever they want. And it doesn't mean a man can be a "resistor," the kind who constantly evades his family responsibility through silence, or complaining, or slipping away, or pretending not to know better, or becoming a workaholic. Plenty of men are like this. When I first heard about the men's movement I shared my excitement about it with guys I know. I only learned later that, to some of them, the "men's movement" simply meant their wives should get off their backs. Such inflexibility has nothing to do with true male domestic style.

I once took Shilly-Shally to a pre-school birthday party at a local motel pool. Among all the mothers and Chrissy the preschool teacher, I was the lone male. Once swimtime was over, we adults worked on getting the kids out of the pool, into the dressing rooms, and then into the party room—which was something like herding emotionally-disturbed weasels. Chrissy and I ended up working with about four kids. "Now let's see," she said. "This is Enrique's pack, and this is his swimsuit . . . " Backpack in one hand, dripping suit in the other, she paused.

I knew why. Even though we were in the middle of what most people would call a crisis, Chrissy was so conscientious, so hard-working—and so female—that she didn't want to put the kid's wet suit into his pack. I could almost hear her thinking, *There are other clothes in there . . . and the pack itself will get wet, maybe even moldy . . . His mother wouldn't just toss these trunks in . . . Let's see . . . Is there a plastic bag around here somewhere? Should I hang the trunks to dry in the party room? . . .*

Forgive me—but this kind of thing just drives a guy crazy. The male reaction? *Too many kids; too much to do. Wet suit in pack. Finito.*

Some further examples of Guy Style:

— Men tend to go at housecleaning a little differently. I find my-self adopting a kind of pirate approach, flinging mop or dus-trag about in a dramatic swashbuckling style, muttering things between my teeth like "Wash out, you bastard!"

— Shilly-Shally, playing "Wolf-Cub" on the living-room floor, is delighted when her biology-conscious father brings out her Clickety-Clack Christmas Pony and tells her it's a "dead horse." "Uuuummm!" she says, tearing off the sequined sad-dle and pretending to devour the body. Later she brings me her Lambchop puppet, says with fierce joy, "I killed it! The shepherd said NO! But I just ran away! . . . " (My apologies to Sherry Lewis—but she did name it "Lambchop.")

— I've taught Shilly-Shally that after you use a paper towel in a public bathroom you ball it up and shoot baskets at the litter bin. She's getting pretty good.

— Sometimes I have to refer to my own male training in order to understand my wife and remember her directions. She insists, for example, that clean towels be placed at the *bottom* of the towel pile, since those placed continuously on top will wear out too fast. I had trouble grasping and retaining this till the day I realized, *Hey! It's just like rotating tires!* Now I remember; sometimes I even do it.

— Specific sports training can be helpful too. A little kick-boxing or karate is great for closing kitchen cupboards when your hands are full (or just for the fun of it). Well-developed periph-eral vision helps you track your four-year-old in crowded de-partment stores. And the basketball ready-position is perfect for dealing with toddlers in open spaces, since it allows for good lateral movement and keeps your hands in front of you for pants-grabbing and vase-catching. (Remember, of course, to "stay between your man and the basket"—in this case, between kid and philodendron, kid and magazine display, kid and Hummel figurine, etc.)

— A friend's little sister used to complain during camping trips that boys had all the advantages when it came to relieving themselves in the wild. Hearing this, my sons and I began referring to the penis as "the camping tool"—and the name stuck. (Sure beats "wee-wee," "pee-pee," "weenie," or my personal favorite, "the Washington Monument.")

I think Guy Style can bring wonderful new qualities to parenting. For one thing, it gives children modeling from fathers *and* mothers, which will help kids balance their own personalities and allow them to understand masculinity in a fuller way (and femininity too, of course!). There's also often a stronger element of the physical in the way some fathers parent, which is very healthy for kids. Many mothers, for example, at least in my experience, overreact when their children get little cuts or bruises.

I find too that men are often looser about household rules. This can create problems, of course; some males don't realize the importance of certain rules for kids. And some are *too* rule-bound, especially about behavior, which just doesn't jibe with the natural psychological anarchy of childhood. But many American children are way too fenced in, locked away behind You can't, Don't ever, etc., and fathers tend to ease this. Men can be very good, too, about not sweating the small stuff. And, perhaps because of the boyishness in most of us, we often bring a strong sense of fun to parenting; we play around a lot—and that's great.

But maybe the most important point here is simply that a child with two such parents will feel that much more loved, whatever style of parenting comes into play.

We also shouldn't forget either that any guy who knows how to sing a lullaby, comfort an injured kindergartener, and earn his

wife's domestic trust is bound to have found some emotional lib-
eration in *himself*. (Not to mention, by the way, that chicks really
dig that stuff.)

The wife who learns to accept Guy Style will find herself re-
paid a hundredfold. But that's not the end of it. The emergence of
Guy Style helps bring a further opportunity to a marriage—this
one the responsibility of the husband.

One Saturday Shilly-Shally and I were playing near a fountain
in an open-air mall when a little girl of eight or nine came running
up to the water's edge. With its descending steps and shallow
basin, this civic beautification was also a behavior-management
challenge for every parent whose kids encountered it. The little
girl quickly slipped off her shoes and tentatively stepped into the
water, looking back at her dad. He just smiled.

Shilly-Shally was shooting me one of those "Why can't I . . .
?" looks when a woman's voice suddenly split the air: "Christy!!
Get out of there!" The mother had arrived; though she was still
fifty feet away, her feelings were quite clear. The father immediately called back to his wife, "It's okay!"

There was no anger in their voices. But this was definitely
contention, that moment of mother-father disagreement we all
face again and again, when the different orientations of the sexes
come into stark contrast and a decision has to be made. But the
way this one turned out shouldn't have surprised me a bit—because what almost always tips the balance in these cases is *knowledge based on experience*.

"Get out of the water, Christy," the mother repeated as she
approached. And then, as if intoning a verse from the Bible, "*You
can't see broken glass in water!*"

What could her husband say to that? What rejoinder could
even *begin* to erode the confident and obvious truth of such a
statement? She had him dead to rights, and whatever response
he'd contemplated died on his lips. You know how in those nature
documentaries two animals are having a fight and suddenly one

decides he's beaten and wanders off to graze? It was just like that. The mother repeated her warning, knowing it was the clincher, and then added, in that quiet but insistent voice parents often use when ironing out differences in public, "Besides, people throw garbage in there . . . " The father just looked away.

In family life this situation is played out over and over. And it's my impression that more often than not, the wife prevails— not because she's pushy but because she's usually the one who *knows*. She knows because she has the orientation and experience her husband lacks; she's thought about such things because they keep coming up in her life.

I'm not saying that a woman never gets drunk on her own domestic power, never gives her own preferences or theories the weight of unbending law. As far as I know, terrorists have not yet begun filling our public fountains with broken glass. You have to understand, though, where a woman's coming from. She doesn't see these housekeeping/childrearing standards as "hers"; in fact, she probably doesn't see them as relative or particular at all. In fact, to understand your wife you must first understand Plato.

This famous Greek philosopher believed that for every particular thing we see on Earth, chairs, for example, there exists a single, perfect version in the Beyond. Somewhere, he said, there's an ideal chair, the chair of all chairs, the Primary Chair which all ordinary physical chairs are just lesser versions of. This is how your wife approaches household tasks. She knows, for example, that there's an ideal Clean Sink. It doesn't exist in our world, but above and beyond it. She knows this not through logic or experience but through the mystic intuition of her soul. When you claim that you've cleaned a sink—but you haven't scoured it with abrasive cleanser till the tile foams and your forearms ache—she just laughs. She knows you've fallen embarrassingly short of the perfection of the One Clean Sink.

When my wife catches me doing some chore in a less than impeccable manner, she often takes over with, "Here—give me that!" I'm bathing Shilly-Shally, for instance, when my omniscient spouse happens by. "Oh, not like that!" she'll say, snatching the soap and washrag. "Look—you take the soap—scrub some onto the rag . . . " Then she lathers the cloth so fast and hard her whole body shakes. I'm thinking, *Hey, I can get the kid clean my way!* . . . Well, to tell the truth, I do tend to forget to wash behind her ears— and sometimes her neck. So here we are again—once more my wife has the clincher. The kid needs to be washed all over; there's just no way around it!

The upshot of all this? Any man who expects his wife to accept Guy Style—must himself be ready to give Gal Style the respect it deserves.

And what better place to end than on a note of mutual respect between husbands and wives? Because that's really what makes marriage work—that and the passionate celebration of those differences that make the union of man and woman so intricate and pleasurable. Sex itself is the central metaphor here, the simple physical foundation of all the great good the sexes can be for each other. I feel nothing but gratitude to a universe that has made us so different, then propelled us into each other's arms; I'm delighted that Zeus' aim was off. Otherwise men and women would have only identical smooth surfaces to present to each other—and that would be boring, to say the least. As it is, we can't be complete without joining ourselves to the very things we consider foreign and difficult. The beautiful paradox is that doing so makes us greater than we would be in the ease of untroubled solitude.

It's not easy—but so what? We'll make out okay. After all— we're not about to stop practicing.

CHAPTER THIRTEEN

The Smoking Ruins of Your Sexual-Romantic Life

A Father's Love Poem

I touched her thigh
Thought, My oh my.
Just then we heard the baby cry.

"Dad, did you used to be a man?"
—my daughter, age 4

THE OTHER NIGHT I had a heartbreaking dream.

My wife and I, somehow, miraculously, were alone in a private place. The intoxication of this intimacy was too much for us; we began to kiss, long and lingeringly at first, but gradually with more and more excitement. Soon we were down on the bed in each other's arms, passion sweeping us away, and I began to undress her. But just as certain highly interesting articles of clothing came off . . .

. . . a whole busload of tourists arrived. Talking, gawking, and dragging luggage, they trooped right past us on their way to their rooms.

On waking I realized bleakly that you simply couldn't find a better metaphor for the sexual-romantic life of people with children. The irony, of course, is that the "tourists" are of our own making. My wife and I love to be together, to talk, to share, to do things as a couple, to make love and then talk some more: to act, in short, just like lovers, which, despite our many years together and the mob-like presence of our kids, is exactly what we are.

What we've actually become, however, is Lovers Interrupted by Tourists.

You're new parents? Congratulations! But you can't eat your cake and then keep on eating it. You got to make the child; that's about all the uninhibited sex you're going to have for a while. And romance, which is rich and slow and time-consuming, is even more problematic. My wife and I go out on dates with all the frequency of Catholic clergy.

But don't despair. In five years or so your kids will be in kindergarten. Of course, even then you'll both have to take a day off work to get any privacy—either that or sneak around like teenagers. Meanwhile, though you'll be sorely tempted, this is not the time to order one of those pay-per-view channels that feature mostly naked people involved in a lot of heavy breathing. It would just be too frustrating.

Can it really be that bad? you ask. Is having kids *that* restrictive?

I've heard about those couples whose children fall asleep at seven and sleep all night, leaving plenty of time and privacy for extra-curriculars. But even that kind of time, with the fatigue factor added in, can't match the romantic freedom of the childless couple. And for many of us, kids-who-crash-at seven—and then stay in bed, without coming back out for a drink of water, a hug, or whatever other pressing request they can muster up—is just a beautiful dream. Besides, if you've got older kids too, as we do, that pretty much covers the twenty-four hours.

Remember that amazing night when you . . . and then she . . . and right there on the living-room floor? Remember those long walks, those unhurried meals at quiet restaurants, those soul-baring discussions stretching deliciously into the wee hours? Watch as such memories fade into myth, cherished tales from the Golden Age of Childless Concupiscence. These days I find myself pushing my wife behind the kitchen door when the kids aren't looking, just to steal a serious kiss or two, like a high-school kid might do near his locker.

But is this any harder for the domestically involved husband than for the other kind? In my experience it is. For one thing, a man who spends real time with his kids often faces frustration, boredom and loneliness that men usually don't encounter out in the "real world." Since he's deprived of adult companionship for significant periods of time, he needs someone to talk to, someone to share with—someone who understands.

He may also entertain doubts about his attractiveness (which is the most natural thing in the world, and of course plagues mothers too). His time with his children brings no salary, no tangible rewards, no social status, no agreeable sense of immediate victory or involvement in the exciting and busy life of the world at large—and he worries that he's becoming some kind of drudge. He dresses down more often (for practical reasons), may shave less often, finds his clothes stained with peanut butter, ketchup or Play-doh—and though this isn't necessarily the result of laziness or slovenliness on his part, he sometimes *feels* like an unambitious putz. The sense that his brain is "turning to mush" (as I've heard many a housewife say) doesn't help either.

Being a real part of your family's home-life can also present certain obstacles to maintaining sexual pizzazz. The long hours can burn you out, make you feel dull. And it's harder to find time for exercise, with the added problem that the house is full of food, and eating is one pleasure you can always indulge in the presence of children. Ever heard that one about how bending over doing housework will flatten your stomach? What a crock. You'll realize, in fact, that it works exactly the opposite way. Once you become a parent, the gene pool wants to keep you right there with the kids, so it works to *reduce* your attractiveness to the opposite sex. Evolution needs you down on the farm, and it only uses gay Paris temporarily—to lure you to the farm in the beginning.

Domestically involved men may even begin to question their own masculinity, feeling less manly because so many people view their lifestyle as irrelevant, even unmasculine. Needless to say, if a guy lets all this get to him, it can certainly complicate his sexual performance.

When you're home with kids a lot you'll probably notice signs of this change in your sex-life. Emptying the wash machine one day, you'll find some of the clothes knotted together, loose threads and sweatshirt drawstrings tangled tightly around the hooks of one of your wife's bras—and you may think back fondly to a time when, maybe in a backseat somewhere, unhooking her bra offered you a completely different kind of challenge. Struggling to unknot the sodden clothes, you'll sigh forlornly to realize that, under present conditions, this is about as close as you're going to get to her lingerie.

In fact, there's a whole new set of conditions now governing your sexual-romantic life.

First, there are three basic ways your children disrupt it:

1. By waking up
2. By being awake
3. By having been awake so long that when they finally aren't, you don't want to be either

Second, finding time to make love will be much more difficult now because it hinges on so many factors. *All* your kids, for example, must be either out of commission or gone from the house, without the possibility of suddenly reappearing (no one will enjoy an unintentional "ambush")—and then you and your wife must be relatively free of work, worry, pain and fatigue—and of course it helps if you're on speaking terms at the moment—and then you both have to be in the mood—and willing to work rather quickly—etc. (I've heard there are couples who simply shut the bedroom door even when the kids are around—but I believe this only happens with serious old-time hippies and a handful of very progressive Unitarians.)

This is fate at its most complex. When all the factors actually do line up right, you have a Window of Opportunity—unless of course the pressure *itself* gets to you and slams the window shut. And that can happen.

Third, of course, is the whole science of male-female differences. When it comes to love-making and the behavior that leads up to it—a behavior greatly complicated by the presence of children and all the chaos they bring to your life—re-thinking some of the basics can be helpful. At this point in your life, you either get efficient or go without.

For one thing, you as a male should realize that, biologically speaking, you're not as different from your wife as you might think. The old idea that only women have complicated plumbing and hormone-induced behavior just isn't true.

Yes, hormones do affect female behavior; go ahead—call Ripley's. One morning as I was driving my wife to work, she asked me rather forcefully to buy her some wine for that evening. She'd been unusually tight-lipped for a day or so; I couldn't understand it. Suddenly there were tears in her eyes, right there in the front seat in the bright morning light. She began to explain that she was entering "that time of the month," but then her voice trailed off. Out of frustration and the pain of heavy cramping—and a loving if somewhat snarled concern for my physical safety—she ended with a simple warning: "Be careful!"

The poor thing! Biology had attacked her, besieged her, captured, pillaged, and possessed her—she was in the throes of suffering—but her deepest concern was that she might actually murder me! We both laughed till our sides hurt—especially when a truck from the Plattsburgh Motor Service pulled in front of us, with only the company's initials painted on its tailgate in blue letters a foot high: *PMS.*

But men have their own version of hormone-induced wackiness, and it plagues them—and they plague women *with* it—constantly. Male PMS is just as strong as any female's; to make matters worse, it isn't restricted to a particular time. Coincidentally, the medical term is the same as for women—that is, the acronym is the same, though the actual words aren't. Clinical experts refer to it as "**P**estering **M**adam for **S**ex"—and men get just as wild-eyed and lunatic under its influence as women do under their own.

Considering how biology can bedevil *both* sexes, it's easy to see why a fourth condition so often affects the domestically involved male: With all these frustrations and complexities, he's likely to exaggerate his sexual behavior. It's a desperate-guy thing. Such a reaction is natural, I think. The feeling that his masculinity has somehow been compromised, in combination with the frustration of long "droughts," can make a guy a little loopy. It's sure as hell happened to me. Pathetic conversations like the following may ensue:

> (Husband and wife together are changing their bed sheets on house-cleaning day)
>
> **WIFE:** This mattress is about shot. Look—there's a big ridge running down the middle, right between us.
>
> **HUSBAND:** You know what caused that, don't you?
>
> **WIFE:** What?
>
> **HUSBAND:** (matter-of-factly) Well, when we make love, we usually lie crossways. So there it is.

WIFE: There *what* is?

HUSBAND: It's the force. You know. I've got such force that I've driven the mattress up in the middle.

WIFE: (curiosity giving way to disgust) You've *got* to be kidding.

HUSBAND: (with scientific enthusiasm) No, really! You know how in plate tectonics India moved north millions of years ago and collided with the Asian mainland? It caused massive buckling—a whole new mountain range—the tallest on Earth . . .

WIFE: You're gross. Shut up.

HUSBAND: (running his hand along mattress ridge) What you're looking at, baby, are the Himalayas of Love.

WIFE: Disgusting! And don't try that old "him-a'-layin'" joke on me either—you're already sleeping on the couch . . .

I don't want to suggest there's anything inherently wrong with male sexuality—just the opposite. "The lust of the goat," as William Blake says, "is the glory of God." Being passionate sexual creatures is good for us, and it's reality. But a male, without even knowing it, can suddenly turn into a great Triceratopsian horn-doggie. When you start going stir-crazy and bullyragging your wife as in the dialogue above, it's probably time to drop back and think things over.

In fact, there are some telltale signs that you've crossed into the Zone of Exaggerated Sexual Behavior. And if you have, you need to know it. If any of the following apply to you, consider yourself a current citizen of that frantic and foolish country.

TEN SIGNS THAT YOU'VE ENTERED THE ZONE OF EXAGGERATED SEXUAL BEHAVIOR

1. Your average rate of mouthwash consumption increases dramatically.
2. You feel inexplicably aroused when your wife squeezes grocery-store tomatoes for ripeness.
3. Every thirty minutes or so you offer to give her a backrub.
4. You pour her a big glass of wine and say "I know how this relaxes you, darling."
5. Hoping for an early bedtime, you try to exhaust your kids by taking them to the beach, the park, the playground, and to that deafening pizza place with all the giant robotic singing animals.
6. You find yourself cutting *through* the lingerie section instead of around it—even at K-mart.
7. The average duration of your good-night kiss increases by 150%.
8. When the new "Victoria's Secret" catalogue arrives, you take it straight to her and say "Gosh, you'd look *great* in one of these . . ."
9. You keep flexing your muscles and saying "Just *feel* this!"
10. When your wife steps out of the shower, you suddenly recall the naval battle in *Ben Hur* and begin to mutter "Ramming speed!"

So, if these are the trying conditions of your current sexual-romantic life, what can you do about them? Unfortunately, this is a disease for which there is no complete cure. The main treatment is to grin and bear it, no matter how tight your grin may get. But there are things you can do to make the affliction manageable.

The first is the simplest: Husband and wife must be patient with each other. Amid such frustrations, the only serious danger is that lovers, instead of sharing their trials and joys, will turn on each other. That can be a true disaster, and its effects may be permanent.

Another important step, at least for me, was learning simply to be *aware* of when I was entering the Zone of Exaggerated Sexual Behavior. That usually gives me enough control to soften its effects somewhat. "Zone behavior" tends to be counter-productive; you drive your wife crazy, and yourself, and by overdoing it you can even endanger your opportunities by destroying the mood. It's not that I *blame* myself; my lust for my wife is as beautiful and natural as sunlight. Still, there *is* such a thing as an obnoxious male on the make—and she deserves better.

It will also help to remind yourself that "making love" is much more than physical intercourse. You and your wife are not just two bacteria mingling fluids; you have a *relationship*. "Making love" should be defined, I think, as everything that passes between two lovers; the way they talk to each other about the PTA is just as important as how they touch each other in bed. Life with children calls for compromises, but it can't keep you from "making love" in the broader sense, stealing kisses and fleeting caresses, sharing tenderness, loving each other in the uncountable little ways—and in the less dramatic daily way of working together as partners in the mundane but beautiful enterprise of raising a family.

My fourth recommendation is that you think seriously about what masculinity really means to you. Isn't there more to the male than being, as Elvis once described himself, "horny as a billy goat in a pepper patch"? Part of masculinity, of course, lies in self-restraint, and family life continually asks that of us. It's all part of the package. We should consider self-control, of course, just as manly as sexual desire itself.

Re-defining masculinity can also help us overcome some of our male insecurities. It's no disaster for the domestically involved guy to feel less masculine at times, and no man should be ashamed of that. It happens. Don't get all down on yourself if you find you're gaining weight, or wearing sweatpants too often, or, miracle of miracles, if some night *you're* actually the one who's too tired.

But if you can define masculinity to *include* passionate domestic commitment—and if you come to believe this emotionally as well as intellectually—you may find yourself feeling better. Consequently, of course, you'll be less prone to exaggerated sexual behavior, lack of sexual confidence, and other pitfalls.

And there are lots of practical things a couple can do to keep their romance alive. The most important is to actively pursue it! I don't mean all that foolishness about her dressing in saran wrap, or him coming home in a Zorro costume. But of all the crucial aspects of a busy family's life, what tends to get pushed to the back burner? Mom and Dad's love-life. The kids simply can't exist without constant affection and attention, and all the practical chores are mandatory; husband and wife often find that their own relationship is the only thing they can skimp on. But that can be dangerous. Even though it's a lot of work and you're already working hard enough—even though you may not feel like it at the moment—even though you think you've given all you have to give—you must *fight* to be a couple, to have time alone together, to truly share yourselves amid the endless booming distractions of family life.

So find that secret fifteen minutes; investigate the advantages of futons as opposed to creaky antique beds; keep yourselves as attractive as you can for each other; be ready to give yourselves to sudden passion—and ready not to, when that's the more loving alternative.

A particularly helpful strategy for us has been to squeeze "dates" out of unlikely moments. Friday night grocery shopping at least allows something like conversation on the way and back (though punctuated by a kid in the backseat who wants to tell us every detail of her day); besides, we get to smile at each other a lot in the checkout line. Some of our best "dates," in fact, have come as we discussed things over breakfast, or went for a walk, or talked in the car while our kids snoozed during a longer trip.

Even when you can't find time alone, there are little ways to stoke your passion. How many times have our eyes met and lingered on each other for a moment during a hectic dinner, or during the protracted ritual of getting our daughter ready for bed? How many times have we joked with each other, or said excitedly "Oh! I forgot to tell you! . . . ," or danced to a song on the radio during Saturday-morning housework? How many times have we stopped to embrace when passing each other in the hall? How many times has the waking one caressed the face of the sleeping one? And on a seemingly more mundane note: It's amazing how much affection is generated simply by regularly *thanking* your spouse for all the work she's doing.

But there's a deeper way to deal with all this too—and it has to do with reaching past yourself for the empowering vision of the true nature of romance and desire. It comes to me tonight as Shilly-Shally dances for us in the living room, wearing her mother's high-heels and underthings.

In her indefatigable way, our ever-exploring daughter quickly discovered her mother's underwear drawer, and its super-feminine treasures dazzled her. So tonight, with her mom and dad crashed in exhaustion on the couch, she's performing for us an animated and caboose-shaking version of the Dance of the Seven Veils.

Over her jeans and t-shirt she's wearing the wine-red camisole—three sizes too big—and pale-gold French-cut panties I bought her mother in a moment of delusional hope (or perhaps prayer). She dances and sings for us, then runs through the house playing "Beauty and the Beast" ("Do you like my party dress, Beast?" she asks breathlessly, to which I duly answer "Oh, you look lovely, Belle!"), then flings herself on the couch and eats her cracker snack, then whines (like she does every night) about having to take a bath. And why not let her wear the stuff to bed? No one else will be using it—her older brothers stay up late.

Besides, it's important for her to play dress-up, one of the many ways a child practices for adulthood. She's already begun the process that will culminate in her going to the junior-senior prom wearing stiletto heels, black hose, heavy make-up, flashy jewelry, and a tight black dress with plunging decolletage, in that utterly transparent imitation of womanhood high-school girls are so drawn to. And someday she'll meet a guy—the real thing, this time—and fall in love, and marry, and he'll probably buy her a wine-red camisole and pale-gold French-cut panties, which they'll put to good use—and that will eventually produce children, perhaps a daughter—who will then run around the house with her mama's pretty things over her jeans and t-shirt. And some night she and her husband, crashed on the couch, will realize just as I have tonight that right before their eyes stands the living symbol and embodiment of their sex life.

For it's the inevitable nature of love to bear fruit.

One day while dusting I happened to notice a little blotch of ink on my wife's white desk-blotter—and immediately saw it as an island. Putting the dust rag down I began doodling with a ballpoint pen, naming the bays and peninsulas in tiny print, imagining us walking the island's forested hills and surf-washed beaches. For a time I was lost in that most common of fantasies indulged in by busy parents: just the two of us, alone and free in some far-off place, with all the time in the world to catch up to our own hearts. I could almost hear cruiseship-commercial music in the background.

How good it felt to escape the constant demands of being somebody's father (that is, the sometimes-overwhelmed father of three very intelligent and energetic young somebodies)—and to escape with the one I love! So in my waking dream the two of us hiked, and swam, and made passionate love, and read books without being interrupted to change bandaids or make sandwiches, and slept deep, unbroken sleep. And the ripe fruit just tumbled from the trees.

A week later, dusting near the blotter again, I saw that my wife had added her own doodles, sketching in a house on the island, a library, a swimming pool. So I contributed a few more touches of my own. Without exchanging a word, we'd entered a secret world together.

Week by week the dream-game continued. The surprising thing, though, was that even though we were together in our fantasy, we gradually grew lonely—just as our love in the real world created a kind of loneliness in our early married life. As dreams do when they're taken seriously, our blotter-island reverie slowly became more realistic and practical. The island seemed empty without our kids playing in its breakers, or running its trails, or flinging mud at each other with plastic sand-shovels—so we'd soon added a tree-house, a play center, and a stable. Eventually we penciled a beautiful, bustling city onto the mainland coast, then built a wonderful school just across the channel from our dock—only noticing then that our tranquil island fantasy had begun to resemble the close-quartered, high-tempo, demanding life we're currently living in the real world (except that in the fantasy, of course, we had lots of cash).

What happened to the two lovers reading beneath a tree or sleeping naked in the afternoon sun? The same thing that happened in reality: Our love blossomed—it overflowed. Sitting at the desk with pen in hand one cleaning-day morning, I realized that we'd fantasized ourselves right smack into the middle of the lives we'd wanted to escape from.

Romance is far too powerful and beautiful a force to be limited to two people. It could never be accurately represented only by roses, candlelit dinners, gifts of jewelry, and the pleasures of the body. Romance stirs through the world like wind, and through our own bodies and hearts, a great waking of lives, a lord of the air bringing profound sweetness and imperious commands. All our human smallness bends before it; not even a woman's "evil-twin" PMS or a man's constant lustful-coyote howling can keep its deeper powers at bay. And it teaches a profound lesson: that beyond sex and passionate expressions of love, the most romantic thing of all is simply to be there for each other, to be good to each other, to lovingly share our lives.

So here we are in this life of ours, lovers disguised as Mom and Dad, with jobs, a car, a house, kids to look after and fuss with and all the rest. And this, we know, is the true life of romance, however unlikely that may seem.

Still, that doesn't keep me from whispering a line from Yeats in her ear, as we're folding the day's last basket of laundry:

> *To an isle in the water*
> *With her I would go . . .*

CHAPTER FOURTEEN

The Male As Domestic Warrior

"When a man is deprived of the power of expression, he will express himself in a drive for power."
—Jose Arguelles

"'A hero,' said Jack Molay, 'is not only someone who acts. A hero is also someone who endures.'"
—Stephen Dobyns, *The Wrestler's Cruel Study*

LAST JANUARY I opened the paper one day to see the headline "DAD DIDN'T FEED OR CLEAN KIDS FOR THREE DAYS."

This man's three children, all under five, were in terrible condition. The one- and two-year-old each had blisters and sores because their diapers hadn't been changed; the four-year-old "had eaten his own feces." During the police visit, the father complained that his wife had left for the weekend. The arresting officer asked why he hadn't looked after the kids himself. His answer? "I don't do that."

This case is extreme, of course. The excuse, however, is all too familiar. Some guys use it regularly, expressing it either in words or in non-verbal ways. I once asked a friend of mine—a very *good* man—about his wife's post-partum depression. "How's she sleeping?" I wondered.

"I don't know," he said.

"What—you don't talk about it?"

He gave me a funny look. "Well, I don't say *How did you sleep?!*"

This is a hard-working, highly-skilled guy, a superb athlete and excellent businessman, the kind of man who knows how to get things done, and who also has a great sense of humor. But this kind of domestic awareness just wasn't modeled for him, and consequently he couldn't even imagine it.

When I was first married I bought into the same attitude myself. "I'll do a lot when I'm a father," I'd tell my young wife, "but I'll *never* change a diaper!" Maybe she was tempted to ask that proverbial question: *Did I think my own was odorless?* Eventually she let me know just how wrong I was, pointing out that *someone* had changed *my* diapers (Gee, Mom—can I ever thank you enough?). So I became the brave man I am today, never hesitating to descend into the netherworld of an active backside. Still, I'm ashamed to say that at one point I "didn't do" diapers.

So I wasn't surprised at a Parents.com poll showing that, although in 63% of American households both mothers and fathers change diapers, in 35%, mothers usually do—and in only 2% do fathers generally take on this oh-so-symbolic task. A more recent 2010 survey by Pampers found that 69% of men said they changed diapers as often as their wives, with 11% saying more often. But while this shows increasing male involvement, it must be pointed out that only *31%* of mothers agreed that fathers share diaper duty, and only 4% said men did more. American family life, one suspects, is still a work in progress.

And the problem of the uninvolved father can go much deeper. The counsellor Richard Rohr says, "I have found father hunger to be the single most prevalent wound in the human soul—and one of the most painful," a conclusion he reached partly from his work with convicts. Psychologists call it the "father wound" and show how it leads to great hurt, especially for males, and often to misguided, even self-destructive attempts at winning the love and respect the father never gave.

Carl Jung's words, written in 1912, haunt me to the degree that they're still applicable to many guys today. The American man, Jung said, "...is focused almost entirely on his business, so that as a husband he is glad to have no responsibilities. He gives the complete direction of his family life over to his wife...This is what you call giving independence to the American woman. It is what I call the laziness of the American man. The lazy part of his life is where his family is." And that approach has led, David Yount points out, to our current state of affairs, which psychiatrist Anthony Clare characterizes this way:

> "...the whole issue of men—the point of them, their pur-
> pose, their value, their justification—is a matter for public
> debate. Serious commentators declare that men are redun-
> dant, that women do not need them, and children would be
> better off without them."

How could it come to the point where such an idea would even be thinkable? It's clear, to me at least, that we need to make some changes. And what men need most, I think, are some new ways of looking at themselves and their lives.

But today's American male is at times confused. Just who is he supposed to be, anyway?

On one hand, there's clearly a need for change in some men's domestic behavior. A Feminist Dictionary, in its entry for the term "family man," points out that "[t]here is no label family woman, since that would be heard as redundancy." Many of us are dis-tressed, too, at the private failures of famous and powerful males, the domestic lies gradually exposed by journalists and muckrak-ers. Oh, he was a statesman, an artist, a big wig, but now it's revealed that he completely subverted his family's needs to his own ambitions, or that he slept around, discreetly or not, or that he abandoned or abused his spouse and/or children, verbally or otherwise. Somewhere there's a small bleak place where his greatness can't reach, somewhere a wife in stony silence or an angry and troubled child.

But what should the "new male" be like? How do men balance the realities of their own natures with what the modern family asks of them? After all, we're not "bad guys" — we're *men*. And it bears stating the obvious here too: We *should* be men, we have a right to be men!

One problem, which affects both women and men, stems from the effects of unrealistic idealizations of the opposite sex. When men and women are isolated by rigid roles, each tends to develop self-serving fantasies about its "ideal mate." The result? In the absence of realistic ideals, we learn to desire exaggerated and shallow qualities in each other.

My daughter has a plastic "Ken" figure—to go with Barbie, of course—that just amazes me. The little stud-muffin wears turquoise shoes and slacks, a tight gold jacket, a pink turtleneck, and a gold medalion; he's as tan as George Hamilton and has his perfect blonde hair in a huge bouffant. What the hell is *this* about? Here's a version of the "sensitive guy" taken to a logical extreme, so "in touch with his feminine side" that he hardly seems male. And of course he's an exaggerated version of the current "metrosexual," a type that, we're hearing now, is passing out of favor. Judging by sales, Ken's pretty popular with little girls, and romantic ideals can be influenced early. So does *he* represent, in some general way, what American females want us to be?

But then again, aren't there plenty of guys who'd be happy with a real-life Barbie? I fantasize about marching in front of Mattel corporate headquarters chanting

Free the women! Free the men!
Deliver us all from Barbie and Ken!

And stereotypes about "masculinity" persist (just as they do, of course, for "femininity"). I recently heard a well-known TV comedian declare, "I want to celebrate *men!*" and my heart beat a little faster. *This is just what we need!* I thought. But what's manhood to him? Home repair, fixing cars, and following pro sports teams—so narrow a band of behaviors that his "celebration" of masculinity is in some ways just the same old stuff. Other "tributes" to men show what I consider a similar narrowness. In a popular magazine a father is highly praised because, while his wife deals with their newborn, he "pitch[es] in to help out with an older child's care"; the wife adds gratefully that "He's managed somehow not to comment on my appearance—even when he's met at the door by a wife wearing sweatpants and covered in leaking breast milk and spit-up."

Holy machismo, Batman!—as if this guy is going beyond the call of duty simply by doing his share and showing basic courtesy! The unspoken assumption here seems to be that you just can't expect more from a male.

In our society, the word "mother" is still widely used when "parent" is more appropriate, as if men can have nothing to do with children. You see the same phenomenon when a father himself refers to watching his kids as "babysitting." Another example will underscore the point. Back in '95 I looked at an issue of *Healthy Kids* Magazine (from the American Academy of Pediatricians, no less) and counted all the pictures of adults with children, in ads and articles, and divided them into three categories. 15 of the pictures showed mothers parenting; 6 showed fathers; only 2 showed Mom and Dad parenting together. But surely things have changed since then? Well, the June 2012 *Pregnancy* magazine was revealing. There were 7 images of men alone with a child or children, and 7 of a man and woman with children. But there were 23 of a woman alone with a child (I'm not including the 37 pregnant women without males). And this, if you can believe it, was their "Guy Issue"!

A split in our traditional view of males can be traced way back, and certainly to earliest American times. On one hand, there's the venerable Benjamin Franklin, ultimate man of achievement. His image is everywhere, and he certainly was a remarkable human being. But a current biography discusses his capacity for anger, and his estrangement from his oldest son William, a Loyalist. Nor was Franklin above philandering.

On the other hand we have the fictional Rip Van Winkle, remembered as a shiftless, hen-pecked husband who magically escaped a shrewish wife. But the story says too that *he* was the one who played with the village children, who taught them, laughed with them, was their companion.

This is the either/or that to some degree affects every American father today. In our tradition, a male is sometimes seen either a man of action and thus naturally distant from homelife and his children—or, if he truly shares himself with them, as unambitious, even as a wimp or ne'er-do-well, someone who just can't handle the male achievement role. And this stereotype can get even darker. A woman I know told me that the male teacher she had for third-grade back in the 70's aroused suspicions in her family: Was the guy just desperate for work? Aiming to be principal? Gay? A pedophile?

Somewhere between these two poles we American males have to find ourselves. And we've begun to look. As early as the late 80's *The New York Times Magazine* reported that "millions of fathers now are experiencing . . . stresses as they try to fulfill longtime career goals and satisfy new family demands."

It's men themselves who have to decide how to work this out. My friend Marie tells me how her husband Ron is gradually learning to do the domestic tasks she asks him to; her eyes often tear up as she gratefully recounts his progress. As moving as this is, however, it often leaves me frustrated; there's still that stereotypical truth we hear in joke-form about wives having to "train" their husbands. The right to define fatherhood—and the responsibility—should rest with the men who must live that role. A man should act out of *intrinsic* motivation in this regard, not just extrinsic reinforcement or direction from his wife or anyone else.

A good place to start is with our feelings about "adventure."

As a boy I longed for it. "Adventure" to me always included some thrilling challenge that also involved the possibility of danger—a journey or exploration, especially of the natural world—usually some kind of warfare or lesser violence, or at least athletic competition in some form—and of course glory. Such longings aren't exclusively masculine, I know, but they certainly moved my brothers, my male friends and me. We expressed them first in play and later in high-school sports: We were going to be pirates, or raft down the Mississippi, or drive cross-country and discover the true America; we'd take our run-and-gun offense all the way to the state championship.

Only as an adult did I realize the deeper truth about adventure: In the real world it's much more profound, potentially more dangerous, and—once you look past all the overblown color and drama we get from the movies—far more ordinary than I'd ever imagined. Starting your own business is an adventure. Being a firefighter, a political whistle-blower, an artist, or a single parent is an adventure. Any risky, profound attempt at significant achievement is in fact adventurous—and adventures occur *within* us more frequently than outside us.

Parenting, it follows, is one of humanity's most essential adventures, a supreme endeavor, and we need to learn how to see it in that light.

A second point is to consider the ancient male ideal of "warriorhood."

I often have dreams in which my children are physically threatened and I react with rage and violence to protect them. There is, it seems, a guardian instinct woven deeply into the male; I know mothers have it too, but in my experience they aren't as pre-occupied with it as fathers are. It's not that all men are phys-

ically aggressive, or even brave, but such qualities seem to reso-
nate deeply with males.

In the modern world, though, physical aggression is often
prohibitively dangerous. There are far too many guys who still
think they can resolve conflicts with their fists, or with weapons.
But trying to vilify or eradicate basic maleness is no way to address this problem. It makes more sense, I think, to expand our
"warrior" urges, as Robert Bly uses the word—to set them burning more quietly and more constantly—to help men become,
along with their wives, both the public "warriors" they've been
all along and private ones too, fierce protectors and supporters of
family life.

Maybe the best way to accomplish this is for men to consider
the true threats to their families. What are the chances your child
will be kidnapped or attacked by a criminal? These things happen, but they're relatively rare (in most places, that is). What are
the chances, though, that *any* child will develop school problems,
grow up without self-love and confidence, abuse drugs or alco-
hol, become bulimic, workaholic, neurotic? Such quieter threats
are far more common, and more dangerous.

The modern male warrior will direct his protective rage
against these ordinary dangers. He'll pour devotion over his kids
so their hearts can grow strong. He'll work hard to help them love
reading and do well in school. He'll put up with some of his sons'
Oedipal behavior because he knows they have to go through it;
he'll help his daughters learn to accept and appreciate their physical appearance. And he'll be pro-active in his protectiveness. He'll
do, in fact, whatever it takes to keep his kids growing, safe and
happy.

Do you love your wife and children? Will you strive to be
heroic in the way you express that love? I'll give you heroism—
the hardest kind, and perhaps the most fruitful. You can become
one of that secret and fabled brotherhood, the Order of Knights
Domestic. It won't be easy. You'll have to deny your own de-

sires, face boredom, frustration and drudgery. Will you kneel at vigil all night in the chapel, broadsword beside you? No—your vigil will be at the bedside of a cranky kid covered with chicken pox. Your great enemy won't stand armed and glowering before you; it will lurk within you instead, in your own weakness or selfishness, and around you, in all that threatens your family, visible or invisible, in all that can harm them or limit their fulfillment.

But why even use the word "warrior" to begin with? Because there *is* a war. Walking downtown recently I saw a sticker on a lamppost that read, "Every minute 30 children die of disease and inadequate health care—and the world spends $1,700,000.00 on war." And this of course doesn't even mention the wounds of spirit that afflict so many families. The *real* war is always being fought. It's a war against indifference, abuse, human inertia—against poverty and emotional numbness—against ignorance, intolerance, violence and wasted lives. And it's a personal war for you; you're a soldier in it simply because you're a parent.

A third step for the new definition of fatherhood is obvious, at least to me: Men must *commit* themselves to family life.

A woman I know who does janitorial work at my gym tells me that cleaning the men's bathrooms is always much worse than the women's; for one thing, she declares hotly, "Men—don't—flush!" Most guys, we have to conclude, don't perceive such things as having anything to do with them.

I wish I could claim *I* always behave like I should. (I do flush! Well… usually.) But I still tend to draw invisible boundaries around my responsibility, without even realizing it. Don't get me wrong here—I'm a realist: There's stuff I do because I choose to do it, but there's also stuff I do only to keep from getting in trouble. And I suppose that'll never change completely; the male psyche can only handle so much "maturity," after all. I'm trying hard. Still, only in the last few years have I woken up enough to begin replacing the toilet paper in the bathroom. Macaroni and cheese is another example; though I've been making it for my kids since the 80's, I still have to the check the directions every time to see how much milk and butter to add. I'm a grown-up; I've memorized my address and social security number. But knowing off the top of my head how to make macaroni and cheese? No, that would be too much like a commitment to food preparation. Not my department.

Some men, in fact, can be profoundly stubborn about such things, and may go for years uncommitted, or half-committed, floating along as their wives carry the brunt of responsibility for homelife. I know of a guy who, though he has three kids and doesn't want more, refuses to get a vasectomy—on the grounds that he shouldn't have to go through the discomfort! How does that kind of "discomfort" stack up against his wife's pregnancy, labor, episiotomy, giving birth, post-partum letdown, night feedings, and the struggle to return to normal weight—and all of it times three? The guy apparently doesn't regard reproductive control as his concern. Maybe he could use a good snipping.

I see six general levels of domestic involvement in men. Check out the following and ask yourself where you fit. (It doesn't really matter whether you work full-time, part-time, or not at all; the point is what you're like when you *are* home.)

LEVEL 1: THE UNINVOLVED MALE

Won't do housework or care for children; that's "women's work." Selfish and self-isolated.

LEVEL 2: THE PASSIVELY UNINVOLVED MALE

He's not consciously or openly resistant; he just doesn't care, and he can't be bothered. Though easier to live with than the Level 1 guy, he's ultimately just as bad, only quieter.

LEVEL 3: THE BEGRUDGING CONTRIBUTOR

If asked, he'll do some—but he doesn't like it and resists or complains, or expresses his reluctance in subtler ways, like by doing a crappy job. One of his main strategies is simply to "screen out" or not pay attention to crying kids, dirty dishes, etc. In many cases, his wife eventually gives up and just stops asking.

LEVEL 4: THE "TABLE-CLEARER"

He's somewhat involved and does some work—though not his share. But what he does is his basis for considering his wife lucky to have him. Inconsistent.

LEVEL 5: THE "BIG KID"

He helps a lot, is always willing. But really hasn't taken full responsibility for his share; must be "programmed" for everything, continually pointed in the right direction. In some ways a further burden on his wife; she wishes he'd figure out for himself what needs doing. On the other hand, the "big kid" is usually really trying, and will gradually move to Level 6. (Some wives, too, ambivalently prefer to *keep* a husband at this level—or keep him there simply by unwisely and compulsively insisting that *everything* be done exactly her way and her way only.)

LEVEL 6: THE PARTNER

He looks for and willingly accepts his responsibilities, identifies himself as a father and husband, takes pride in his domestic role. He doesn't consider himself amazing but simply a man doing what should be done. When husband and wife are true partners, of course, they'll disagree more about how their homelife should proceed. But good partners work such things out.

If you're at Level 5 or 6, your commitment will reveal itself in new behavior and new knowledge. Take the following quiz to get a more detailed picture of where you actually stand.

MALE DOMESTIC COMMITMENT TEST

DIRECTIONS: For each "Yes," give yourself one point. (You *are* allowed to respond "Yes—but I didn't like it".)

1. Have you ever actually spoken the words "No problem—it's only urine!"?
2. While busy in the house, have you ever put your child's dirty socks or underwear in your pocket for later deposit in the clothes hamper?
3. Over time, has *Barney* gone from an attack on your senses to mere background noise?
4. Have you ever said to your wife, "Please get out of my kitchen"?
5. After your child tells a long incoherent story about a puppy/super-hero/jungle animal/cartoon character, have you ever said, "Tell me more!"?
6. Has your response to a child's vomit shifted from vomiting yourself to worrying about stains on the carpet?
7. Do you know *why* we separate the lights from the darks?
8. Have you begun to pay attention to ads for garage sales and consignment stores?
9. Can you say, without flinching, "I'll be right in to clean your bottom"?
10. Have you begun to actually care about what happens on *SpongeBob SquarePants*?
11. Have you found yourself listening with interest to housekeeping tips?

12. Have you ever actually cleaned the condiment shelves in the refrigerator door?

13. Have you come to realize that granola bars are really just candy with oats in it?

14. Have you ever proudly created a smiling-clown face out of bits of cheese on a piece of baloney?

15. Have you ever found yourself saying, "Oh well, might as well clean it while I have the chance!"?

SCORE:

13–15	You're officially a Good Man. (Don't be alarmed; does not lead to testicular shrinkage.)
11–12	You're part of the family.
8–10	Still struggling. Keep it up.
6–7	Lots of room for improvement.
3–5	A New World awaits you. Start paddling.
0–2	Hopeless sexist bastard. Your penance: Listen to Helen Reddy's "I Am Woman" fifteen times in a row. Time to nut up!

Adventure, warriorhood, commitment—and along with these another crucial quality: a new orientation.

As a kid I read a science-fiction novel about a huge asteroid hollowed out and made into a starship. During its centuries-long interstellar flight, the people in the different walled sections of the asteroid-ship forgot about each other. The cooks no longer knew about the engineers; they simply put food trays on the conveyor belts that disappeared into the walls. On the other side, the engineers never cooked for themselves; they ran the ship and the food simply came out three times a day and they ate it.

This is pretty much how it is for some American men.

I don't mean to exaggerate. Lots of guys will fix themselves a sandwich now and then, and we all know where the can-opener's kept—it's a beer thing. But as a group, do we really *think* about the maintenance of house and kids?

Even fathers who sincerely want to be domestically involved find they still have to re-orient themselves. After all, as I keep saying: It's not like we were trained! The set-up for most of us was pretty simple: When it came to domestic stuff, Mom took care of it. In fact, many males were downright encouraged to let someone else do the daily practical stuff. And even if our mothers resented it, they still did the work, and usually didn't go to the trouble of teaching us to do it for ourselves. We knew, just as dogs do, that food and drink would be provided; we got to the point where we could just manage to roll over when we wanted our bellies scratched.

My wonderful neighbor told me the other day how, spiking a bad fever and feeling disoriented, she went to bed. Later she woke, the fever worse and her thoughts getting scrambled. *I can't die!* she found herself ranting. *I can't! No one but me knows how to cut the boys' sandwiches!*

My brother-in-law, a brilliant and wonderful guy, is now a high-ranking officer in the Air Force. But an incident from his younger years exemplifies how domestically disoriented men can be. Jim had come to visit my sister Jane (his fiancee at the time) and of course brought a suitcase. When Jane opened it later, it was crammed with dirty clothes. "I know how he thinks," she told me. "It was time to go to the airport, and he knew he should have a suitcase, with clothes in it. So he stuffed some clothes in and off he went." As a dutiful girlfriend, Jane washed all the clothes, folded them neatly, and put them back in the suitcase. Jim took the suitcase when he left.

The next time he flew in to see her, Jane again opened his suitcase. Inside were the same clothes she'd washed—folded and arranged just as she'd packed them two months earlier. Jim had gone home, set the suitcase down, and hadn't touched it till it was time to leave again. You have to wonder what he wore in the meantime—maybe his old football and baseball uniforms.

Lots of guys help with the dishes, which includes, of course, wiping off the stove. But for most men, this means only the open areas. The typical guy just "doesn't do" burner-pans. Grease and crumbs and charred food and God knows what else fall down into the pans. But that's no-man's-land.

Most women don't recognize these boundaries. "The burner-pans get dirty!" they may say. "How come *I'm* the only one who cleans them?!" But the husbands forget; there's no place in their heads for this new knowledge to stick to. Later, when someone turns on the stove and the crusted egg droppings begin to smoke, the man says to his wife, "Hey! Something's burning!"

She'll want to scream, "That's because there are two months' worth of crud in the burner-pans that you never bothered to clean out!" But like as not, his innocent ignorance will exasperate her into silence, and in future she'll clean them herself.

This whole go-round occurs because men just haven't learned how to think about homelife. Some guys have trouble getting out of that typical male fog in which the only truly powerful thought is "Okay, what fun thing do I get to do next?" Men have to break this cycle for themselves. And habits of dis-orientation may be the greatest obstacle. As Proust says, "The voyage of discovery lies not in finding landscapes but in having new eyes." It's almost like learning to accept some strange behavior from another culture. After a while, it makes perfect sense—but at first you don't get it, and you feel clumsy, and you sometimes resent having to change. And at times you even give in to infantile frustration and give up, then just roll over, hoping someone will scratch that belly of yours.

I've only recently realized another huge gap in my own domestic orientation: the whole area you might call "procurement." Struggling by myself to get the fitted sheet on our bed the other day, I suddenly realized that I've never in my life thought about actually going out and *buying* sheets when the old ones wear out. As much as I've improved, there are still things I automatically leave to my wife.

But it really isn't manly to be such a punk when it comes to domestic life. Some fathers, for example, are disgusted by their children's bodily fluids, even fearful of them. So where's their machismo? It's like that old joke boys tell each other:

> **FIRST KID:** *You think you're strong?*

> **SECOND KID:** *Yeah.*

> **FIRST KID:** (Spits on ground.) *Pick that up.*

Even Schwarzenegger said, once he became a parent, "All of a sudden all those things that normally gross you out, they don't gross you out at all."

There'll be other signs, too, that you've expanded your horizons. The re-oriented male won't habitually leave laundry unfolded or dishes unwashed at night, because he now understands the principle of "It-Won't-Go-Away" (also known as the "Those-Clothes-Aren't-Just-Going-to-Fold-Themselves" Law). The re-oriented male will cringe when he hears his young son singing from the bathroom, "No matter how you shake or dance/The last three drops go down your pants." (He doesn't object to the song, mind you; he just realizes the kid may sing it someday for Miss Carrie at pre-school.) He'll understand why there's a whole industry based on household advice—why there are magazines with articles like "Two-Step Teriyaki" or "Making Your Bathroom Say 'You'!," and stories about women turning jerks into nice guys—and why Heloise is in the paper every day, even with that hair. And he'll find himself surprisingly grateful for home-use products that get the job done, are easy to use, and don't cost an arm and a leg.

With your new orientation you might find yourself noticing deeper things too. You may recognize with shock that popular old movies like Disney's *Peter Pan* or *Mary Poppins,* even *The Sound of Music,* are, among other things, serious attacks on traditional fathers. Each presents the typical dad as a virtual enemy of the rest of the family, a blustering power-mongerer everyone has to appease, obey, or try to manipulate. As you watch, you may feel you've broken a kind of code—the code of an "enemy" you didn't even know you had—a code of offhand remarks, rolled eyes, secretive complaints, and the unspoken understanding between mother and children that it's best just to stay out of Daddy's way. You may notice in *Peter Pan* that the same voice-actor plays Mr. Darling the father *and* the sadistic Captain Hook.

As you re-orient yourself, you're likely to discover a whole new pantheon of male heroes. Men like Morel de Villiers, mayor of a French village in the late 1800's, who established laws and hospital policies that reduced infant mortality "from thirty per hundred to zero." Men like Edmund Muskie, who may have lost the Democratic presidential nomination because, while publicly criticizing an attack on his wife, he had the guts to cry on national TV. Men like offensive tackle David Williams, fined $111,111 by the Houston Oilers when he missed a game to stay with his wife the day after she gave birth. Or Andrew Vachas, a lawyer and writer whose war against child abuse has cost him, among other things, a bout with malaria and two broken jaws. Or the novelist Charles Gaines who, after his writing life "estranged" him "from . . . his role as father and husband," chose to turn back to his family and build a house on Nova Scotia with them—and then wrote honestly about the experience and about his own failings and new discoveries. Or Charles Ballard, who initially went into the streets of Cleveland to help teenage fathers and now runs the National Institute for Responsible Fatherhood and Family Development, helping young men to finish school, work past anger, and assume their duties toward their children and wives. Or Mandy Patinkin, who gave up a role on an Emmy-winning TV show because the demands of the job were destroying his family life. Or Dan Mulhern, the state of Michigan's "First Man"; after his wife's election to the governorship, Mulhern said (in a reporter's paraphrase) that "it's difficult but important for men to take on the kinds of support roles that wives of high-profile men have filled for years." Or the Air Force colonel I know who, with almost 20 years in the service, turned down a career-climaxing battalion command because it meant an overseas posting that wouldn't work for his wife and children.

Not only have these men done heroic things, but they've done them without the affirmation that accompanies traditional male heroism; I think of writer Shana McLean Moore's words in my local paper:

> "...dads such as mine and my daughters' who will never get the media attention of their notorious peers. Their fame is earned, instead, in the hearts of their wives and children..."

Your new orientation will bring you much joy and wisdom too. "Having children," a woman writer has said, "opened up my world more than anything else"—and this can be just as true for men. The re-oriented male begins to see how utterly dependent the world is on how the young are raised and taught. He learns whole volumes about joy and play and a looser idea of time. He begins to understand the necessity of certain forms of drudgery, how such work is good for him, how his love for his family and his pride in himself are shaped partly by that kind of labor. He begins to understand something of what it has traditionally meant to be a woman, and what a woman's life is like; he looks at his wife with "new eyes." And he gets a huge kick out of his kids—for one thing, the way they're always making him laugh.

Another new insight may be a re-defining of "success." The male role in our culture is based largely on achievement—outward, measurable, socially rewarded success. But success in the domestic sphere is a very different kettle of fish. For one thing, it takes decades before you can see the long-term results of your parenting. For another, society gives little or no reward to parents and/or homemakers. But maybe the hardest thing for the traditional male is the *invisibility* of the work. When you do your job right in the working world, there are usually tangible results, and sometimes praise and/or monetary reward; at home, however, there's nothing to show for all your efforts except more or less contented kids and a relatively clean house—in other words, the status quo. Those piles of toys you picked up? The gallons of mud you wiped off the floor? The endless loads of laundry you washed and folded? The boredom you alleviated in your children, the fights you prevented, all the effects of abuse and neglect that your kids will never know? No one but you will see these things. Much domestic success consists simply of breaking even, or just avoiding disaster. And not even your spouse will see all the potential disasters you prevented, all the bad you made good. The rest is fostering the slow, quiet, steady growth of the child, which is only half-visible even to the full-time parent—but which, in time, is exactly what creates the world we all live in.

The domestic warrior accepts this reality, strengthens himself for it, knows he's fighting for a magnificent cause. And he may also learn something profound about human happiness: the simple fact that you can't always tell you're happy even when you are. The domestic warrior learns to look past hard work and boredom and see that the truly important things are going as they should; this makes him deeply happy. Sometimes, for example, my wife and I get a little crazy about some of the more disgusting bathroom work we have to do, at certain moments bristling at the indignity of it. But as I'm plunging a toilet or flushing after the forgetful, I often find myself remembering Yeats' words:

"'Fair and foul are near of kin,
And fair needs foul,' I cried . . .
' . . . Love has pitched his mansion in
The place of excrement;
For nothing can be sole or whole
That has not been rent.'"

Even if he doesn't have time to meditate or reflect—hell, even to sit exhausted in a chair with his mouth hanging open like a recently thumped cod—the commited father may begin to feel the underground river of love that nourishes his marriage and his children. Being with kids—and some of the "dead-end" qualities of the job—may teach him too, as Jung says, that

" . . . the greatest and most important problems of life . . . can never be solved, but only outgrown . . . [With a] broadening of . . . outlook . . . the insoluble problem los[es] its urgency. It [is] not solved logically in its own terms but fade[s] when confronted with a new and stronger life urge."

So the domestic warrior must learn to think and act in new ways. But there are some distinctly "old-fashioned" qualities he must develop too. The most important, I think, are courage, faith, and the willingness to work.

For one of the best depictions of fathering I've ever read, consider Dr. Seuss' *Horton Hatches an Egg*.

I can't say if the childless Seuss meant Horton the elephant to represent fathers committed to homelife. But the parallels are uncanny. Horton promises to watch over a mother-bird's unhatched egg while she takes a break—only she never comes back. But Horton won't abandon the child:

"I meant what I said
And I said what I meant . . .

An elephant's faithful
One hundred per cent!"

His vigil is beset with difficulties. There are physical trials when winter comes. (As one real-life parallel, consider the recent *New York Times* article reporting that "Young families with children have significantly less money than their counterparts did a generation ago . . . "). Horton also faces psychological trials; the other animals mock him for sitting on a nest (much as some people look askance at the domestic male). Horton gets frustrated, and like any active person "want[s] to play." And when hunters sell him to a circus, he's displayed as a curiosity (as stay-at-home dads sometimes are). But maybe the toughest thing is just the endless work and lack of stimulation:

> Then Horton the elephant smiled. "Now that's that . . . "
> And he sat
> and he sat
>   and he sat
>   and he sat . . .

I see the whole breadth of my fatherhood in that one line.

Just when the hardest time is over, though, just when the child is most lovable and when being a parent is dramatic and exciting, the mother-bird shows up to claim the egg. But what hatches is "an elephant-bird," a truly integrated child—and Horton is of course its real parent.

Fatherhood requires hard work and courage, and a powerful conviction that all of this is good, deeply good, that parenting is sacred and crucial and fruitful, worth far more than the effort you have to put into it.

Being a parent, Marian Wright Edelman says, is "the most important calling and rewarding challenge you have." In homes across the country, real American men are already serving as true warriors in the most crucial fight of all—the battle for human fulfillment and happiness. It's *natural* for the male to love his family, to find in himself a passion so great that it will deny itself for the beloved. Men can understand just as easily as women do what writer Elizabeth Stone felt when she wrote

> "Making the decision to have a child—it's momentous. It is to decide forever to have your heart go walking around outside your body."

So how do we define manhood? Whatever else you may say, say this: A man takes care of his own. If that means getting up in the middle of the night with a sick four-year-old, he'll do it. If it means standing up to some thug on the street to protect his family, he'll do it. If it means compromising or postponing his own career, looking past his own fulfillment, he'll do it. If it means trying to balance work and homelife, he'll face that maddening, hectic struggle too. He'll take on anything that threatens his family, and he won't let go until things are right—even if it takes years. He'll understand that, as Bill Cosby says, " . . . a father's job is *not* to get tired of what he has a right to get tired of . . . "

He'll push himself to do the little things—to find the "right" kind of cheese puffs, to wash behind the kid's ears, to read that pamphlet on "Middle Ear Fluid" the pediatrician gave him, to sit down in the living room for another of those endless tea parties his four-year-old loves—because he understands that in parenting, as in other art forms, excellence lies in the details.

A *man* isn't afraid to really listen to his wife and learn from her. But he doesn't surrender his dignity and independence to her either, not even in domestic affairs, no more than he would expect her to give up hers for him. And he's not afraid of what "some people" may think. He's not perfect, and he knows it; sometimes he loses his temper, or gets tired, or discouraged, or just sick of everything. But he pushes himself. This is his warriorhood.

And men are changing. I account one little sentence my dad said, in fact, as a sign of this change—and as one of the triumphs of my life.

One night when our sons were young, we were having dinner at my parents' house. As we tended to the boys, my dad suddenly remarked, apropos of nothing, it seemed, "You know, if I died I'd want to come back as Tim and Cilla's kids."

I've stored this in my heart like a prize, an Olympic medal. It meant he not only accepted our very different style of parenting but admired it—a kind of validation that, coming from him, made my heart sing. I also felt a sadness behind his words, glimpsing, perhaps, his own wistful desire to have been loved with the kind of overwhelming tenderness we showed our little boys.

But there was even more in that simple sentence: a kind of openness or humility which came through his imagining himself in such a vulnerable role. *Dad*?! The Pillar?! The two-fisted doctor and paterfamilias who shamefully apologized after his heart attack for "letting the family down"?! The King of the Jungle casting himself as a baby, a toddler—as my *son*?! This was something new, something powerful, something positively Christian—like the King of the Universe humbling Himself to become a human infant.

Maybe it's because my father was growing old and saw the possibility of relying on us physically some day, in that parent-child reversal age can bring. Maybe it's because he saw a way past the rigid male role he'd always lived by, and had suffered for. Maybe it's just because he loved us. But one thing came through clearly: A strong, dominant, conservative male of the old school was looking at parenting in a whole new way.

The new domestic warrior, unfortunately, is rarely praised like this, and no one gives public awards for the labor and bravery parents show. I didn't need my father's approval—at least I didn't think I did—but when it moved me so much, I realized something very simple and very true, something I'd learned in

Catholic grade school, something that cuts to the heart of what's most difficult, and most rewarding, about fatherhood.

The cathedral workers of the Middle Ages, an old nun told us, *built for the glory of God. But the cathedrals were enormous. A sculptor might find himself on a scaffold near the ceiling, chiseling an angel's face onto a pillar, a face no one could possibly see from the floor below.*

But he'd do his best work, make it perfect—because he knew God could see.

Whether he's religious or not, this is what the domestic warrior lives by: He does what's right. Someday his work will blossom in the lives of his grown-up children, but that's far off. For now he makes it right because it should be right, he gives his best out of an indefatigable love.

And because his own manhood will accept nothing less.

CHAPTER FIFTEEN

Our First Goodbye

"I sigh that kiss you,
For I must own
That I shall miss you
When you are grown."
—Yeats, "A Cradle Song"

HERE IN THE NORTH COUNTRY, just south of the Canadian border, late summer doesn't bring the Dog Days. The sun is hot, of course, and humidity often rises with the heat; we keep our table fans humming, eat popsicles, go swimming in the lake. But then a cold front passes through, often out of northern Canada, and temperatures in our little city drop into the 60's, even the 50's, as the air dries out. Everyone notices a cool autumnal sparkle in the late-August air. *You can feel it,* we tell each other. *The Change is coming.*

And this year Shilly-Shally goes to kindergarten.

For weeks now I've noticed a gradual tightening of my heart. As summer warms to a close, there are lots of things to do. We take her shopping for shoes, clothes, a lunchbox. We spend a good half-hour in the school-supply aisle at the grocery store, where the smell of paper, pencils and glue reminds me of my own childhood excitement at such things. I wonder if my eyes got as bright as my daughter's do now.

Deeper preparations are occurring too, some of our own doing and others on the part of nature itself. Our little girl is changing. Her language abilities have sky-rocketed lately, and she's been writing with anything she can get her hands on: pens, pencils, chalk, magnetic letters—she's even shaped her food into little words. She's grown more independent too, adding new skills to her repetoire almost daily. She's learned to skip, to hold her breath, to do the dog-paddle, to make her own sandwiches, to draw jolly animals with human heads and faces. She's learning too how to better go about getting what she wants; when I pulled out a bottle of diet cola the other day, which she's not allowed to have yet, she put on that big-eyed seal-pup look and said, "Dad, I want something to drink—something *black*." And her longing for playmates has only intensified; she just learned what "recess" means, and it sent her into spasms of excitement. As far as school goes, she's as ripe as a late-summer apple.

(I also see her approach that other major watershed of childhood: She's actually losing interest in the Hokey-Pokey.)

I'm looking forward to this Change for my own reasons. Kindergarten is a kind of finish-line for hard-working parents; never again will your child be quite so dependent, quite so needy, quite so constant a presence. A kindergartener is, relatively speaking, a low-maintenance kid. Shilly-Shally will be in school till 2:30 five days a week; I have plans for that time, plans I've waited years to realize. My wife's as excited as I am, since she'll have more time too; the Change will bring us much more freedom for adult pursuits. *All* of them, in fact; she mentioned the other day that she can start wearing her teddies and camisoles now—that is, if she can find them in Shilly-Shally's dress-up drawer.

But beneath all this runs a deeper, sadder strain, something we all feel as autumn approaches and the bloom of summer swells toward its demise. Soon the great ragged lines of geese will begin passing overhead; hearing their joyous cries, we'll know they're on their way again. A few leaves have already begun to turn, yellow and red in the endless groves of green. The fall will soon follow, sweeping everything away as it always does—sweeping, in fact, one whole world away—and sweeping my baby with it, as she slowly becomes someone else. It won't be long till, in the silence of the house, I'll long to hear her voice.

And just now this is much more difficult. Our older son is a high-school senior, our younger only a few years behind him. The approach of *that* goodbye and what it means—the natural culmination of their births and childhoods, of all we've been as a family—is almost unbearable to my wife and me.

When a parent closes up the house on the way to bed at night, he or she often feels a deep and heart-easing sense of security. Turning out lights, locking doors, knowing your children are all safe asleep in their beds, everyone happy and dry and warm and accounted for, and all under the one roof—as you climb the stairs yawning, this brings a profound satisfaction. But one day soon our son will leave for a new life, and I know I'll never have quite that same feeling again. Maybe that's why I dreamed last week that he was lost in the wild, the Out There—only there were two of him, the young-adult version and the little boy he used to be. Soon he'll have to look out for himself, be his own father and mother. And, despite the great confidence we have in him, that scares and saddens us.

Our acceptance comes from knowing that they must go, each of them in their time, that college will be so good for them, that their happiness and excitement will fill us too and buoy us up— and from the hope that they'll come back to us, in whatever form that may take. But there'll be whole forests of sorrow between then and now, and our grief has already begun. In its own way, Shilly-Shally's move to kindergarten is just as profound and irrevocable.

"Everything," I heard a character say in a movie, "is on its way to somewhere." As our sons grew we watched them change, saw how they gradually lost interest in some of the things we did together, even as we found new things to share. And of course this has already happened with Shilly-Shally, and will only continue. But gradual growth comes into sharp emotional focus when a single dramatic change looms before the family, and a child's first entry into school—and last exit therefrom—are probably the most powerful ones. I know that, in some ways, I'm losing my Sweet Companion.

To a father like me, kindergarten is what weaning must be for a nursing mother. For the first time my daughter's dependence on me, with all its intimacy and intensity, will be lessened in a sudden and significant way. And our bond is a very emotional one; a few days ago, when we went out to draw with our new sidewalk chalk, she and I sat down and spontaneously began writing each other's names on the cement.

My wife and I also feel a keen regret as, with our daughter, we ourselves slowly leave early childhood again. Shilly-Shally took us there, let us re-visit that earthly paradise, just as her brothers once did. But now she's leaving it, further away with each passing hour, each new day, and the gates of that bright land are gradually being locked against us, since, as adults, we can only enter in the company of a native guide.

None of this is easy. As the warm days pass, I realize with a sorrow vast as autumn that our child will never again be who she was. Suddenly, quietly, a haiku by Shiki comes into my mind:

> *Backward I gaze.*
> *One whom I had chanced to meet*
> *is lost in haze.*

But then one morning I wake to bracing cool air at the window and think, *Come on, Tim, snap out of it! Jeeze—the world goes on!* It's silly to let my sorrow paralyze me, and it isn't fair to my family. Besides—what am I really so sad about?

Yes, our children are growing up; that's what children do. I did too. And what about all that our children have already given us, all we've done together? Do I overlook the shared life of this family just because that sharing and living will now take different forms? Part of being a good parent is realizing that, at times, your desires are contradictory; you'll want them to stay, for example, even as you'll want them to go. It's only human.

But it's also human to stand back and try to see the whole picture. As Shilly-Shally grows older, another emotion is outpacing my sorrow: excitement at who she's becoming. Even during the pregnancy my wife and I endlessly discussed that thrilling mystery: *What will she be like?* Now, right before our eyes, she's beginning to blossom toward the answer. And when we consider how bright, passionate, loving and fun-loving our sons have become, we get an inkling of what's in store for her.

I'll miss the little girl Shilly-Shally has been, and I know she'll never be quite the same whimsical, life-crazed creature again. Our easy intimacy will grow complicated as she moves toward womanhood, our unspoken agreements challenged as she asserts her own will. But I see all the signs of a wonderful human being in the making, and one with her own definite flair; my daughter, as an old Irish story puts it, " . . . has her own way, and has it entirely." I know too that she's learning how to love, how to find faith and wonder in the great challenges of the world. And hell—she's a lot more fun these days; we play checkers all the time, for example, but lately she's expressed a tentative interest in actually learning the rules.

And suddenly I find myself in a much deeper Moment. Carrying an armload of folded laundry, I pause at the front door; my three children, two giants and a half-pint, are out working on sidewalk chalk-drawings. For a moment I just look at them. Then a terrible question rises unbidden in me, spoken in my own voice but as if by someone else, some stern and powerful judge: Have I done right by these kids?

This same question came to me with great force just a few weeks ago when I dropped our sons off for school.

As they walked toward the building in the morning light I happened to glance at them—and suddenly a vision came. There they were: not only the two hulking high-school boys whose impact on our grocery bills is so alarming, not only two young men who shave and like thrasher music and hike Adirondack peaks and write editorials for their school newspaper—but also two little boys walking with me to Redbud Island to mess around by the river, wearing the little backpacks they've loaded with cookies, action figures, and (though none of us mentions it) stuffed animals.

As I sat there in the car watching them trudge off to another day of class, all the years suddenly fell away: We were just as we were then, a father and two bright-eyed, silly-hearted little boys for whom play was passionate seriousness—and whose sun in the sky was the look on my face. For a moment those little ghosts walked right beside me, talking and laughing and throwing stones into the river of time.

In that visionary moment I didn't look only into the past, longing for what used to be; I looked joyously too at the men my sons are becoming and saw the roots of their adulthood, saw child and adult simultaneously, and the existential river that inextricably links them. I found myself rejoicing simply because they're alive, felt in a single passionate instant every ounce of my love for them. Then those questions arose, with a haunting force I couldn't ignore: *Have I been a good father? Will they be okay? Have I given to them sufficient to the depths of my love?*

When this moment comes to a parent—and it *will* come, sooner or later—you see one thing with utter clarity: Your children are unspeakably precious, your love for them overpowering and almost helpless—and they *must* have the best you can give. In this searing moment your sadness at their growing away from you seems almost inconsequential, a sorrow whose true face is pure joy. But if you weren't the parent you should have been, if you didn't give enough, if you missed out on being with them, if selfishness or laziness or mere inertia kept you from actively loving them and helping them—then that sorrow can open a bitter wound in you which even the long, slow power of time will never heal.

In that moment of burning regret, all the job problems and promotions and mortgages and new cars and salary considerations, all the various practical successes and frustrations of adult life, go completely transparent. Suddenly all those things are no more than leaves on the trees, growing and falling. If you've let them come between you and your child, you'll suffer for it—and you'll hate knowing what you've thrown away, knowing you can never go back and set things right.

My wife and I will sorely miss our pre-schooler. But I know that, tonight, after tucking our new kindergartener in, we'll sleep the sleep of the just—because everything we've done for her or given her, every moment of work and patience and paying attention, every self-denying effort we made, great or small, was just one more sparkle applied to the jewel of this child's growing soul. We realize that life will sometimes be very tough for her, as it is for all of us. But we know she'll land on her feet—and this brings us a peace far too deep for words.

As adults we often get lost in the daily struggle for ordinary contentments, forgetting the larger flow of things. My Shilly-Shally's off to kindergarten, to a greater life; "Everything is on its way to somewhere." I have to remind myself that life is an endless succession of hellos and goodbyes, that every particle of time-space is in fact an infinite hello-goodbye. The mystery of all things brought my daughter to me, just as it brought my precious wife and sons, just as it brought me into the world through the door of my parents' desire for each other. It's as if, standing here at the curb of Bailey Avenue School, looking over Shilly-Shally's head at her teary-eyed mother, feeling things far too ordinary and profound to be said, I'm also looking into my own mother's and father's eyes, the three of us finally understanding each other perfectly—though my mom is, at the moment, two thousand miles away, and my dad died when his granddaughter was still a baby.

And that's what we finally come to understand: that it's all so inseparable. This is life, this is the world—and the only real way for me to live in it, to find my bearings among its immensities, is in a family. What Jane Yolen wrote in "Autumn Song of the Goose" applies equally to human beings; I think of her words as I hear again in memory the joyous honking of a migrating flock as it passes over our house:

> *"We fly but wingtips apart,*
> *No compass, no compass but the heart."*

(Besides—by 2:45 that afternoon, Shilly-Shally's back home and sitting with me at our kitchen table, stuffing Pringles in her mouth and saying in one burst, "You know what we got a hamster in kindergarten it's a girl named Ricky but that's not a girl's name can I put on my blue shorts I want to play with Alex hey is there anything black I can drink with these Pringles?").

So goodbye, precious girl—Goodbye . . .

And Hello!

Afterword

APPLE TREES IN EARLY WINTER

They stand. That's the thing of it.
Gnarled into shapes like constantine wire,
dark-boled and scraggly with
those few leaves not yet ripped away
by wind's ungainly wrath,
they stand.

Here and there a single apple hangs,
its red forlorn in the graying world,
juice past sweetness. The farmer
rarely comes to the orchard now.

If only I could get the trick of this,
this standing, this silent patience.
Sadness in the winter landscape
means nothing to them, it seems, cannot
darken their lives, whatever thoughts
in the slow deep sap they think—

See, they must have bound themselves over
in service to something deeper.

(This poem first appeared in
Adirondac Magazine).

About Tim J. Myers

TIM J. MYERS is a writer, songwriter, and professional storyteller living in Santa Clara, California, where he also teaches at Santa Clara University. Tim earned his master's in literature from the University of Wisconsin-Madison and has 32 years experience teaching, both at the classroom and university levels. He's published 10 children's books (with one on the way) and over 120 poems. His notable works include *Basho and the Fox* ('00), *Dark-Sparkle Tea* (Wordsong), *Good Babies* (Candlewick '05), and *Basho and the River Stones* (Cavendish '04). He won the 2012 *SCBWI Magazine* Merit Award for Fiction.

About Familius

Welcome to a place where mothers are celebrated, not compared. Where heart is at the center of our families, and family at the center of our homes. Where boo boos are still kissed, cake beaters are still licked, and mistakes are still okay. Welcome to a place where books—and family— are beautiful. Familius: a book publisher dedicated to helping families be happy.

Familius was founded in 2012 with the intent to align the founders' love of publishing and family with the digital publishing renaissance which occurred simultaneous with the Great Recession. The founders believe that the traditional family is the basic unit of society, and that a society is only as strong as the families that create it.

Familius' mission is to help families be happy. We invite you to participate with us in strengthening your family by being part of the Familius family. Go to www.familius.com to subscribe and receive information about our books, articles, and videos.

Website: www.familius.com
Facebook: www.facebook.com/paterfamilius
Twitter: @familiustalk, @paterfamilius1
Pinterest: www.pinterest.com/familius

CPSIA information can be obtained at www.ICGtesting.com
Printed in the USA
BVOW071409250313

316381BV00002B/6/P